IMAGES
of America

MADISON COUNTY

On the Cover: Festivities in Jackson commemorating the first-day issue on April 29, 1950, of the Casey Jones stamp included these McCowat-Mercer Printing workers wearing train hats and bandanas. From left to right are (first row) Sebron Morelock, Wilgal Kincannon, Herman Alexander, and Francis "Doc" McCowat; (second row) E. P. Collier, Bill Butler, Melvin Wilson, unidentified, Willie Hogan, J. C. Halcomb, and Esley Farrow. (Courtesy Jackson–Madison County Library.)

IMAGES
of America

MADISON COUNTY

Linda J. Higgins and Scott Parish

ARCADIA
PUBLISHING

ISBN 978-0-7385-6779-2

Published by Arcadia Publishing
Charleston, South Catolina

Printed in the United States of America

Library of Congress Control Number: 2009921628

For all general information contact Arcadia Publishing at:
Telephone 843-853-2070
Fax 843-853-0044
E-mail sales@arcadiapublishing.com
For customer service and orders:
Toll-Free 1-888-313-2665

Visit us on the Internet at www.arcadiapublishing.com

This book is dedicated to Linda's mother, Billie Jennings,
her grandmothers, and Scott's grandfather Earl
for instilling the importance of family, community, and local history.

Contents

ACKNOWLEDGMENTS

We would like to thank Jack Wood, reference librarian at the Jackson–Madison County Library (JMCL) in the Tennessee Room. Without the cooperation and encouragement of Jack and the use of his resources at the library, this book would never have been done. But we would also like to thank the many people, institutions, and businesses who helped by providing pictures and information: Betsy R. Babb, Ralph Barber, Dr. John Barber, Buck Barnett and the Herbert C. Murdaugh Collection, Joel Jackson and the Bemis Historical Society, Billy J. King and the Big Black Creek Historical Association (BBCHA), Ruby Hurt Booth, Lavina Brown, Carolyn Smith Callis, Casey Jones Museum, Lane College, Cecil Cravens, Duncan DeMonbreum, Jim Driver, Doris Freeman, Rosalee J. and Jimmy Gibbons, Griffin Funeral Home, Walter Helms, Helen F. Higgins, Linda Wilson Holder, Betty Holifield, William Holland Jr., Nell Huntspon, Jackson State Community College (JSCC), Billie H. Jennings, Nina May Jones, Norwood Jones, Kisber family, Dr. Victoria S. Lake, Parnell Landers, Denise LaSalle, Madison Baptist Church, Madison County Agriculture Extension Office, Murray May, Billy Mayo, William and Kathleen H. McCommon, McCowat-Mercer, Margaret H. McGill, Mary Jo Middlebrooks, Fulton Mullis, Robert Nolen, Nell Nucholls, Old Country Store, Jane Parham, Joe and Suzanne Patty, Frank Procter, Randy Kennedy and Procter and Gamble Company, Geraldine Rainey, Bill and Judy Ranne, Mary Roberts, J. Phillip Smith, Sharon Baudo Smith, E. Maurice Stansell Sr., Louise Stevens, Victor Sullivan, Mary Jane Tapley, Tennessee Textiles, The *Jackson Sun*, Joan Cook Tomlin, John W. Ulmer, Jackie Utley, and Lynn and John Williams.

Linda also thanks her family, especially her husband, Richard, who served as proofreader; her daughter Robin Ledford, who provided information; her daughter KaCarole Thornton; who listened each day and helped with the tech stuff; and Beth Jones, who was understanding with the deadlines.

We probably missed many key individuals and businesses because our space is limited, and there were some of whom we couldn't get pictures. We're sorry for any omissions, but maybe there will be another book to catch these.

Introduction

In the 20th century, Madison County truly became the hub of West Tennessee. Major highways and rail lines traverse the county and its county seat, Jackson. The main sources of employment in the 20th century were three railroad companies and the industry spawned by the railroads, such as the company cotton mill town of Bemis and, in the mid-20th century, industries such as Conalco, an aluminum rolling manufacturer; an Owens Corning tile factory; and Proctor and Gamble's only U.S. plant that makes the tasty Pringles crisps. As job opportunities abounded, the population grew, and families came from outlying counties, including the family of Carl Perkins, father of rockabilly music, who moved to Bemis in the late 1940s. Carl worked by day at the Colonial Bread Company in Jackson and plucked his guitar by night until he broke through with a record contract in 1955. His first hit recording, "Blue Suede Shoes," was released in 1956 on Memphis's Sun label. W. S. Holland, who lived in Bemis, started out with Carl but moved over to become Johnny Cash's drummer for all the decades that the "Man in Black" entertained. Holland continues to support the International Rock-a-Billy Hall of Fame and appears at the annual Rock-a-Billy International Festival in Jackson the first weekend in August. John Lee "Sonny Boy" Williamson was responsible for popularizing the use of the harmonica in the early blues sounds of the 1920s and 1930s. His music is celebrated each year in Jackson at the Shannon Street Blues Festival. He is a member of the Blues Foundation Hall of Fame. Isaac Tigrett, the founder of the internationally famous Hard Rock Café, descends from entrepreneur Francis Tomlin Tigrett and industrialist/developer John B. Tigrett and grew up in Jackson. Tigrett started his first Hard Rock in London, but when he decided to bring the franchise to the United States, he incorporated in the state of Tennessee and started the venture in Jackson in the Old Hickory Mall, which was part of his mother's ventures. John Luther Jones, also known as Casey Jones, was a famous railroad engineer during the late 1800s. Casey was famous for being on time, and the people who lived along his runs could set their watches by Casey's whistle. He died on April 30, 1900, in the "Cannon Ball" wreck, which was popularized by a folk song that sang his praises for hanging on till the end.

The business climate in Madison County offered opportunities to many women who took charge and were successful as owners and administrators. In the chapter on Outstanding Women in Business, some of the pioneering women in business are recognized.

Some of the sights to see in Madison County include the City of Jackson Nashville, Chattanooga, and St. Louis Depot and Railroad Museum; the Bemis Auditorium, which is now the museum of the cotton mill town; Pinson Mounds State Archaeological Area, with the second highest Native American burial mound in the United States; the historic Denmark Church, a 155-year-old, two-story building with stories to tell about the early settlement of the county, the Civil War, and the fraternal order of Masons; the Britton Lane Civil War Battlefield, just a few miles from the old historic Denmark Church; the Casey Jones Village and Railroad Museum; Lane College, one of the oldest black colleges, with its turn-of-the-century buildings as well as modern buildings; and historic Main Street houses dating from the later 1800s.

Festivals and annual events include the Bemis Reunion Days in May, the Shannon Street Blues Fest and the Miss Tennessee Scholarship Pageant in June, the Rock-a-Billy International Festival in August, the NAIA Ladies Basketball Tournament in March, the West Tennessee State Fair in September, and the biannual Britton Lane Re-enactment in September. Sports have always been important to citizens of Jackson and Madison County. Many citizens have had outstanding careers in sports, such as Ed "Too Tall" Jones, who graduated from Merry High School and went to Tennessee State University. He was drafted by the Dallas Cowboys and played for many years, helping them win several championships.

Baseball has provided opportunities to individuals such as Ellis Kinder, who played with the major-league Red Sox and was posthumously inducted into the Boston's team hall of fame in 2006. Currently citizens enjoy watching the Seattle Mainers AA baseball affiliate, the Diamond Jaxx, at Pringles Park.

Madison County is served by several institutions of higher learning, including Union University, Lambuth University, Lane College, and Jackson State Community College. Jackson State Community College, a two-year, state-owned institution, was founded in 1967 to fulfill the outcry of a great number of West Tennesseans who saw a need for a community college. Lambuth University was originally the Memphis Conference Female Institute and transitioned into a coeducational facility in a beautiful quad-shaped campus on Lambuth Boulevard, where it remains a Methodist-based center of higher learning. The campus of Union University, supported by the Southern Baptist Association, has been at the northwestern edge of Jackson since it moved from east Jackson in 1974. Union's large campus continues to grow. Lane College, founded as a private Methodist Episcopal college by Rev. Isaac Lane, resides in East Jackson. The predominantly black college celebrated its centennial anniversary in 1982. The West Tennessee Business College, which has its roots in the early days of the 1900s, and the state technical school have provided educational opportunities to those seeking a more technical approach.

Jackson's historic midtown area is home of the Lambuth Area Neighborhood Association. The homes and small businesses, largely built in the early 20th century, have been those of many notable people, including M. D. Anderson, Houston cotton exchange broker and founder of the Anderson Foundation, which funds cancer research; Hank Lesh, inventor of radio interface equipment; and Judge Whit LaFon, attorney and uncle of Vice Pres. Al Gore.

Jobs provided income to families and individuals, but community livability in Jackson, Pinson, Beech Bluff, Madison Hall, Bemis, Spring Creek, Malesus, Medon, Denmark, Huntersville, and all the small communities in Madison County rated high in the lives of the citizens. Schools, churches, clubs, and organizations completed the pride the citizens had in living in Madison County in the 20th century.

One

Railroads Bring Jobs

Railroads began operating in Madison County just prior to the Civil War, but many rail lines in the county were destroyed during that conflict. By the 20th century, there were three rail companies doing business in Madison County, and many citizens were employed by the railroads. Rail transit provided opportunities for industry and business development. Railroad companies even gave impetus to industry never before seen in Madison County, such as the cotton mill operation brought here by a combination of the railroad, Judson Moss Bemis, and the county legislative body. The lumber industry benefited from the advanced transportation links. Beare Ice and Coal Company started an ice plant to ice railroad cars transporting fruits and vegetables to northern markets. The president of Mobile and Ohio Railroad Company (M&O), I. B. Tigrett, who lived in Jackson, was instrumental in locating the main engine repair shop of the 3,000-mile line in Jackson. He was called "The Hesitant Hero of Jackson" in the *Saturday Evening Post.* Railroads continued to dominate employment opportunities, especially with the construction of Iselin Yard, which provided jobs to machinists and others whose work didn't involve going out on the trains but keeping them running. The railroads even brought additional industry to Madison County, such as Consolidated Aluminum, Owens Corning, and Procter and Gamble. Consolidation of the Illinois Central and the Gulf Mobile and Ohio rail companies in 1972 symbolized the beginning of the end for the prominence of the railroad in Madison County. For the first 75 years of the century, the iron horse chugged its way through Madison County until the diesel became the engine of choice, and goods began to be transported in trucks on the interstate highways and well-maintained U.S. and state highways. Rail lines contributed to the very existence of some outlying communities such as Bemis, Beech Bluff, Mercer, and Pinson. The railroad industry still occupies a place in Madison County's employment picture, but not as much as at the beginning of the century, when Casey Jones took his ill-fated trip.

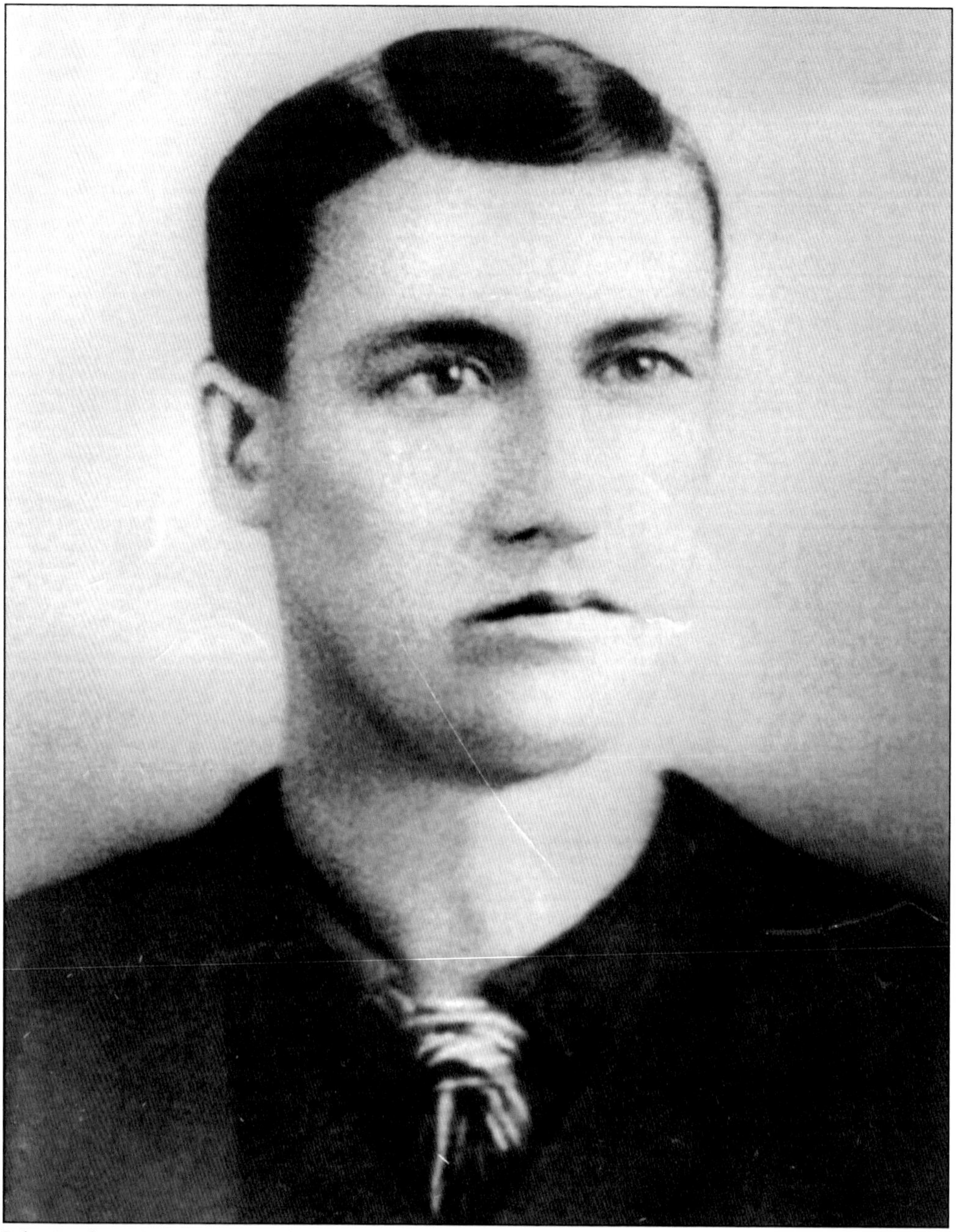

John Luther "Casey" Jones, a locomotive engineer from Jackson, died in an accident on April 30, 1900, when his passenger train collided with another on the Illinois Central Railroad in Vaughn, Mississippi. Jones was the only person to die in the crash. Wallace Saunders, a friend of Casey Jones who worked in the roundhouse in Canton, Mississippi, as an engine wiper, remembered Casey in rhyme and a catchy tune that soon would become a favorite of the fellow workers and eventually the world. William Leighton, who worked out of the Canton yards, passed Wallace's song along to his brothers, Bert and Frank, two vaudeville performers, who spread "The Ballad of Casey Jones" across the land. A professional songwriting team, T. Lawrence Siebert and Eddie Newton, copyrighted the song in 1909. (Courtesy Jane Parham.)

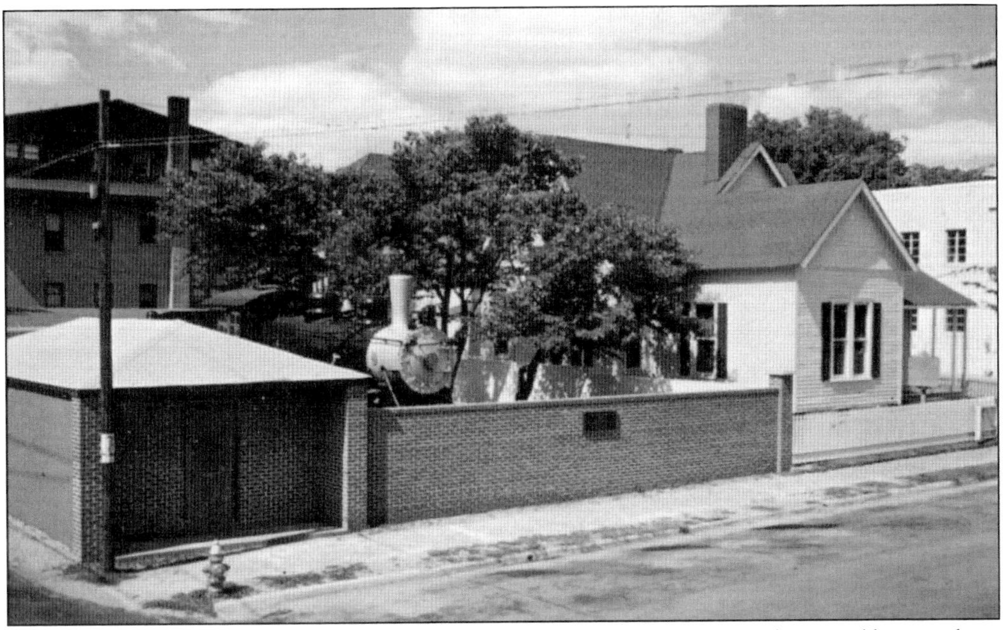

Jackson's first railroad museum opened in April 1956 on Chester Street in the actual house where the famous railroad engineer, Casey Jones, was living when he died. On October 23, 1980, the house and museum displays were moved to their new location at the Casey Jones Village at an Interstate 40 exit; one week later the engine followed. The museum reopened on April 30, 1981. (Courtesy Billie Jennings.)

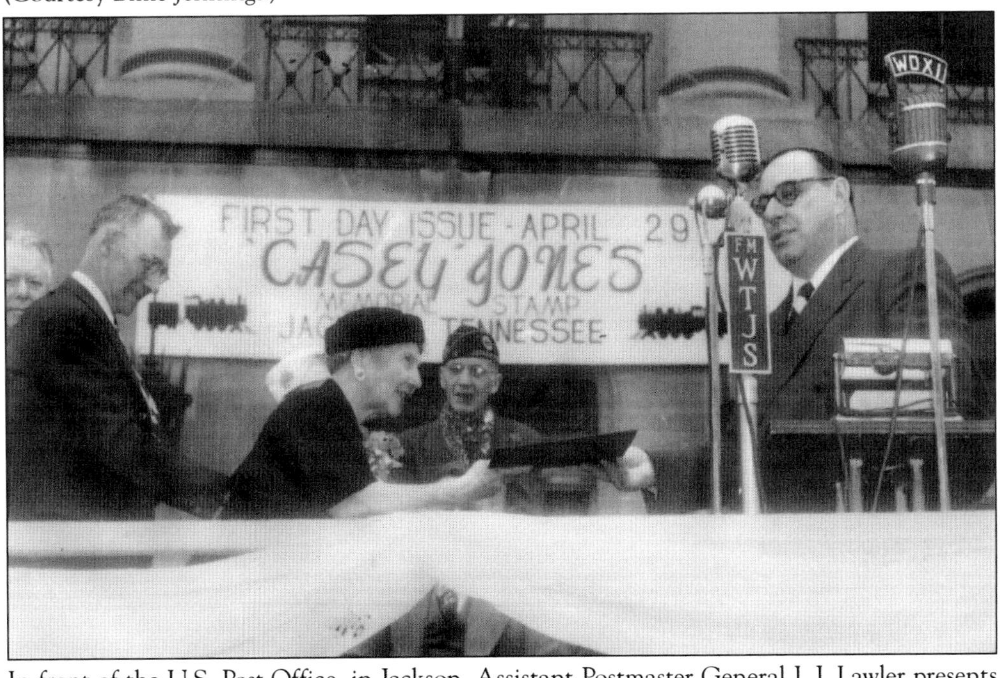

In front of the U.S. Post Office, in Jackson, Assistant Postmaster General J. J. Lawler presents the first sheet of memorial Casey Jones stamps to Jones's widow on April 29, 1950, recognizing the 50th anniversary of the famous railroad wreck of the Jacksonian. The whole town celebrated the anniversary. (Courtesy Casey Jones Museum.)

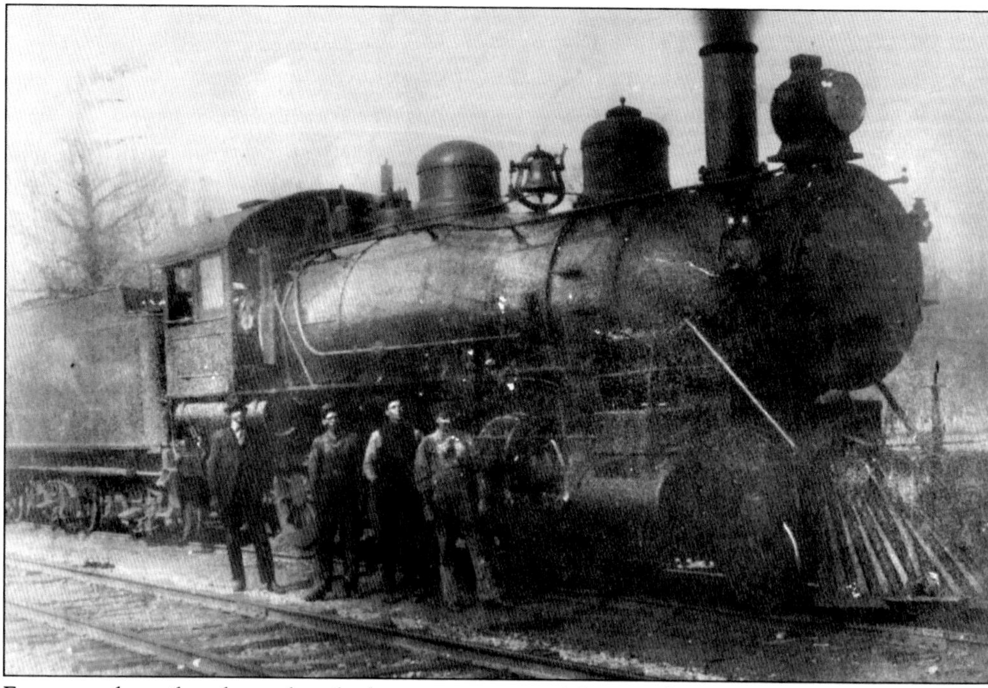

For years, the railroads employed a large percentage of the population of the county and served as a stop for passengers as well as freight. Shown here is a steam engine of the M&O Railroad in the early 1900s with the crew. (Courtesy Buck Barnett.)

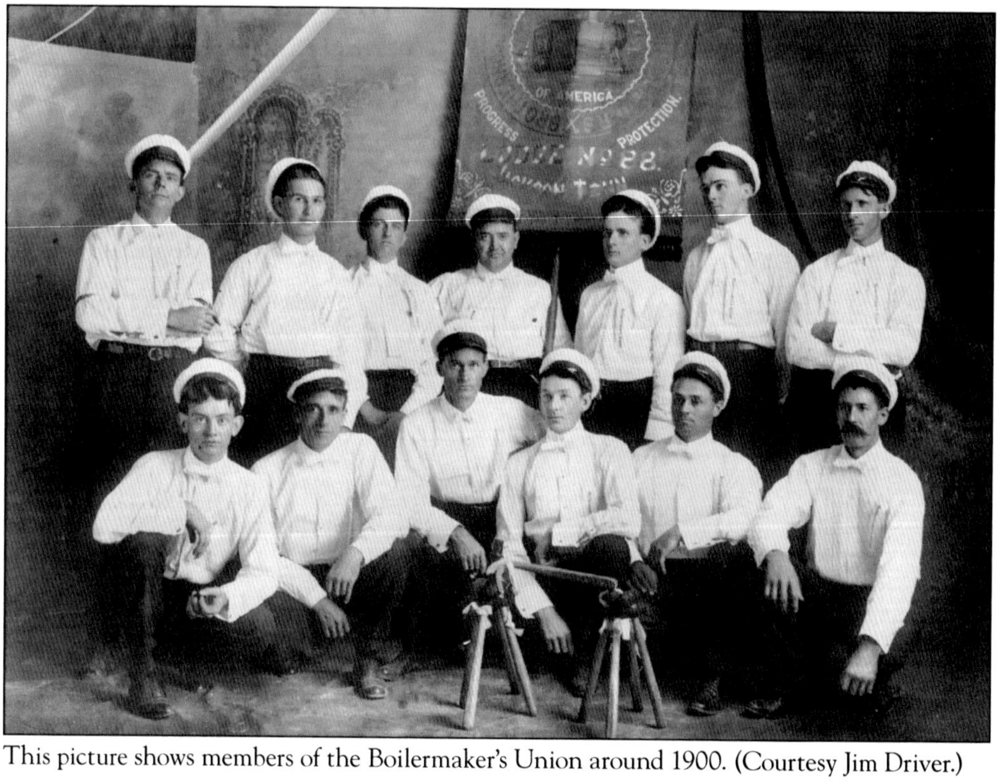

This picture shows members of the Boilermaker's Union around 1900. (Courtesy Jim Driver.)

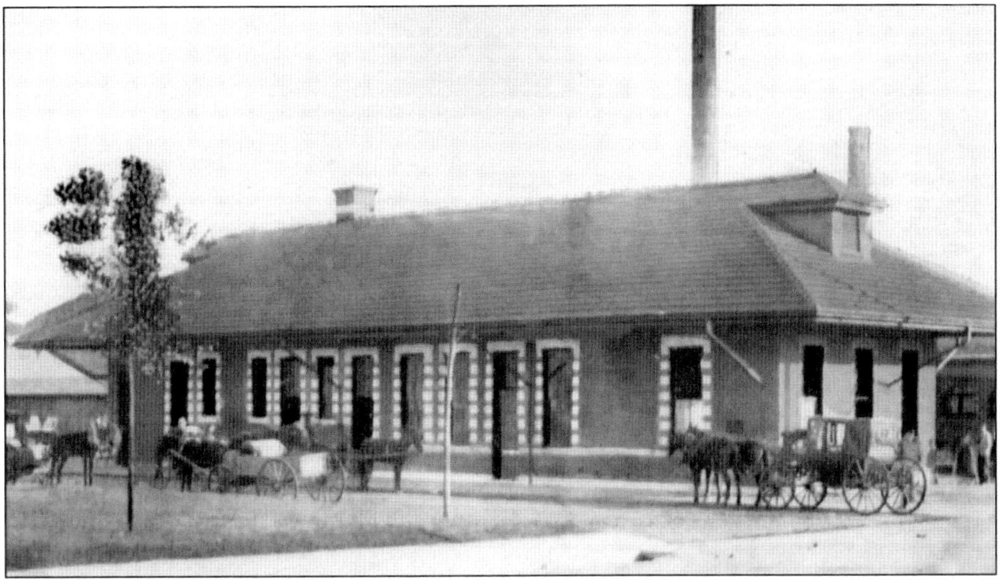

In 1907, the Nashville, Chattanooga, and St. Louis Railroad (NC&StL) built the depot that stands today at 582 South Royal Street. The first depot built in this location was the Tennessee Midland Railroad's, built in 1888. The City of Jackson restored the 1907 depot in 1992 as a lasting tribute to the impact of the railroads on the growth of Jackson and Madison County, and it is listed on the National Register of Historic Places. The depot museum houses a permanent collection that includes photographs, artifacts, and related memorabilia associated with railroad and local history. Also on the grounds are exhibits and meeting rooms, a dining car, and two cabooses. An elaborate working scale model exhibit, built and maintained by the Jackson Model Railroad Club, operates Wednesday and Saturday. Below is the depot around the beginning of the 20th century. (Both courtesy JMCL.)

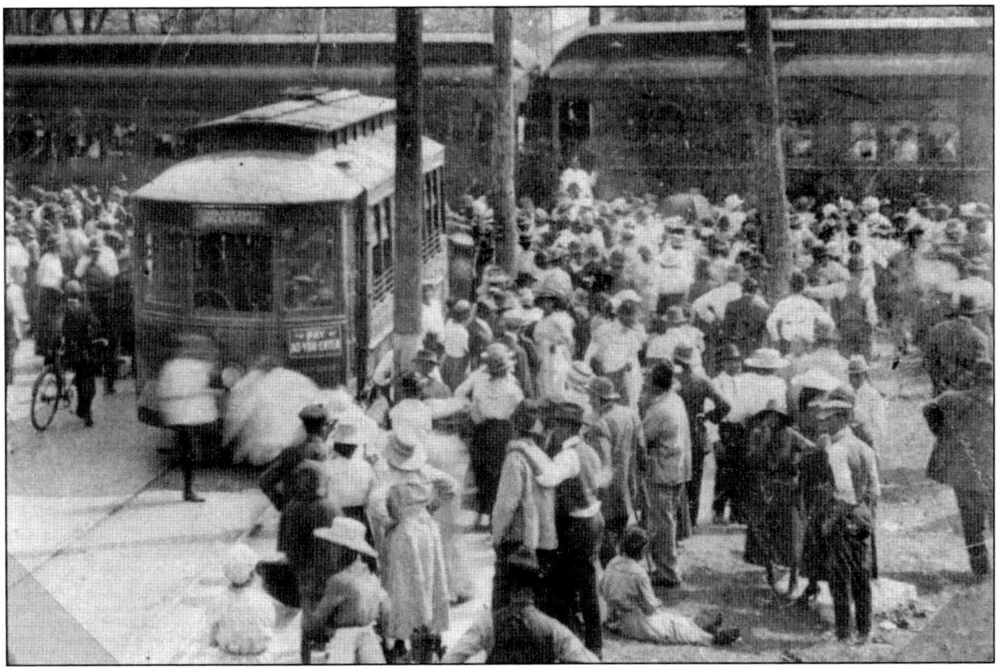

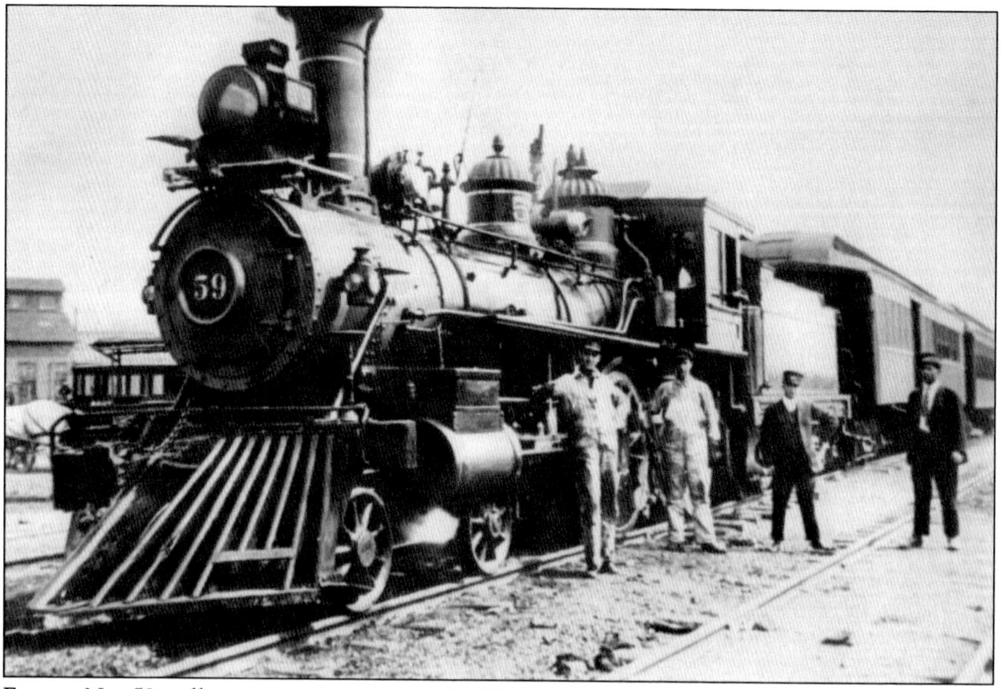

Engine No. 59 pulls passenger cars around 1912. Employment by the railroad was diversified. (Courtesy Jim Driver.)

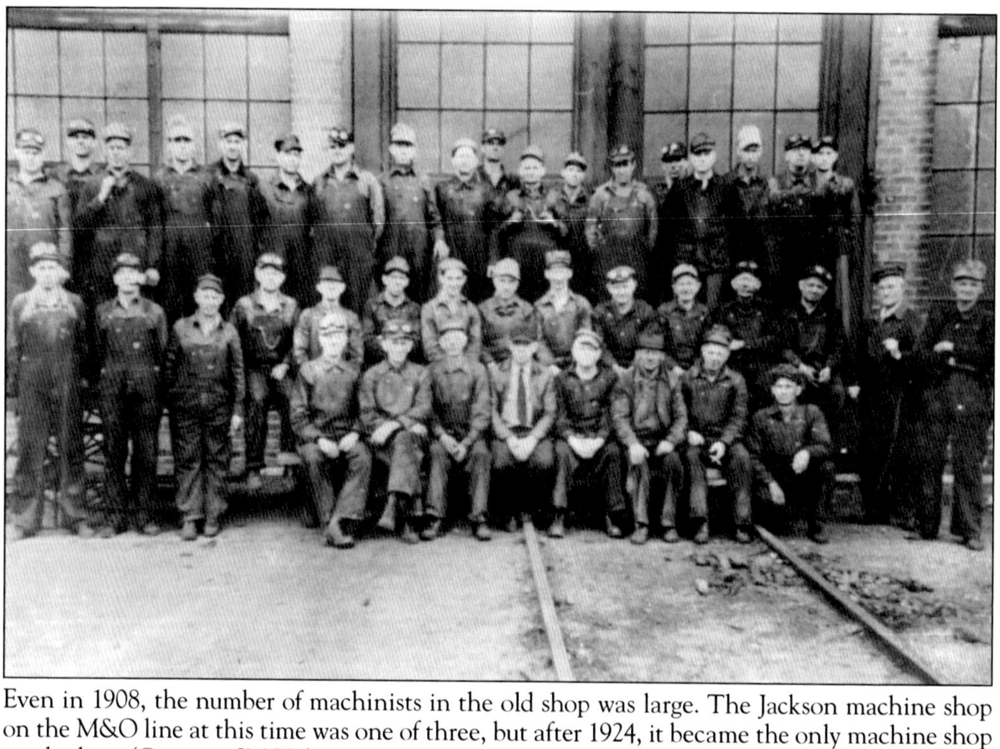

Even in 1908, the number of machinists in the old shop was large. The Jackson machine shop on the M&O line at this time was one of three, but after 1924, it became the only machine shop on the line. (Courtesy JMCL.)

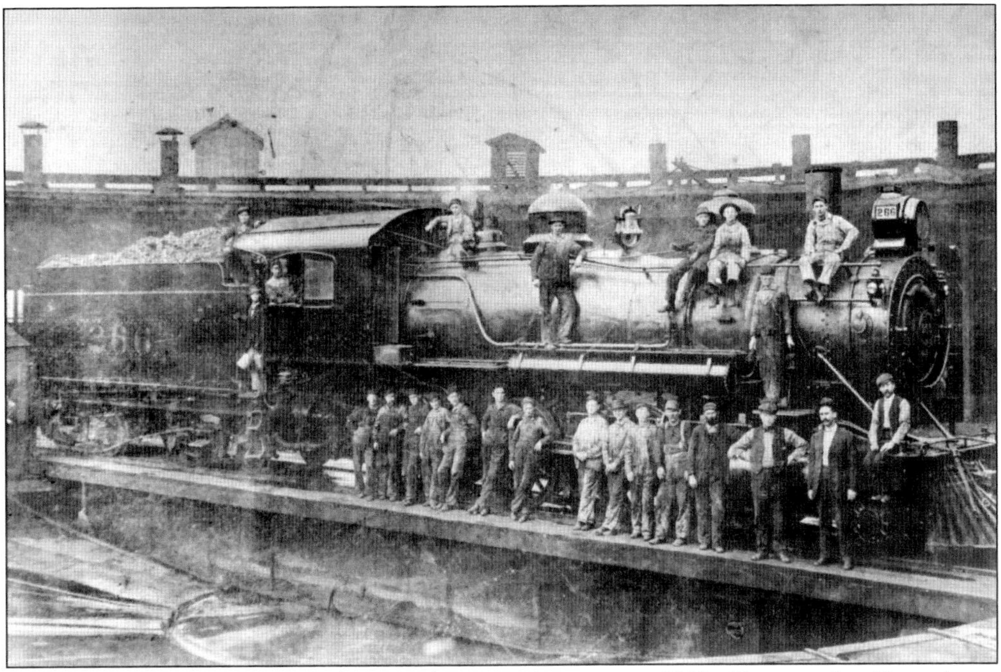

The M&O turntable and back shop are shown as they were in 1908. (Courtesy Jim Driver.)

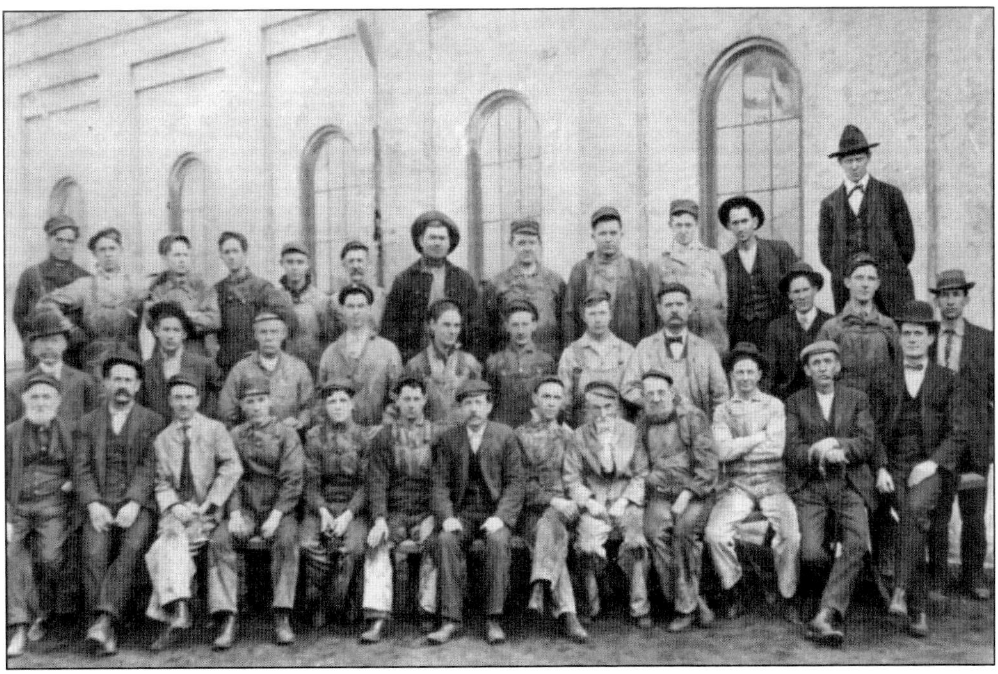

Workers at M&O shop in 1908 are, from left to right, (first row) Martin, C. Jones, Parterage, Mathis, F. Schefold, Ebbetts, Shefold, A. Allen, Parterage Sr., Briggs, F. Turner, Midgett, and Teague; (second row) two unidentified, Purcell, G. Hundson, A. Fail, O. Wilson, unidentified, Gilliam, Oakley, Turney, and J. Dempster; (third row) Carr, B. Little, F. Ryan, M. Casey, I. D. True, J. Little, unidentified, Brooks, Vantrees, D. Coughlin, C. Hahn, and F. Jones. (Courtesy Jim Driver.)

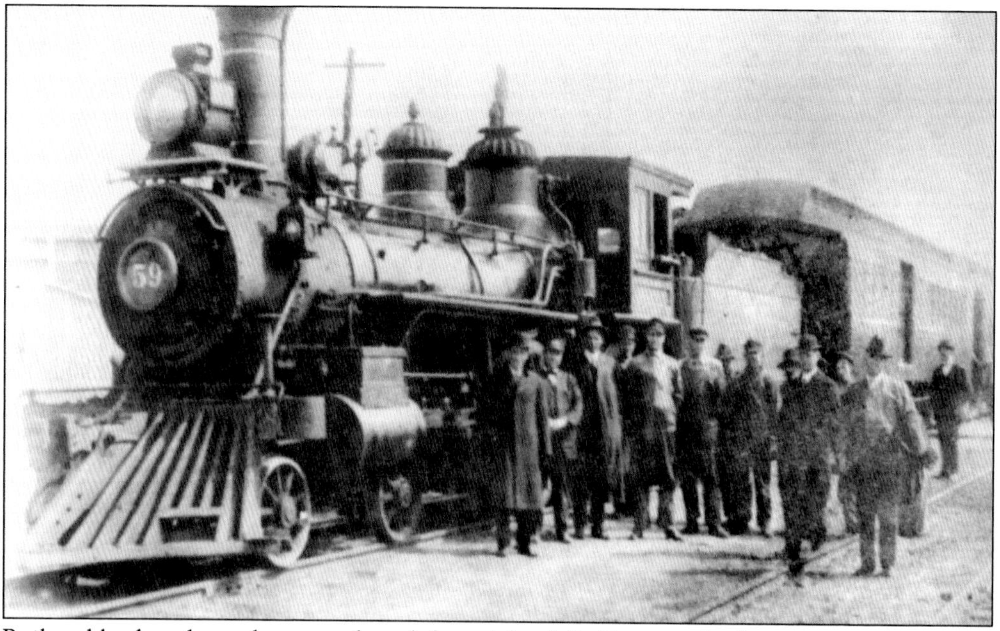

Railroad leaders shown here are, from left to right, I. B. Tigrett, who became president of the M&O Railroad in 1920; Ruddy Hayes, conductor; H. S. Wilson, master mechanic; Roy Groom, engineer; J. O. Williams, fireman; Ed Hunt, machinist; A. V. Patton, assistant to the president; and C. F. Morgan, general manager. (Courtesy JMCL.)

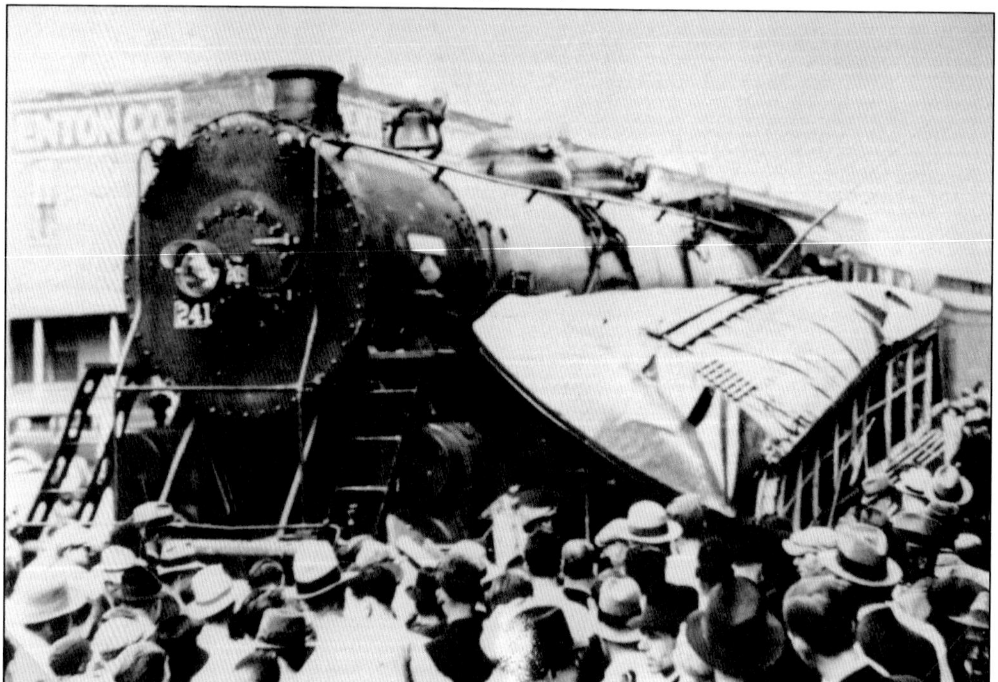

On October 18, 1935, Engine 2419 of the Illinois Central Railroad collided with a streetcar at the Main Street crossing. Guy Toombs, a conductor, said his brakes failed. The engineer was ? Chandler, and Love Freeman was the other conductor. (Courtesy JMCL.)

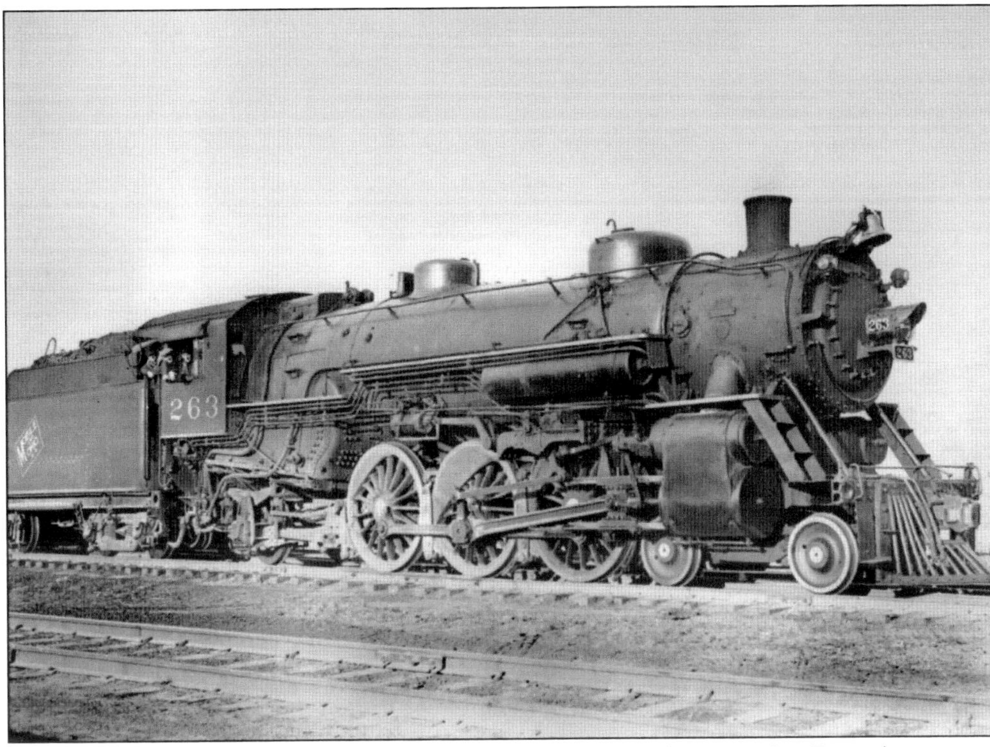

M&O Engine No. 263 was built in 1922. It is pictured in 1939. (Courtesy Jim Driver.)

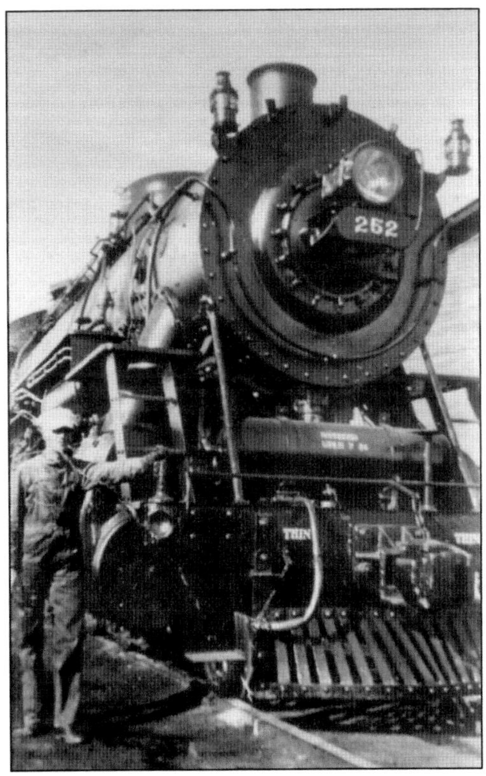

This close-up of a steam engine clearly shows the cowcatcher on the front—a piece of equipment that was needed on early locomotives. (Courtesy Buck Barnett from the Herbert C. Murdaugh Collection.)

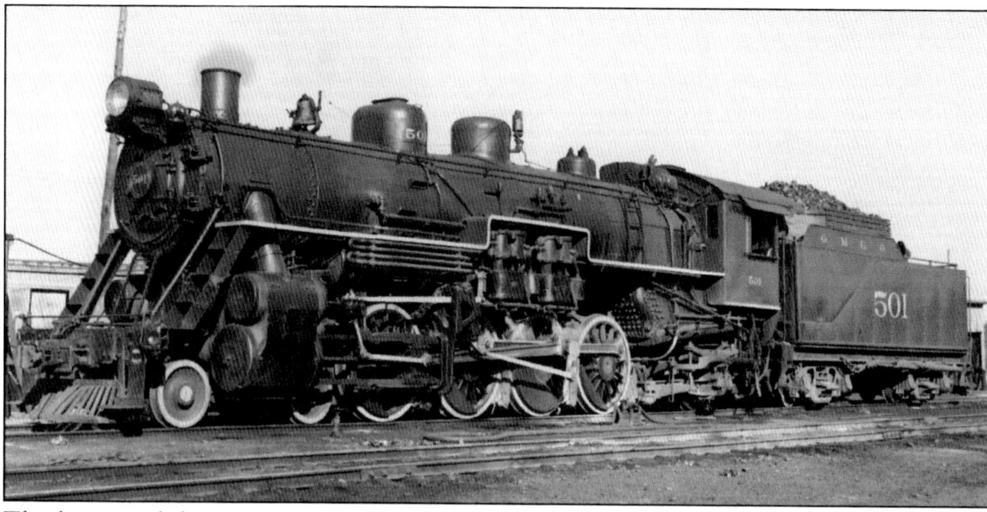

The beauty of the enormous steam engines and coal cars of the Gulf Mobile and Ohio Railroad (GM&O) is shown here in this early locomotive. (Courtesy Buck Barnett from the Herbert C. Murdaugh Collection.)

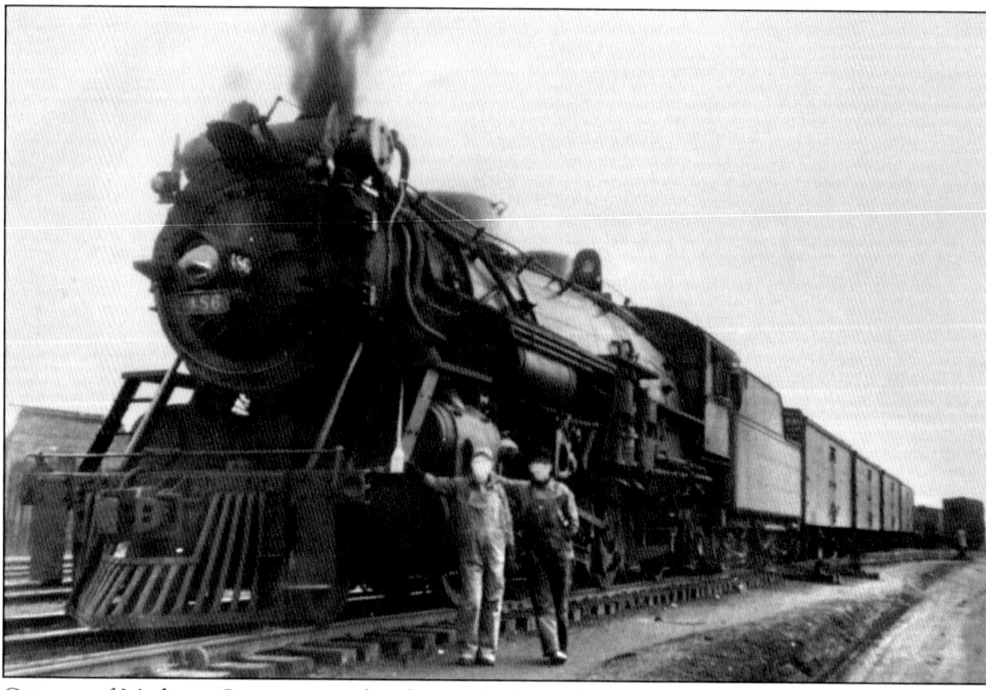

Citizens of Madison County were familiar with the sight and sounds of the steam locomotive. Smoke billows from this coal-fired engine's smokestack. (Courtesy Buck Barnett from the Herbert C. Murdaugh Collection.)

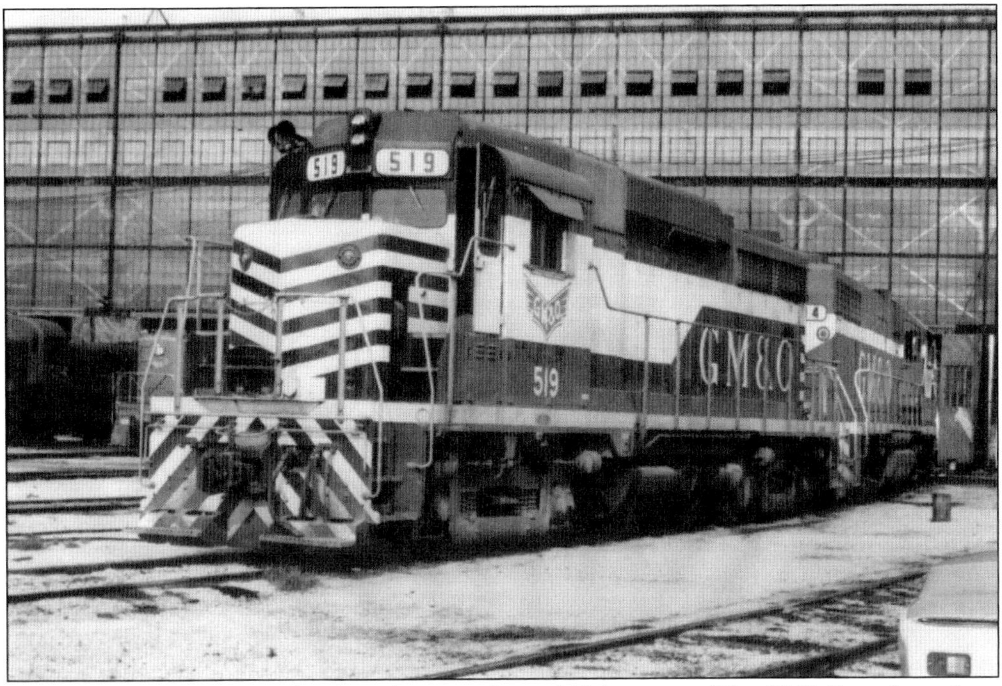

Steam engines gave way to diesel machines in the mid-20th century. The GM&O machine shop, known as the "glass house," is shown in the background. (Courtesy Buck Barnett from the Herbert C. Murdaugh Collection.)

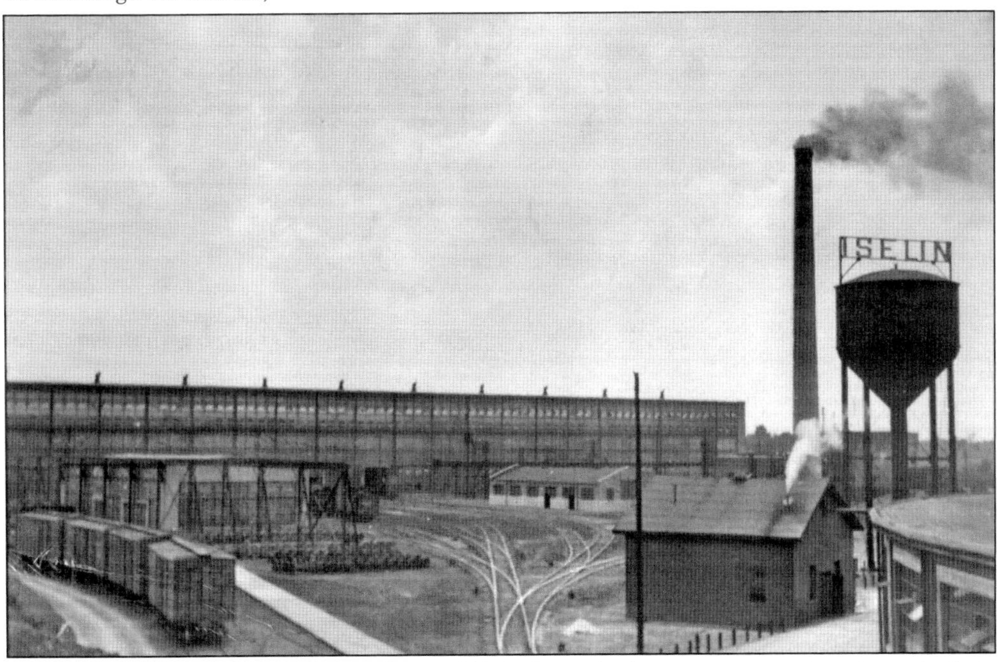

The Iselin Yard M&O shop, shown about 1925, had seen little improvement since it was built in 1855. In 1924, company officials built the first unit of a modern repair shop and engine terminal. The name "Iselin" was chosen in the 1920s to honor M&O directors Adrian and Ernest Iselin according to the GM&O Historical Society. (Courtesy JMCL.)

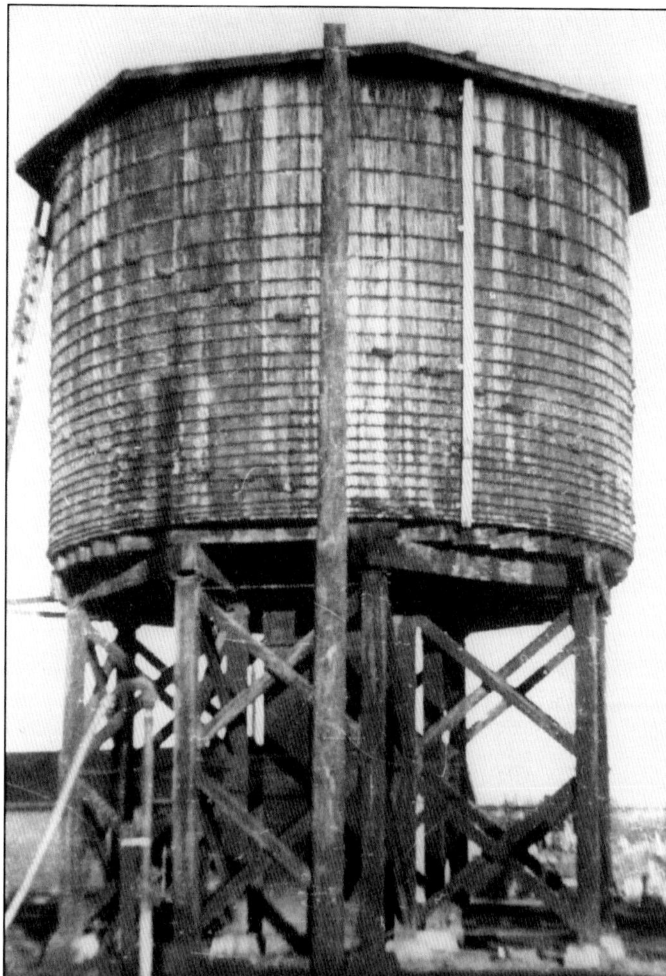

Water towers, such as the M&O water tank at Union Station, shown here, were very important for the steam engines and also for fire protection of the buildings at railroad stops. (Courtesy JMCL.)

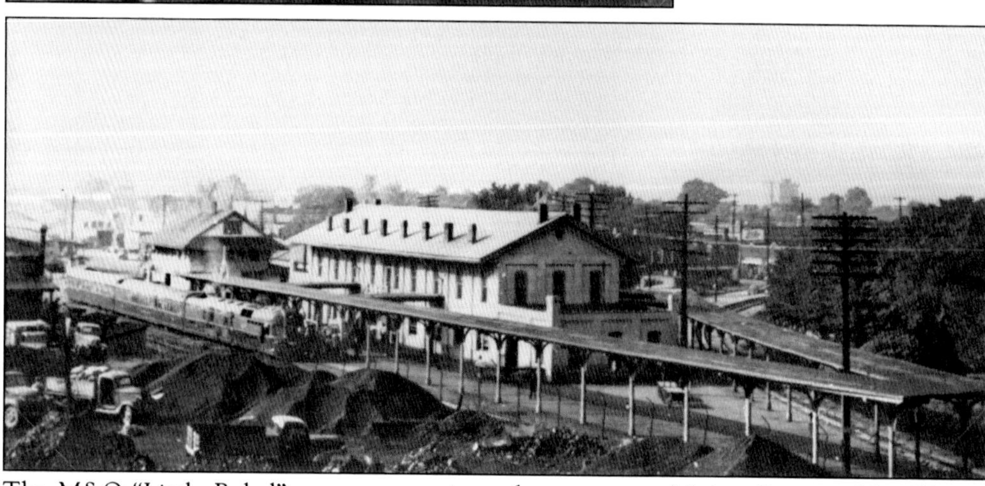

The M&O "Little Rebel" passenger train makes a stop at Union Station. The Illinois Central tracks turn to the right. Both railroad companies used Union Station for a few years. (Courtesy JMCL.)

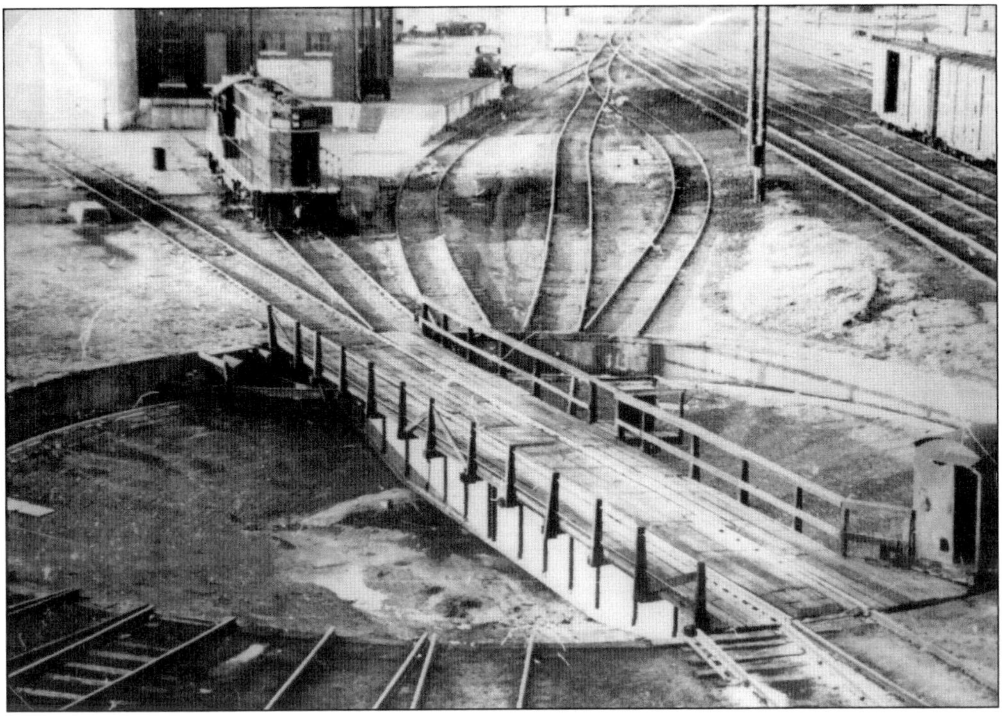

The turntable at the Illinois Central Railroad Shop is shown just outside the railroad's roundhouse. (Courtesy JMCL.)

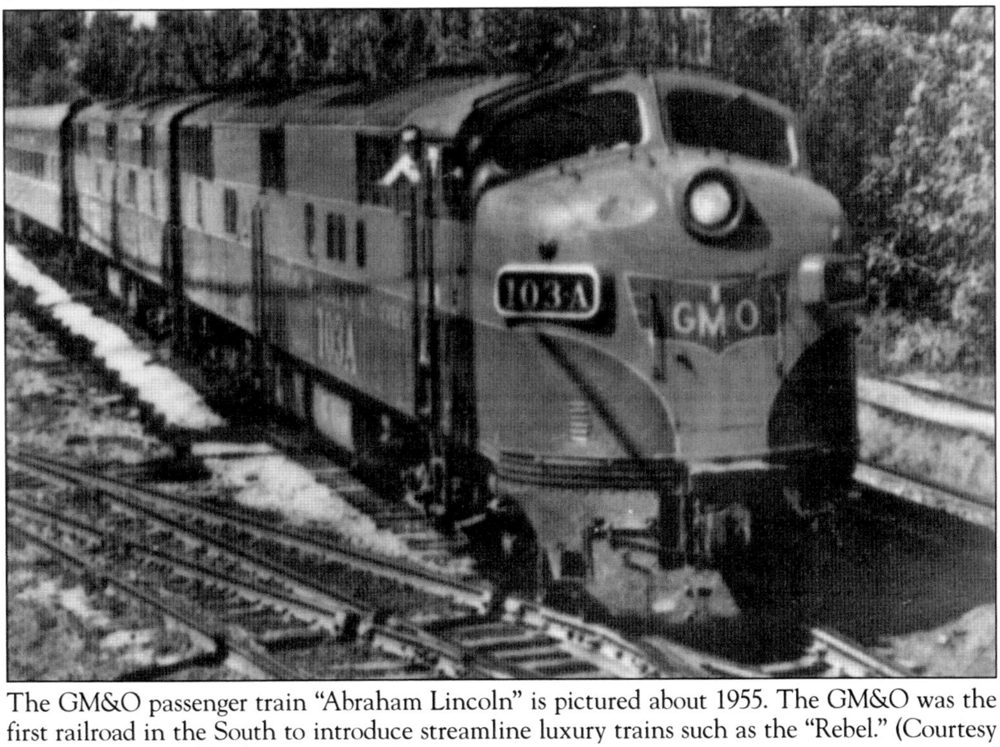

The GM&O passenger train "Abraham Lincoln" is pictured about 1955. The GM&O was the first railroad in the South to introduce streamline luxury trains such as the "Rebel." (Courtesy E. Maurice Stansell Sr.)

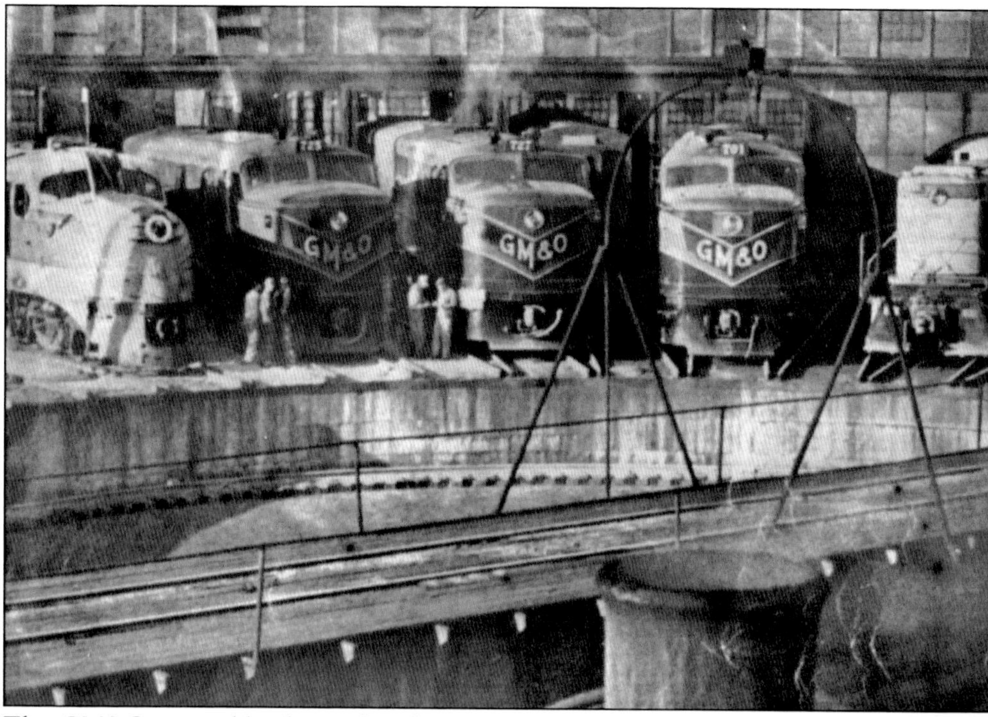

The GM&O turntable shows diesel engines lined up in front of the shop building. (Courtesy JMCL.)

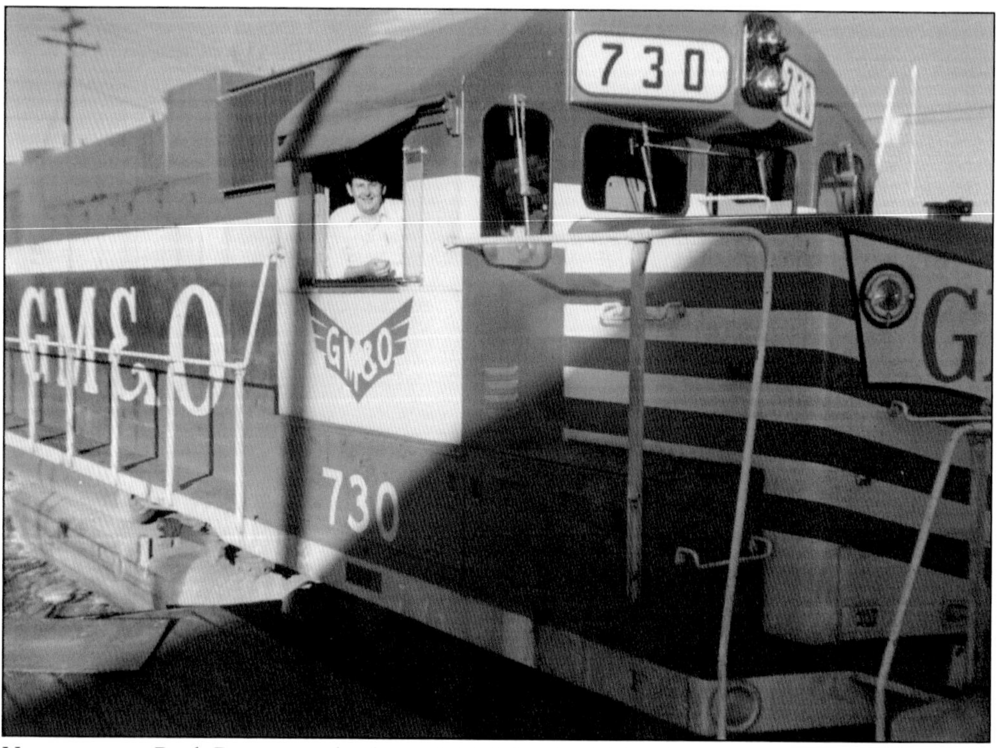

Here engineer Buck Barnett smiles from GM&O Engine 730 in 1972. (Courtesy Buck Barnett.)

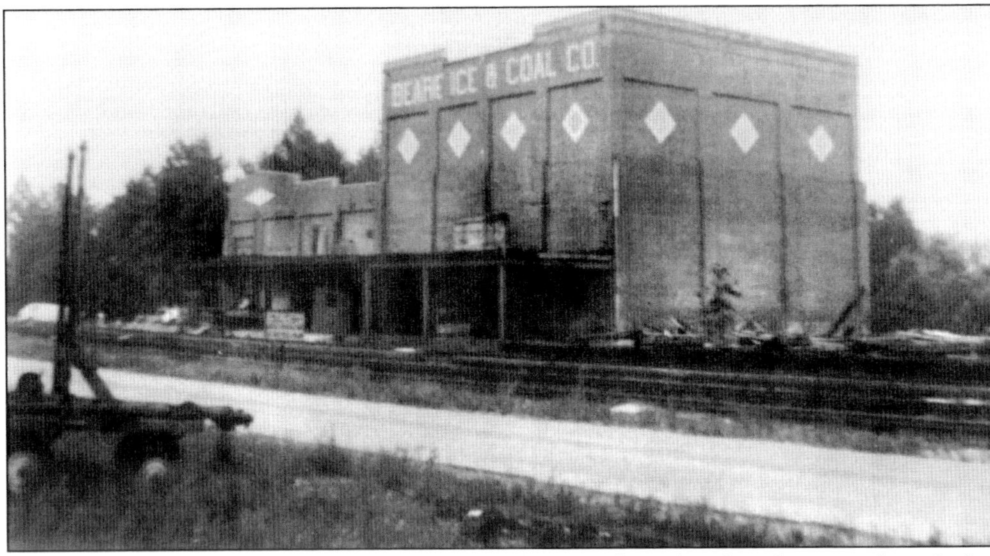

The Beare Ice and Coal Company operated in Jackson on the railroad tracks to supply ice before the days of refrigerator cars and to unload coal that would be sold to homes and businesses in the area. (Courtesy Buck Barnett.)

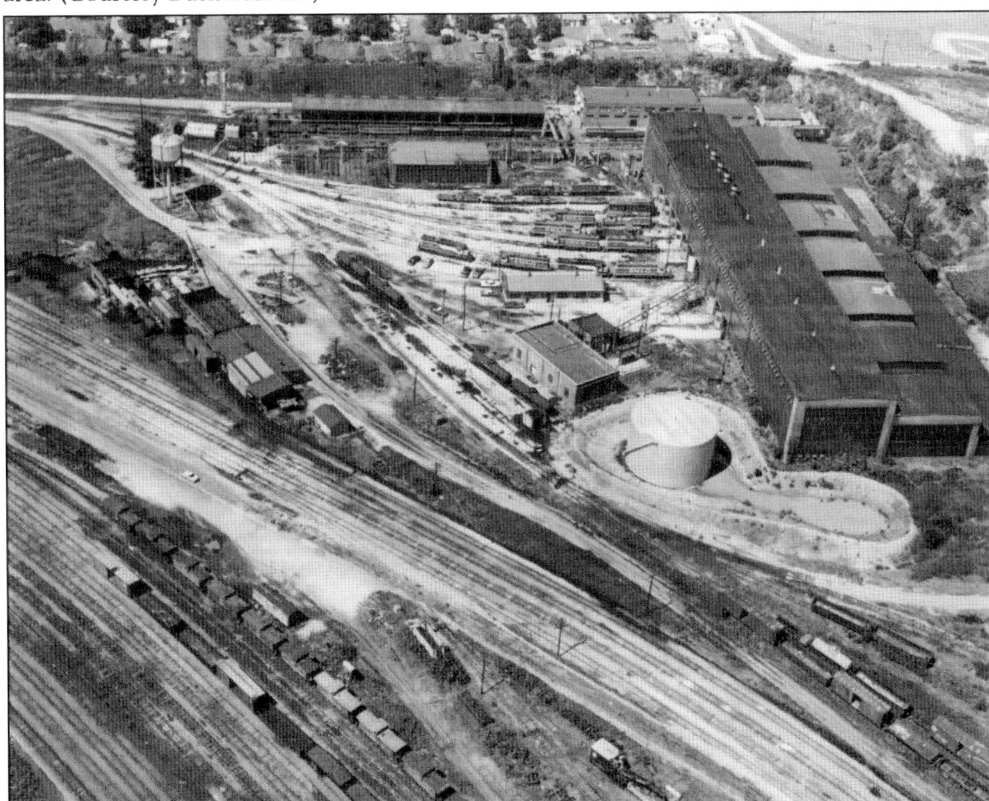

An aerial photograph of Iselin Yard in 1975 shows the extensive impact the yard had on Madison County's business and industrial development. (Courtesy Buck Barnett from the Herbert C. Murdaugh Collection.)

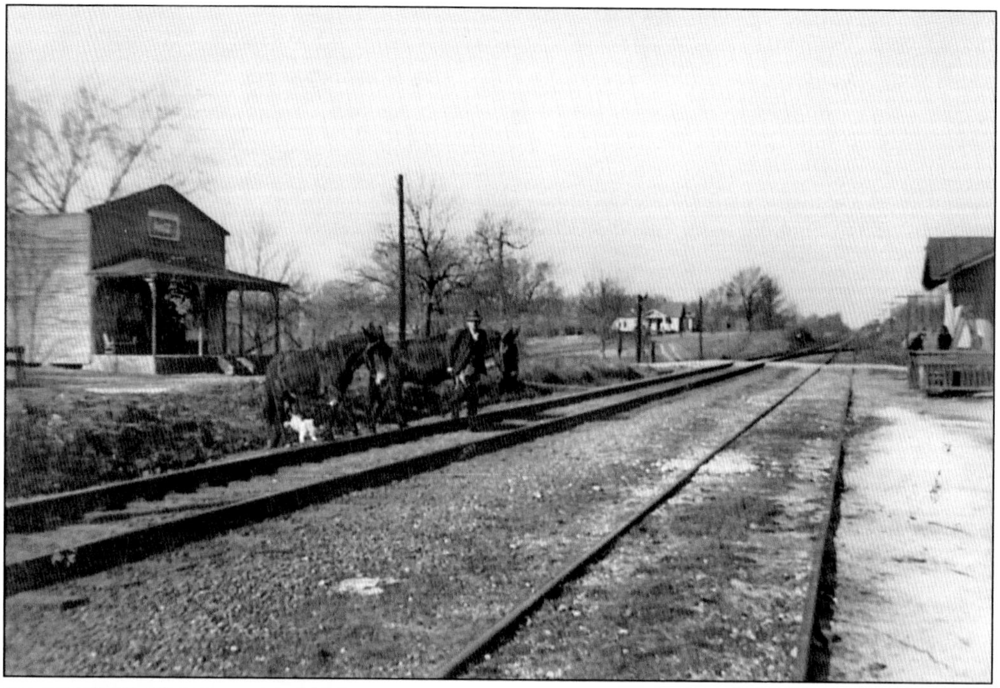

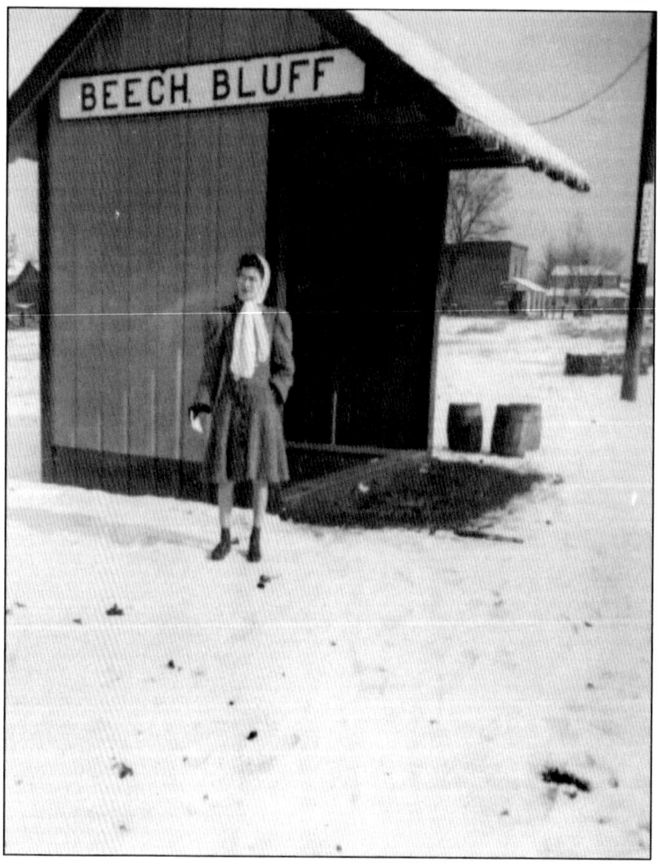

Beech Bluff, on the east-central edge of Madison County, was first known as Homer and was renamed when the railroad was built from 1888 to 1890. The last train ran on this line through Beech Bluff in 1981, and the tracks started being removed in June 1982. Shown in 1921 are, from left to right, S. B. Stayton, W. T. Ross, and George Fuller with mules Tom and Mary on the railroad tracks. The earlier depot can be seen on the right. After the old depot was torn down, the small depot (below) was built in 1944 and used by Beech Bluff residents like Mable May to catch the train to Jackson. (Both courtesy Murray May and Nina May Jones from *'Bout Beech Bluff.*)

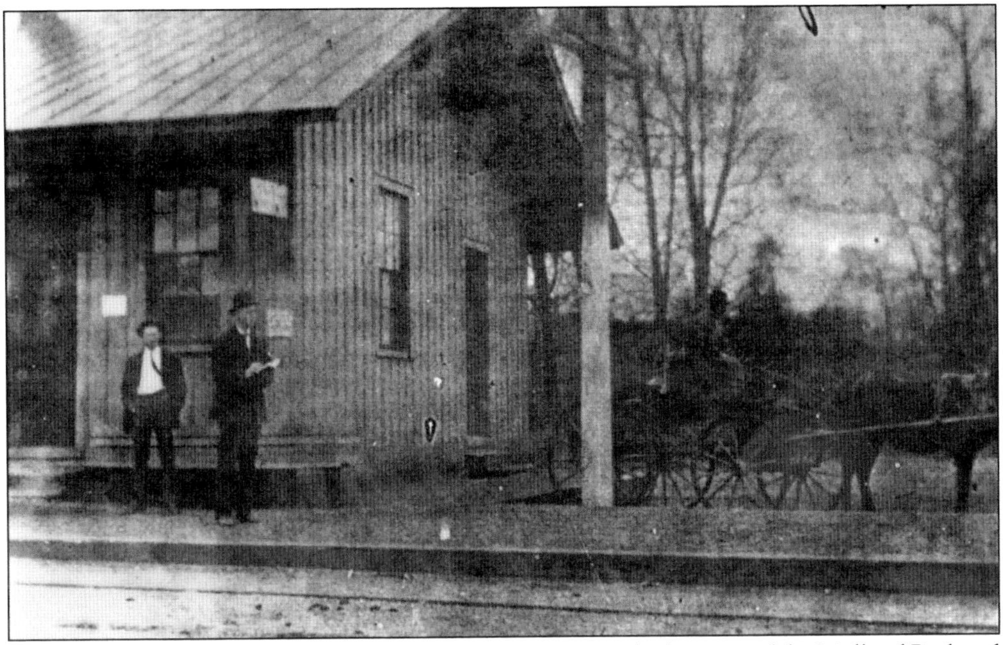

Mercer, a small town in southwest Madison County, came to be because of the Midland Railroad and the farsightedness of T. B. Mercer and his son, T. E. Mercer, who built a store at the crossroads of the stage road and the newly laid rails. When the railroad station was built in 1894, T. E. Mercer permitted his name to be used for the new village. The old depot shown above was closed after World War II and later sold. The tracks were uprooted and shipped away. The water tower (below) was an important addition to the rail yard at Mercer for fire protection as well as water for the engines. Lumber, as shown in this picture, was the largest shipment by rail from Mercer. (Both courtesy BBCHA.)

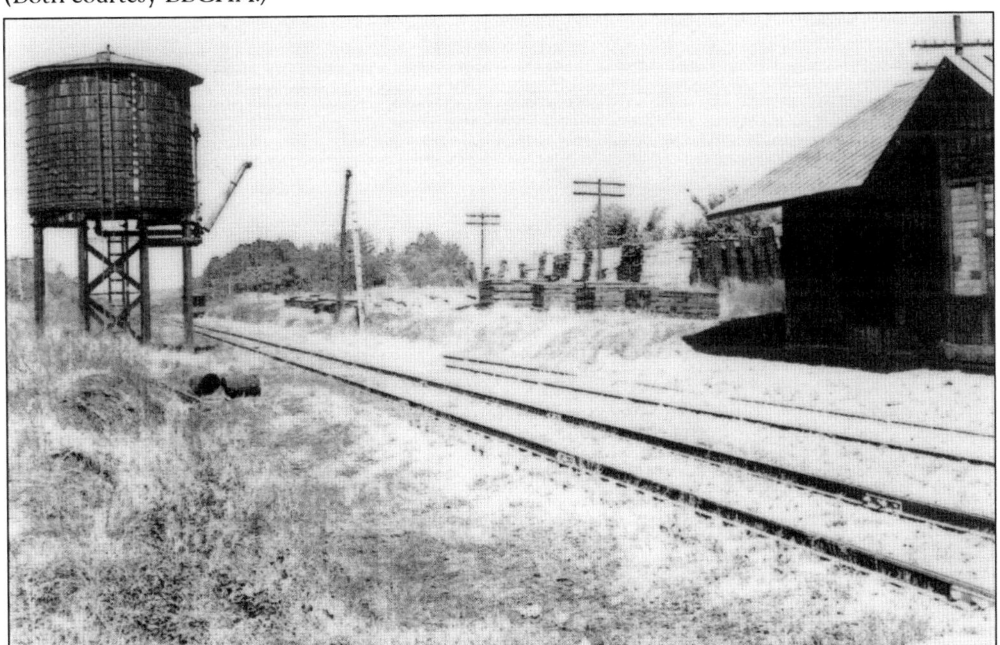

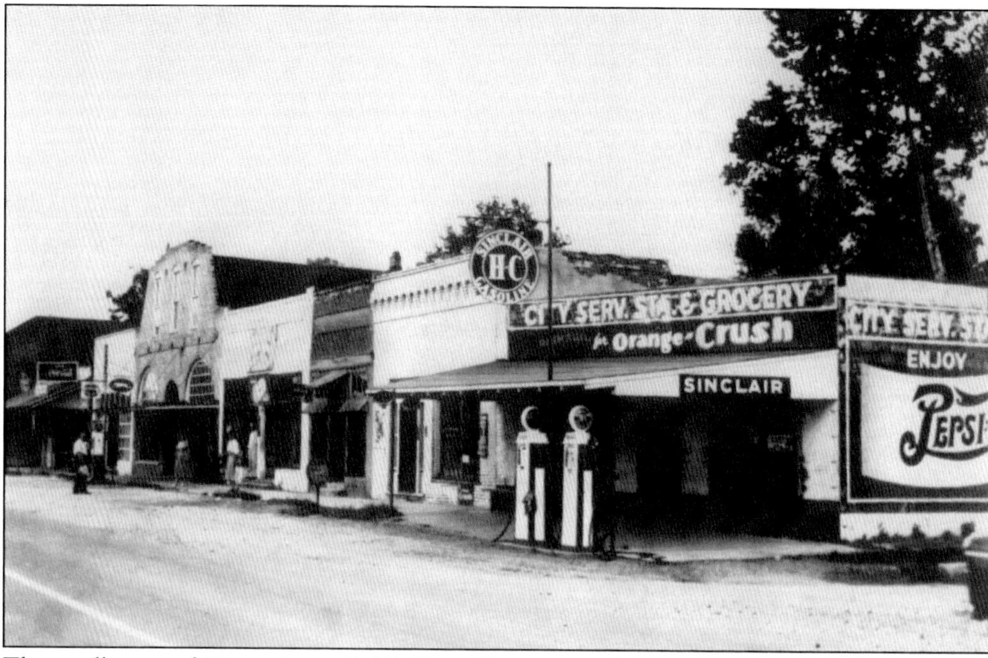

The small town of Pinson in south Madison County was thriving on the M&O Railroad until March 11, 1923, when a F-5 tornado demolished most of its structures. This picture shows the "wide spot in the road" as it looked in the 1950s. (Courtesy Linda Wilson Holder and the Pinson Community Cookbook.)

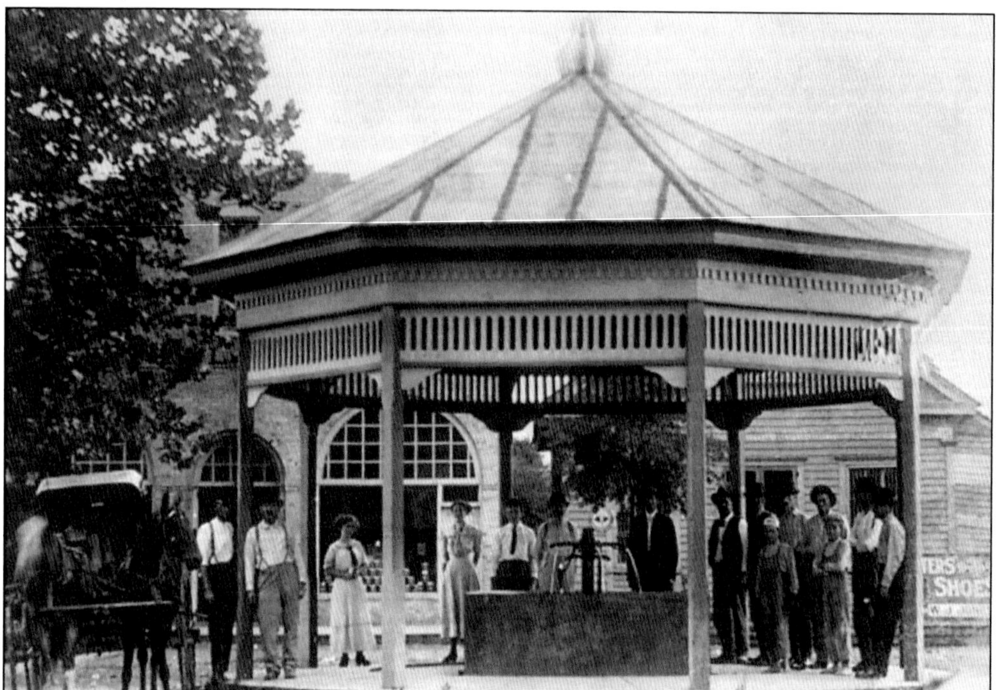

The roadside artesian well that stands by the railroad tracks in Pinson has long been a symbol of the town. (Courtesy Linda Wilson Holder and the Pinson Community Cookbook.)

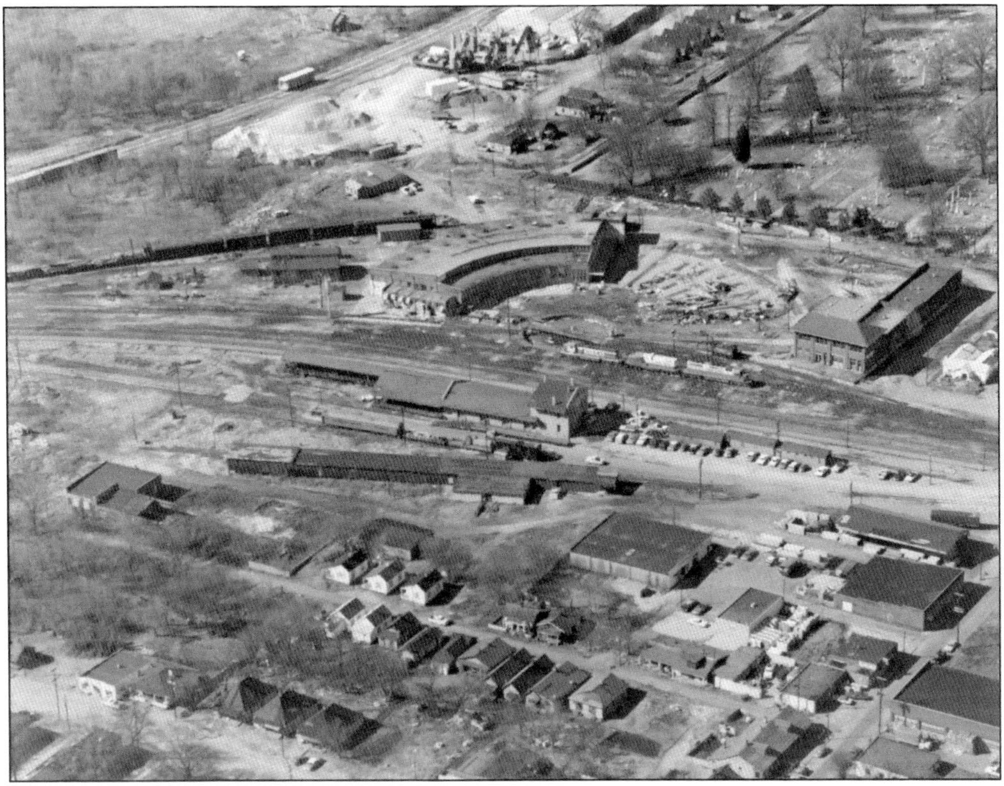

The aerial view of the Illinois Central roundhouse and freight yard in the 1960s shows the roundhouse being demolished. (Courtesy JMCL.)

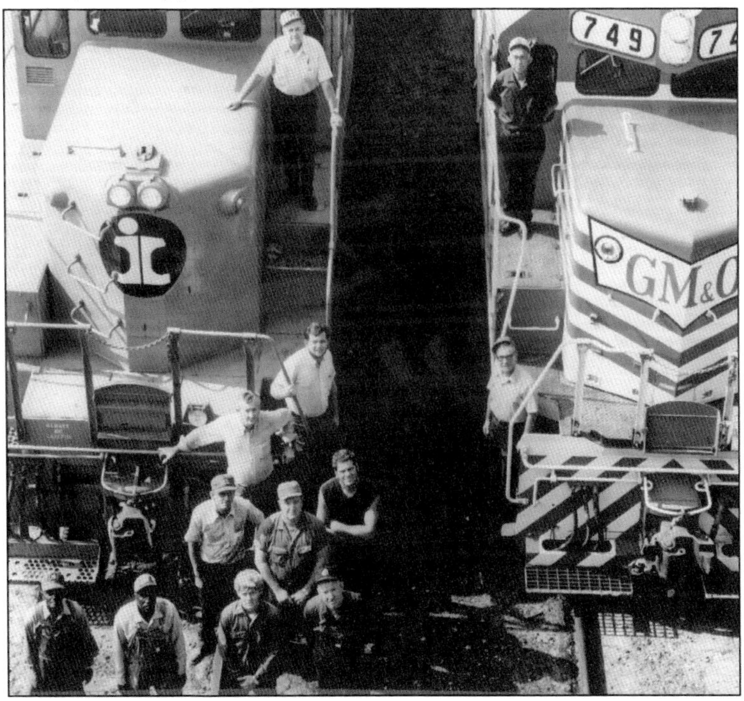

August 10, 1972, is the day GM&O Railroad and Illinois Central Railroad merged. Identified workers are Charles Patrick at the top of the Illinois Central engine and Donnie Stegall (the first one standing down on the Illinois Central engine); other Illinois Central workers are unidentified. Allen Stewart is at the top of the GM&O engine, and Albert Higgins is on the front of GM&O Engine 749. (Courtesy Helen F. Higgins.)

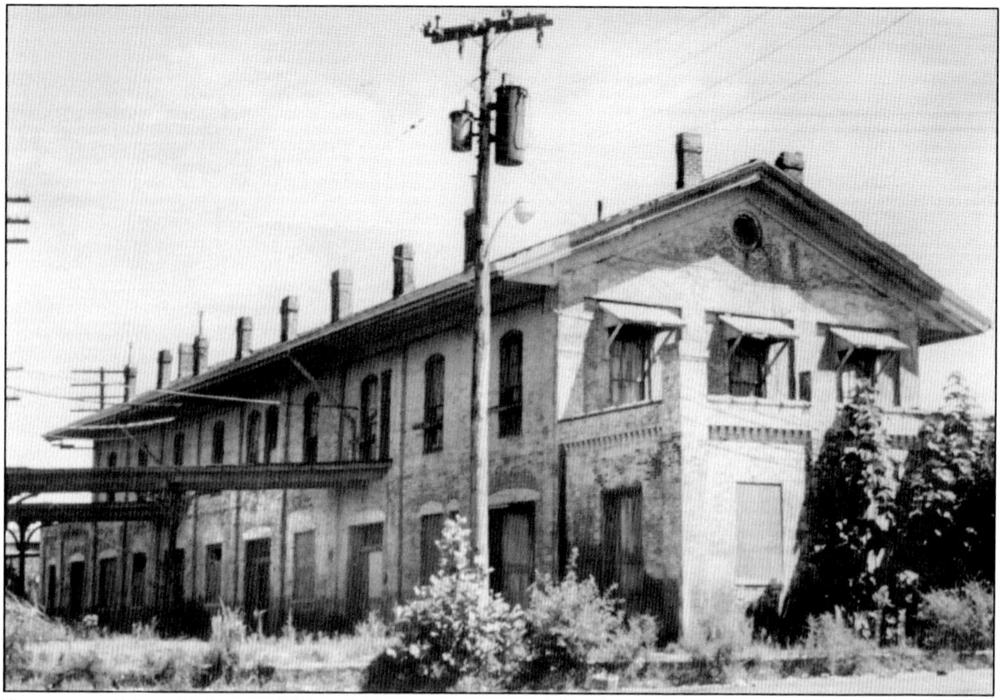

Remains of the old depot off Royal Street are signs of the diminished importance of the railroad. The vine-covered, vacant building caught fire and then was demolished in the 1980s. (Courtesy Norwood Jones.)

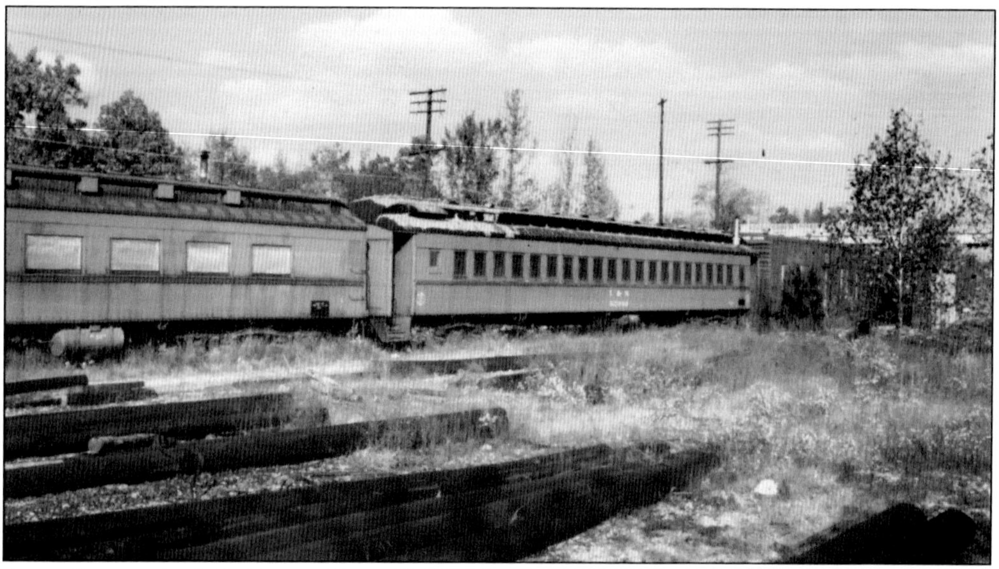

According to the I. B. Tigrett file in JMCL, October 14, 1958, marked the end of almost 100 years of passenger service between Mobile and St. Louis. This 1970s photograph of abandoned passenger cars is a sign of times past because no passenger trains travel through Jackson anymore. (Photograph by William McCommon, courtesy Kathleen McCommon.)

Two

Bemis Cotton Mill Town

In the 1890s, rumors were heard that the Bemis Bag Company of St. Louis wanted to build a cotton mill in the South, close to the raw material, a good labor source, and a rail line that could easily ship the finished product to New Orleans, St. Louis, and other major markets. Officials with the Illinois Central Railroad wanted the industry located on their rail line. Local citizens requested the Madison County legislative body to purchase 300 acres for $6,000 and turn it over to the Bemis Bag Company to construct a 20,000-spindle cotton mill. The first vote was 20 to 15 in favor of the very first industrial land to be purchased by the county. The chair pronounced the motion had died. However, in the afternoon, it was pointed out that the motion did not require a two-thirds majority. Another vote was taken, and the result was 19 to 15 in favor—it passed. Bemis broke ground in the spring of 1900, and the first mill was completed and spinning by June 1, 1901, while construction on worker houses on the north and south sides of the mill took place. The first house was built for the resident plant manager, J. B. Young. Bemis benefited from top-notch, nationally known urban planners and architects in designing the town, and the company also provided community facilities such as the company store, recreation facilities, schools, fire protection, wide streets, and sidewalks, with well-built houses for families.

Jobs provided by the cotton mill and its facilities drew families into Madison County from all over West Tennessee.

By 1950, the Bemis Company had 1,400 employees and was the largest employer in Madison County. Population in the little mill village reached 4,000. By late 1960s, the Bemis Company had sold most of the company-owned houses, and the area was annexed by the City of Jackson in 1977. The Bemis Company sold the mill in 1980, and in 1991, it closed as a cotton mill. Today the mill building is used as a warehouse.

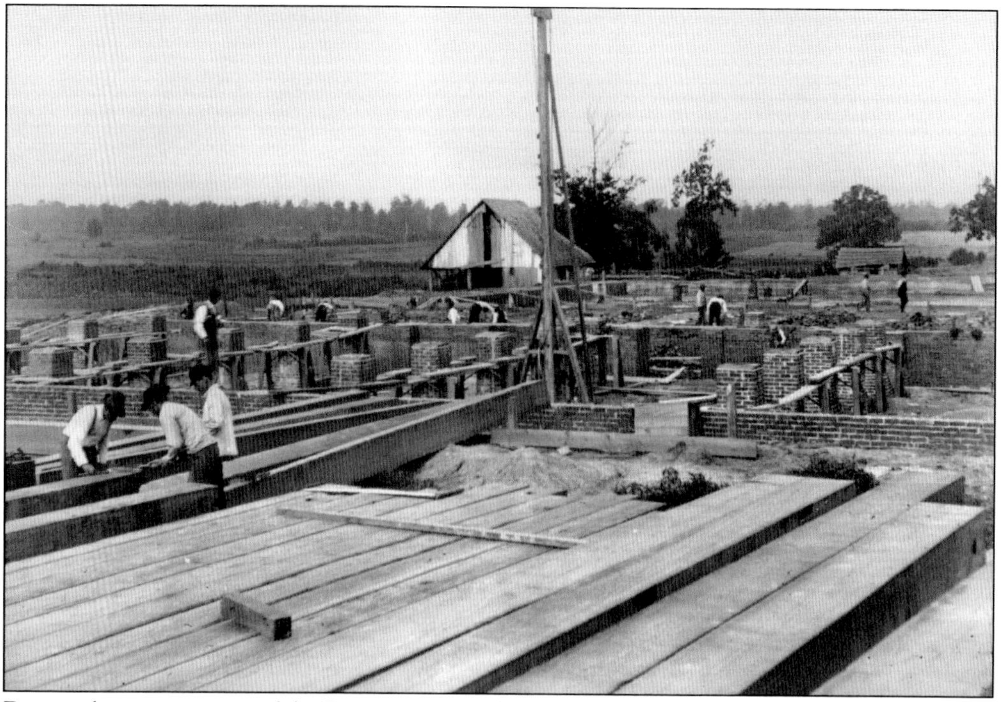

During the construction of the Bemis cotton mill in 1900, bricks for the four-story building were made at the construction site. In the beginning, no road existed to the construction site from Jackson, so workers were brought by rail in the morning and taken back at night. (Courtesy Tennessee Textiles.)

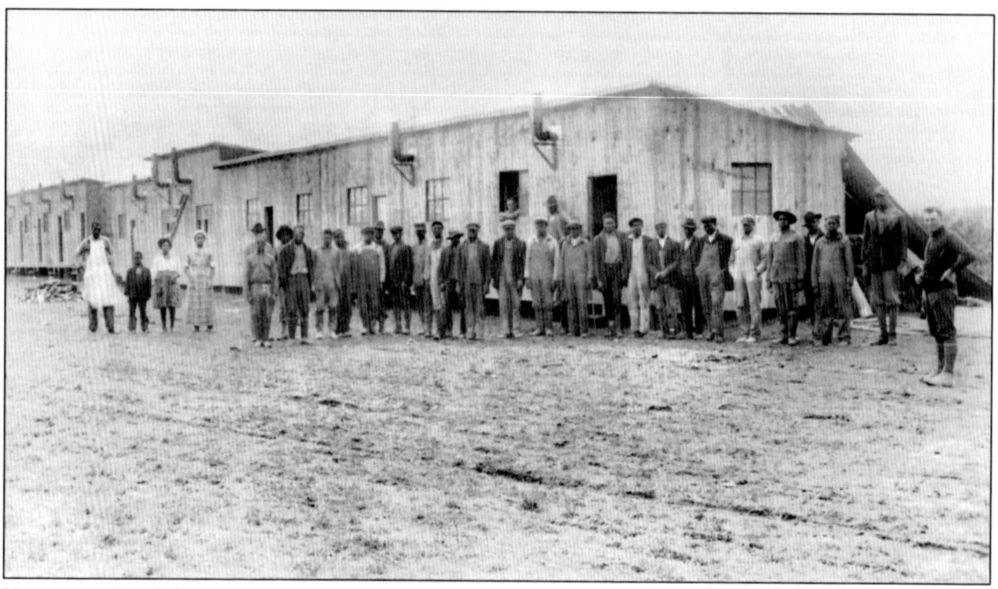

Known as Beulah Camp, temporary shelter was set up for workers in the early days as well as during the 1920s construction spurt in Bemis. (Courtesy Bemis Historical Society.)

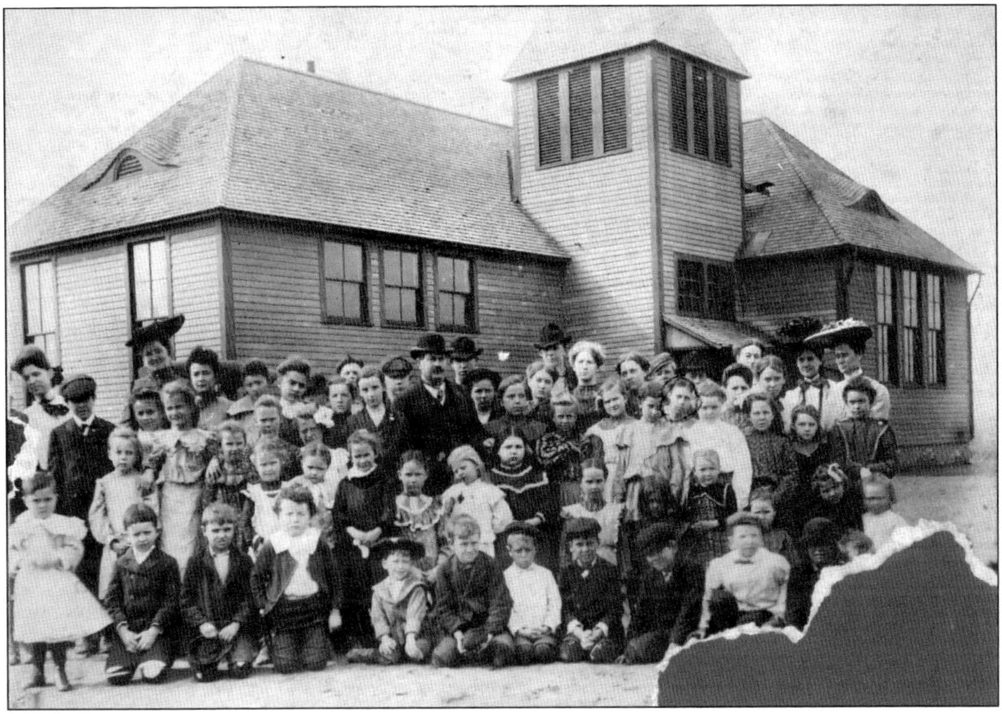

The white clapboard building with a small tower in the center served as the first Bemis schoolhouse. (Courtesy Bemis Historical Society.)

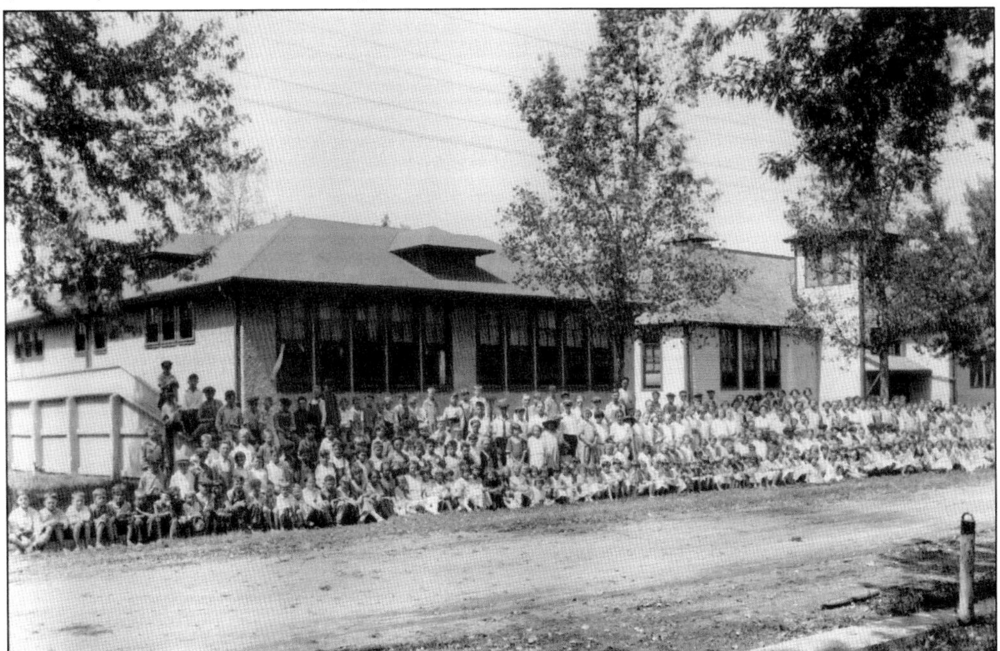

Seen here are 387 pupils in the Bemis schools in 1922. The white clapboard building and the brown stucco building were used in the 1920s and 1930s for the Bemis elementary and high school students. (Courtesy Rosalee Gibbons, Mary Jane Tapley, and Walter Helms.)

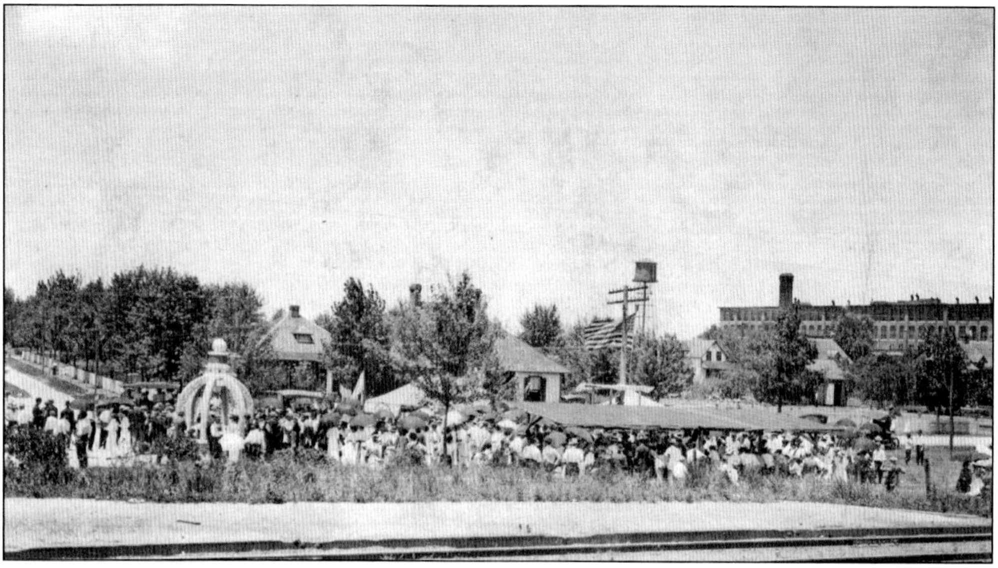

A large patriotic celebration was held around 1914. Above is the water fountain built over an artesian well and dedicated on October 26, 1913. Bemis residents raised funds for the memorial drinking fountain to honor Judson Moss Bemis. The hexagonal structure over the fountain was shaped like a queen's crown. Matthew 7:2 was inscribed on a bronze drum plaque under the spherical dome to express their respect for the Bemis founder. A park, first developed between 1900 and 1905 with many alterations and improvement over the years, is next to the fountain. The picture below, also made around the 1914 patriotic celebration, featured the new and popular Coca-Cola drink. (Both courtesy Betsy Babb and the Bemis Historical Society.)

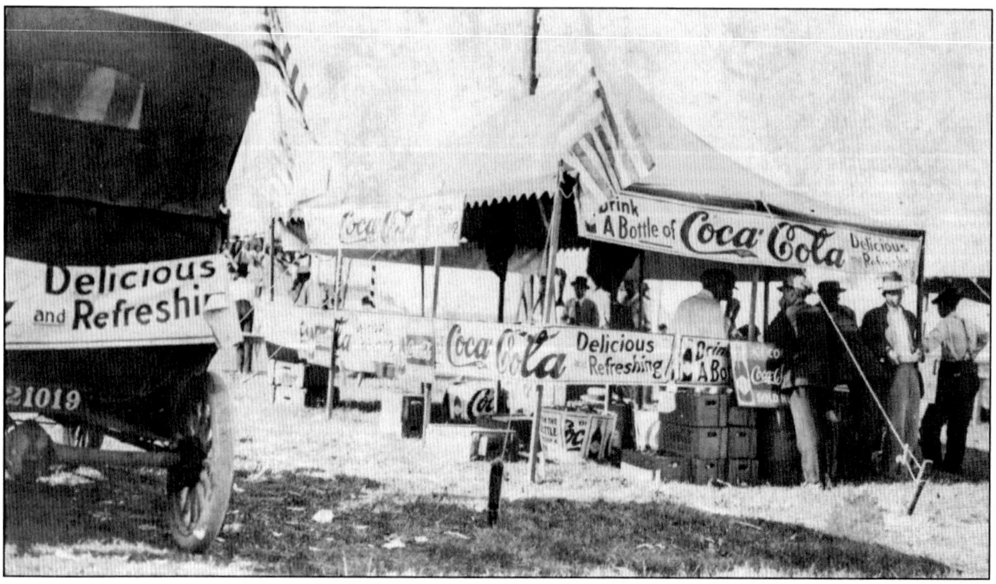

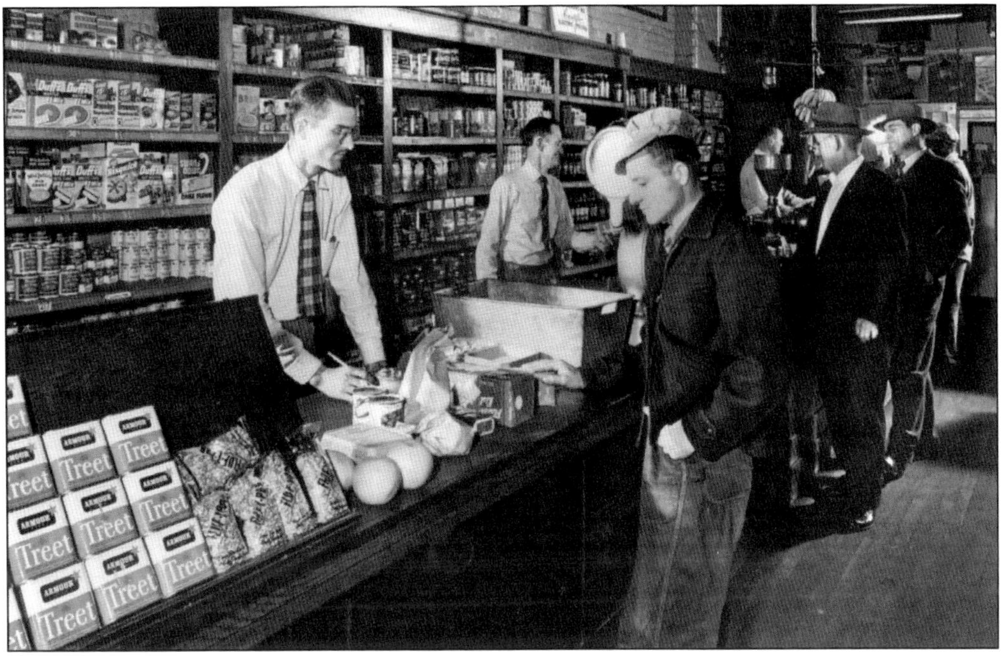

The Bemis Mercantile Store, known as the company store, opened in 1902. Shown here in the late 1940s, the store was a modern grocery with a meat department as well as dry goods. Mill workers were paid in cash, not script. From left to right are Joe Mooney, Curtis Dill, Dave West, Colis Austin, C. V. Hughes, W. C. Johnson, and L. D. Exum. (Courtesy Tennessee Textiles.)

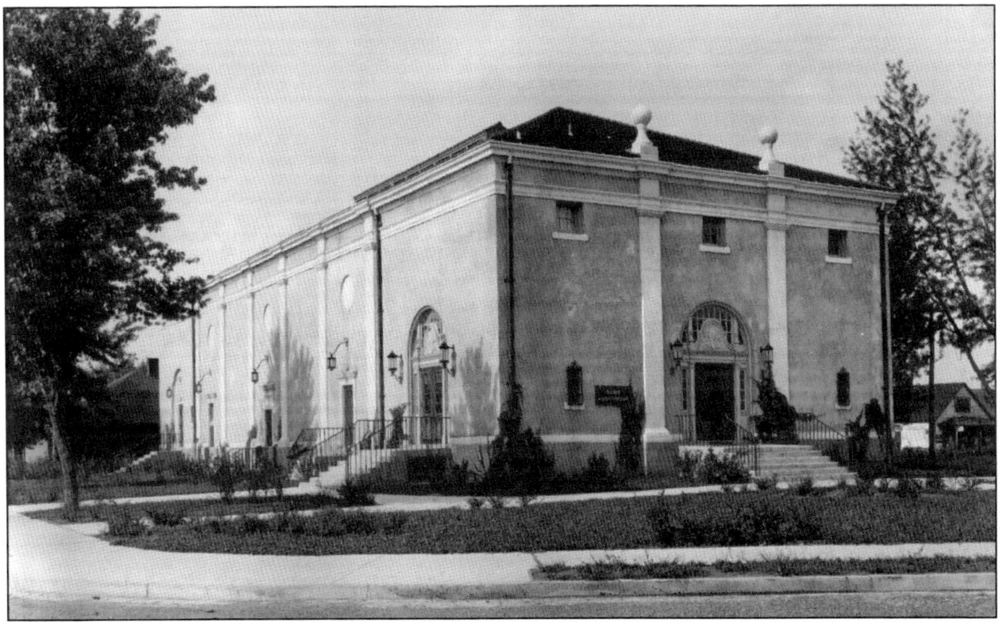

The newly constructed Bemis Auditorium is shown here in 1922. The auditorium/theater was the cultural center of the mill town. This building was designed in 1920 by the famous architect Andrew Hepburn and was landscaped by Arthur Shurcliff through the Boston Housing Company, which was owned by Albert Farwell Bemis, son of Judson Moss Bemis. (Courtesy Rosalee Gibbons, Mary Jane Tapley, and Walter Helms.)

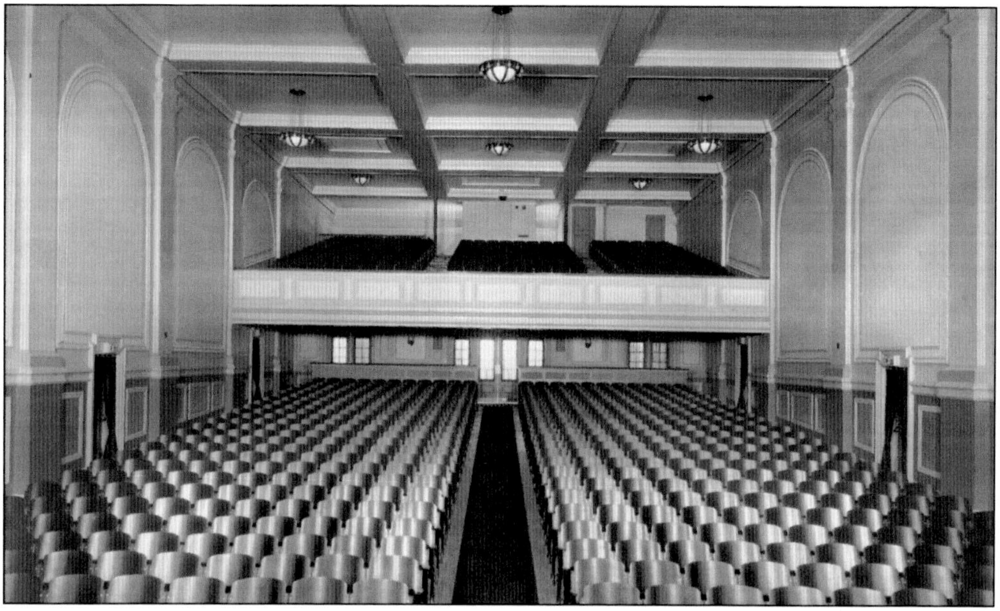

These 1922 pictures show the inside of the Bemis Auditorium, which served as a movie theater as well as a place for plays, high school graduations, and other programs. The picture above was taken from the stage and shows the expanse of the seating, including the balcony. The picture below was taken from the back or entrance lobby and shows the slanting floor, wooden seats, wing walls, and stage. In the late 1990s, Bemis Historical Society was formed, and its first project was to purchase and preserve the auditorium. Now the architecturally significant building is being converted into the Bemis Mill Village Museum. (Both courtesy Rosalee Gibbons, Mary Jane Tapley, and Walter Helms.)

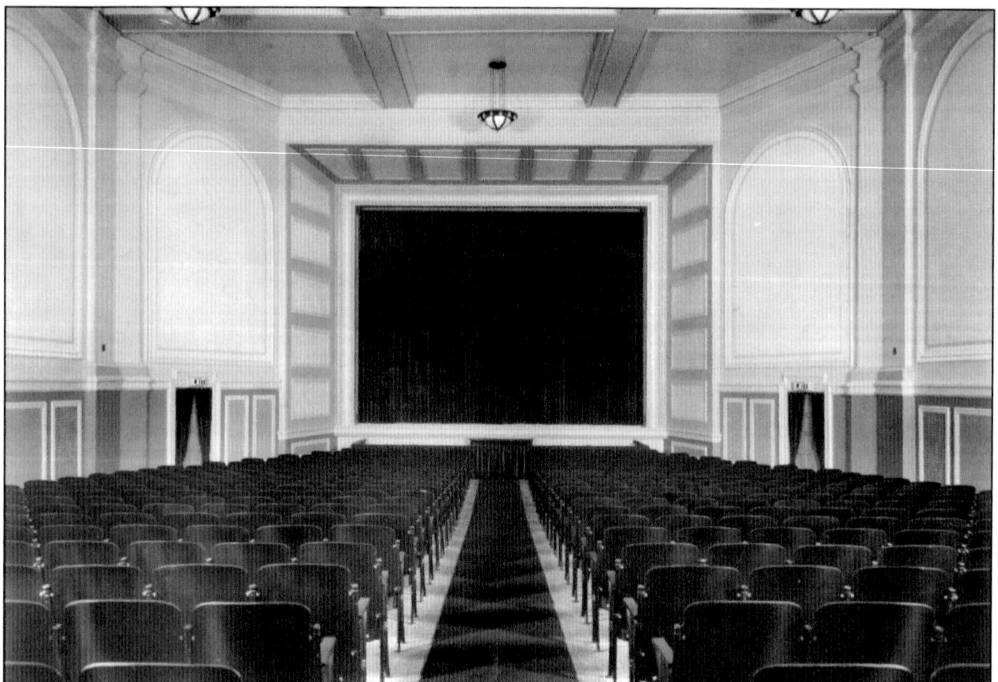

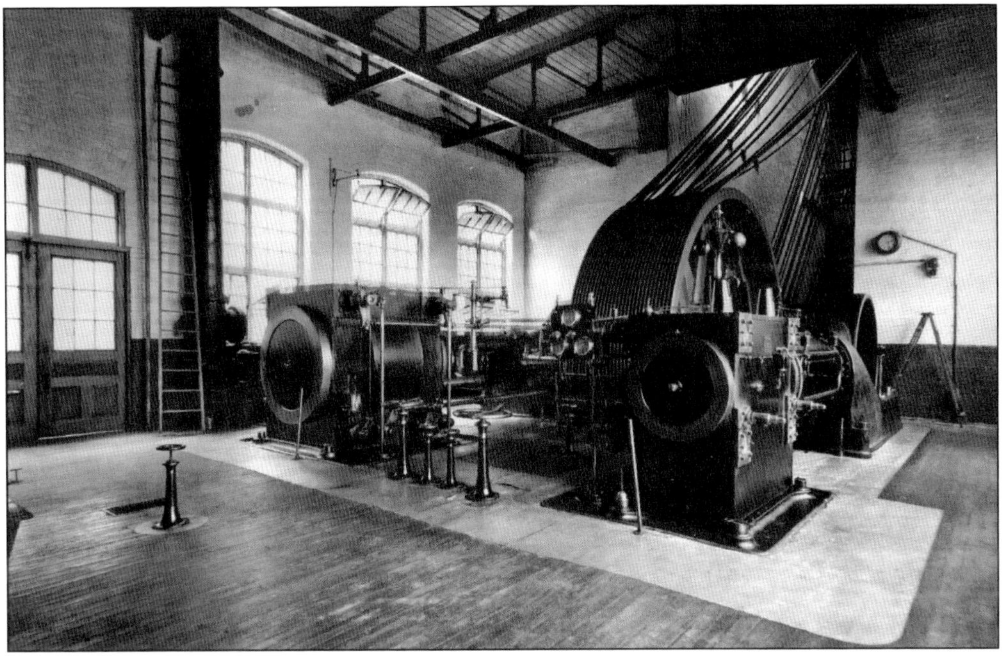

Engine Room Two in the Bemis Cotton Mill in 1922 illustrates the "monster enterprise" predicted by the *Jackson Daily Sun*'s editor in 1900. Each mill was driven by separate cross-compound Corlis engines to eliminate the potential for downtime. This engine, serving the second mill, generated 1,600 horsepower. (Courtesy Rosalee Gibbons, Mary Jane Tapley, and Walter Helms.)

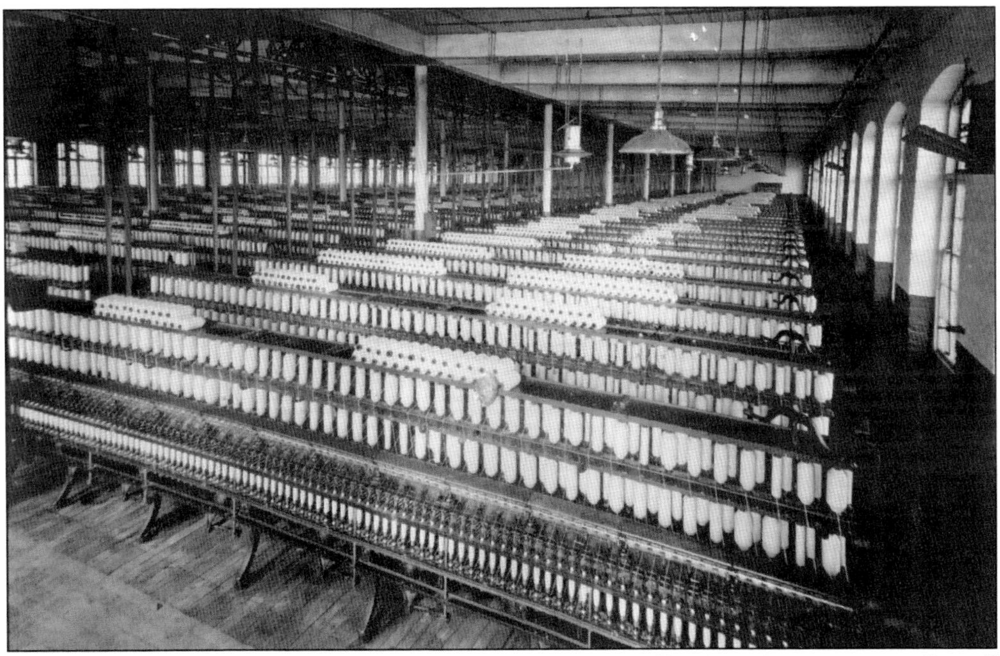

The spinning room, pictured in 1922, shows many more spindles than the 20,000-spindle mill had when it started making cloth in 1901. The completion of Mill No. 2 brought an additional 25,728 ring spindles online for a total of 56,728. (Courtesy Rosalee Gibbons, Mary Jane Tapley, and Walter Helms.)

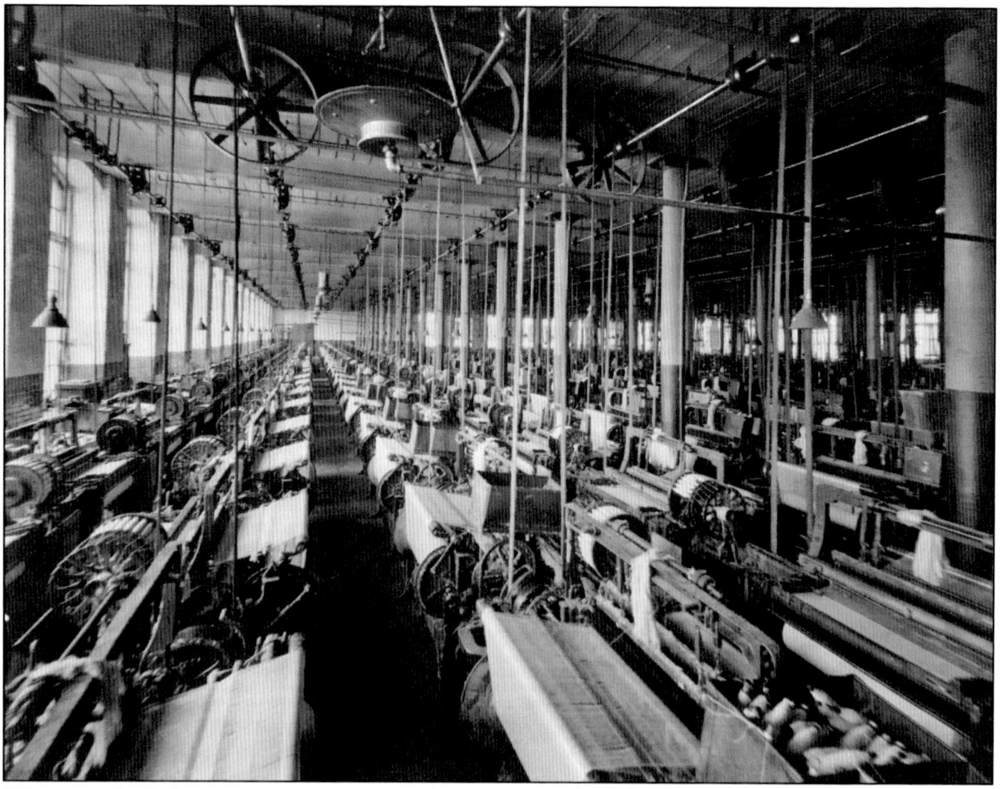

Weaving cloth from raw cotton material was the goal of the Bemis Brothers Bag Company. (Courtesy Rosalee Gibbons, Mary Jane Tapley, and Walter Helms.)

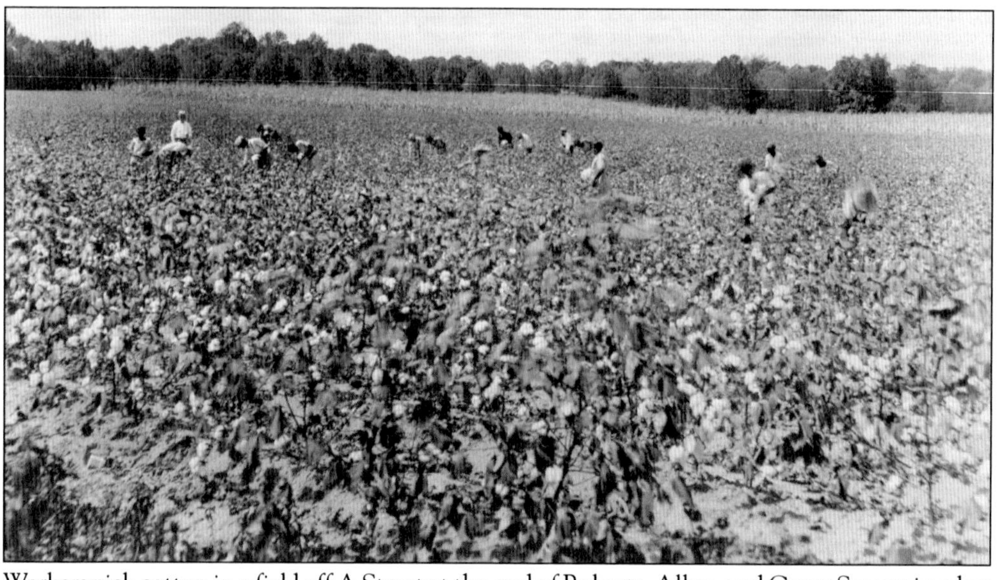

Workers pick cotton in a field off A Street at the end of Roberts, Allen, and Gregg Streets in what was known as "New Town." (Courtesy Rosalee Gibbons, Mary Jane Tapley, and Walter Helms.)

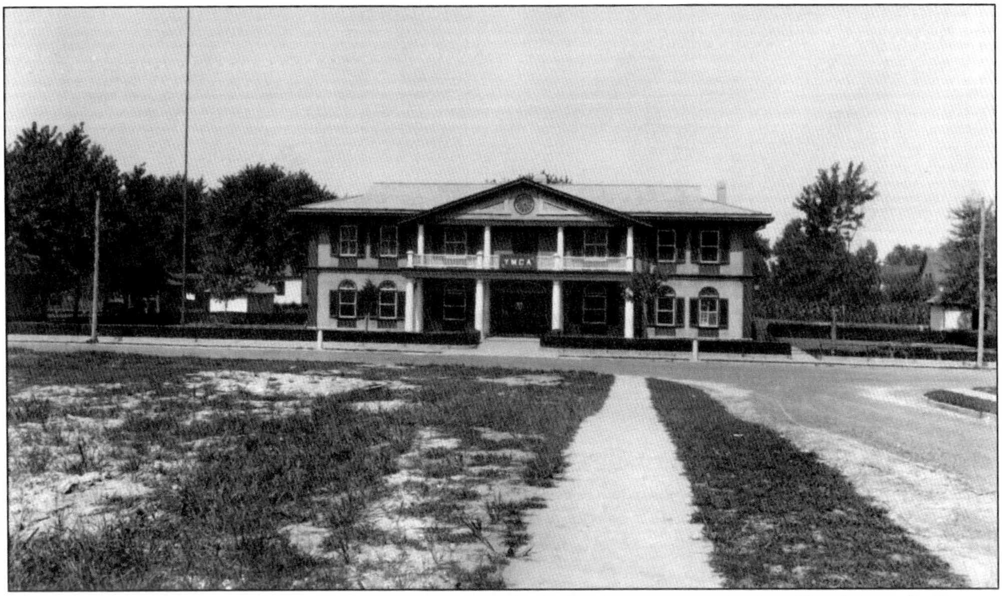

The Bemis Brothers Bag Company not only provided jobs, housing, and school buildings for Bemis residents, they also provided leisure activities through the YMCA, built as early as 1914–1916. The Colonial Revival–style stucco two-story building was for men (below), but in 1939, the company built an adjoining brick building that housed joint activities for males and females, including the skating rink with large gym and recreation room upstairs. Children had a place to go while parents worked. Classes were given to workers who needed to further their education. Various clubs had meeting rooms. The mill had a basketball team, and regional basketball tournaments were held there. The Y taught teamwork, which was good for workers in the mill. (Both courtesy Rosalee Gibbons, Mary Jane Tapley, and Walter Helms.)

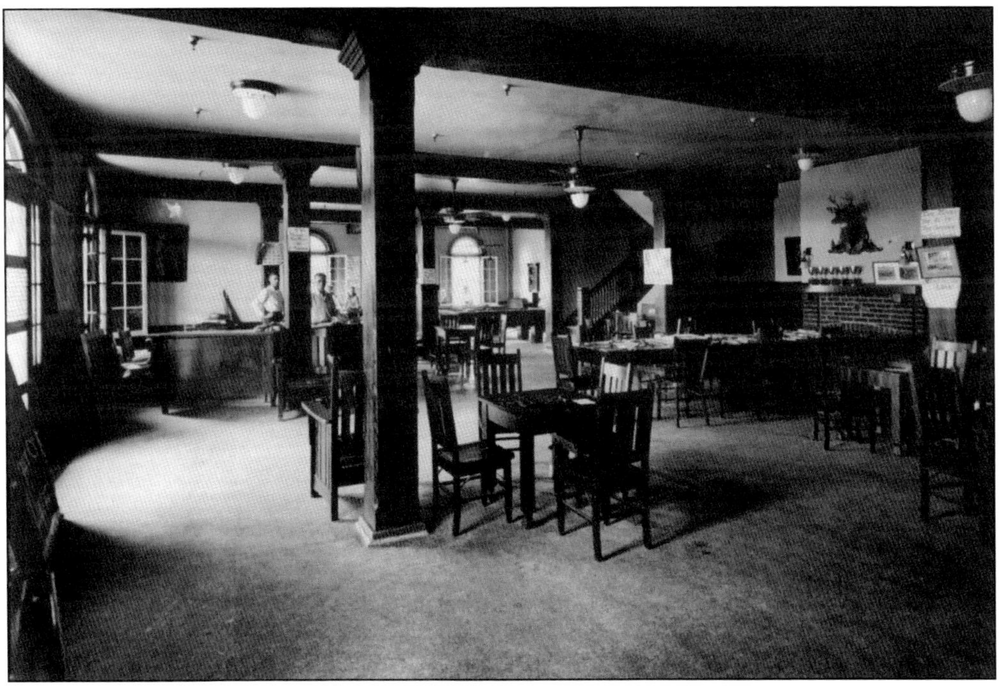

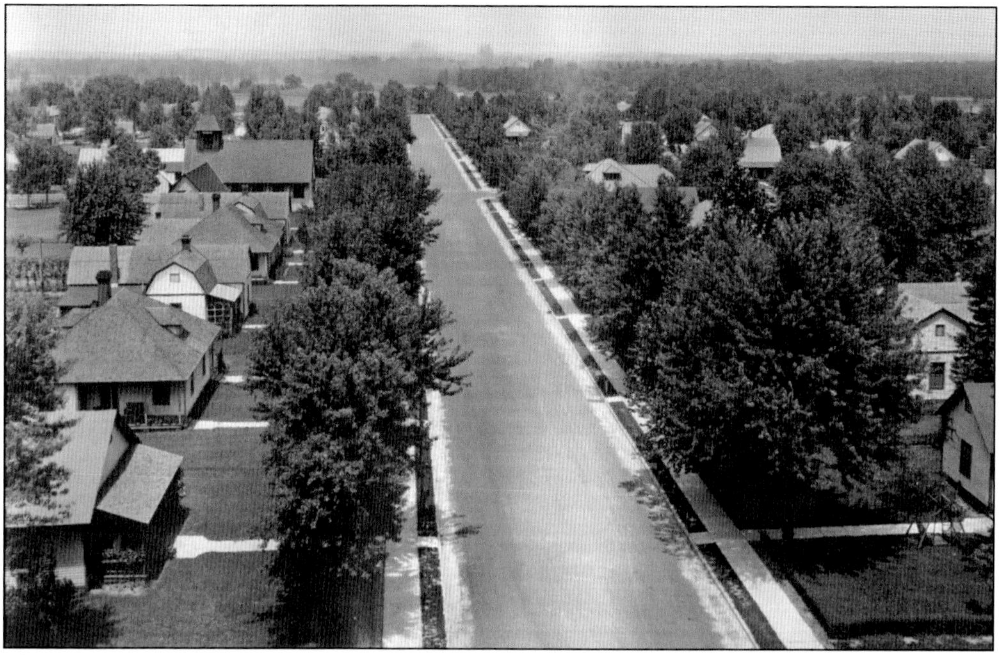

This picture was taken from the roof of the four-story mill looking north on Massachusetts Street. Note the wide, tree-lined streets, the varied styles of houses—no cookie-cutter construction—and the beautiful Tudor Revival and eclectic Gothic Revival church roof and steeple. (Courtesy Rosalee Gibbons, Mary Jane Tapley, and Walter Helms.)

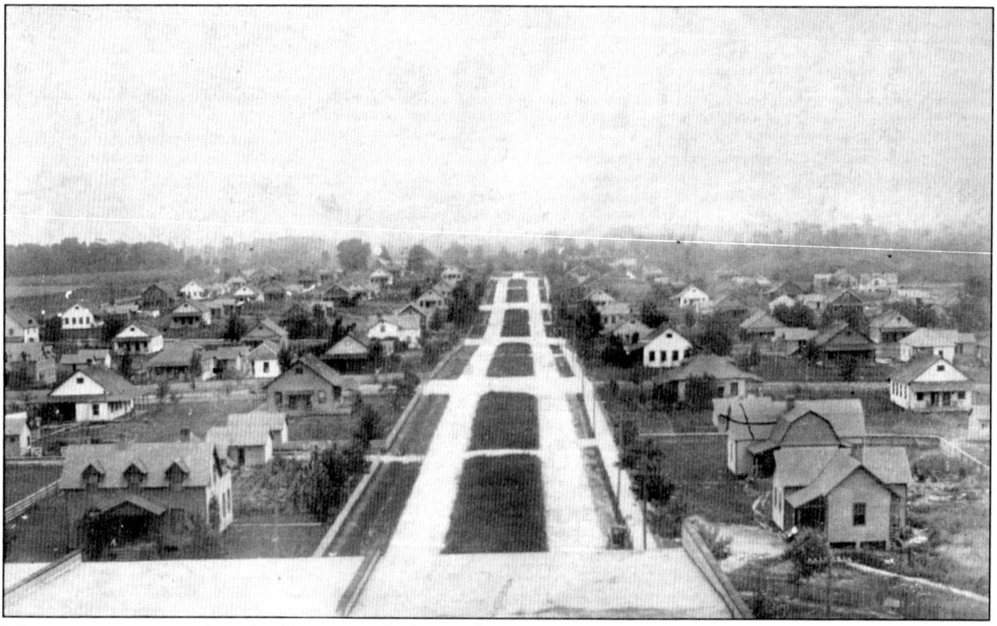

This picture was taken looking south from the top of the mill down the wide Massachusetts Street, with a grassy median and sidewalks. Even though horses and buggies were the mode of transportation when the town of Bemis was built, the modern urban planners designed wide streets with medians and sidewalks that could easily handle the coming automobile. (Courtesy Bemis Historical Society.)

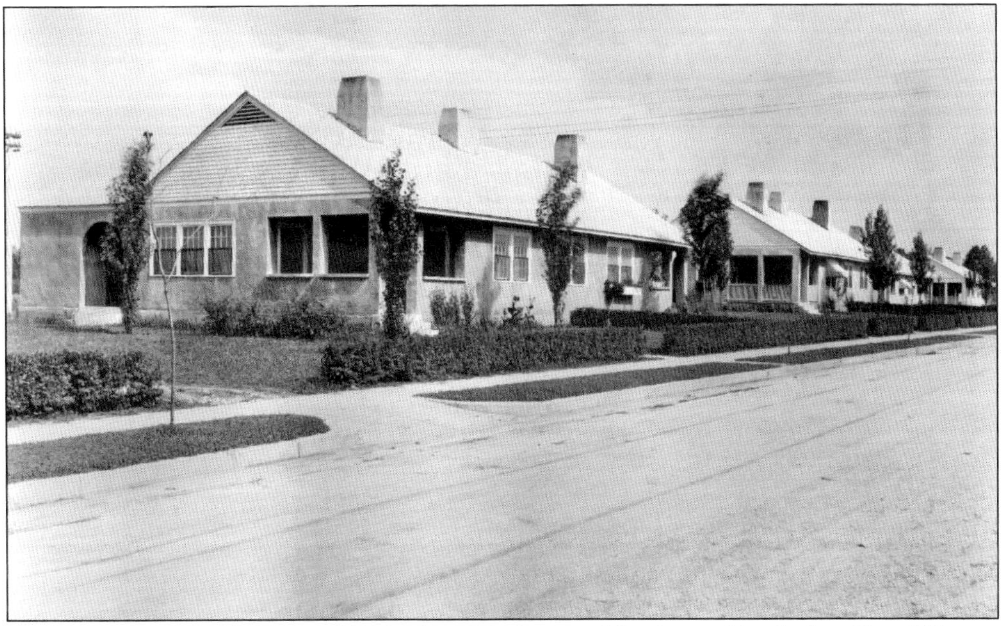

Homes in Silver Circle, designed by Andrew Hepburn and landscaped by Arthur Shurcliff, were built in the 1920 renovation program of Bemis. At first, the houses were stucco, but the humid conditions caused the stucco to fall off, and the houses were refinished with a silver siding instead. Stucco stayed on the auditorium, the office building, and a school building. (Courtesy Rosalee Gibbons, Mary Jane Tapley, and Walter Helms.)

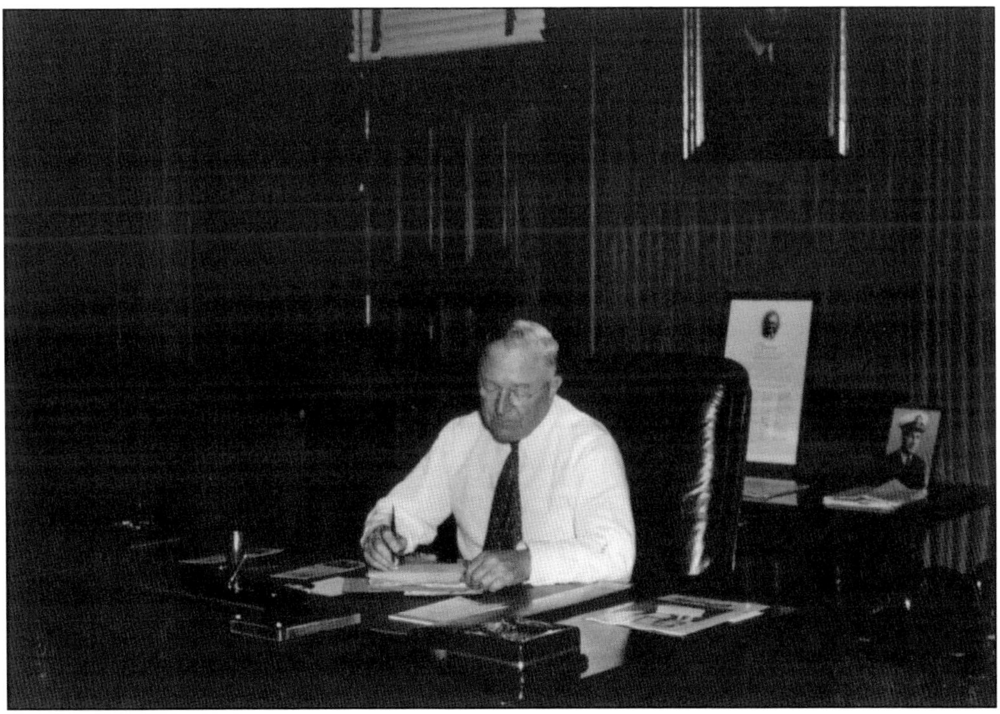

The Bemis general manager shown here is Fred Young, sitting in his office under a picture of J. B. Young, the first manager in the cotton mill town. (Courtesy Tennessee Textiles.)

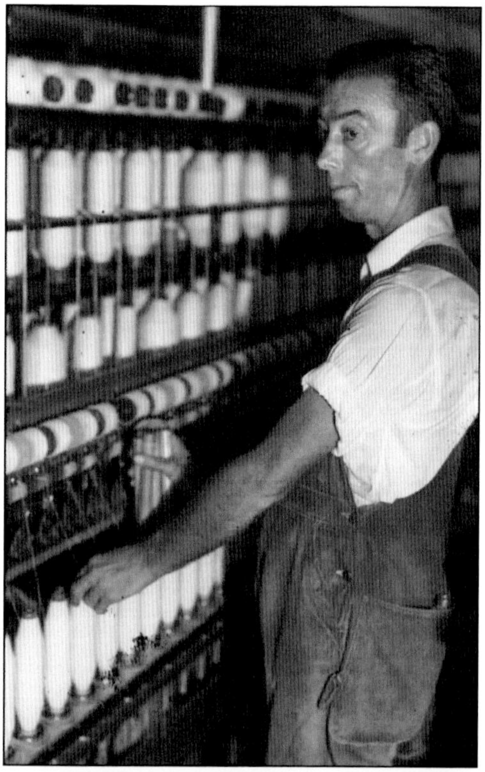

J. F. Davidson was a worker at Bemis Cotton Mill in the late 1940s. (Courtesy JMCL.)

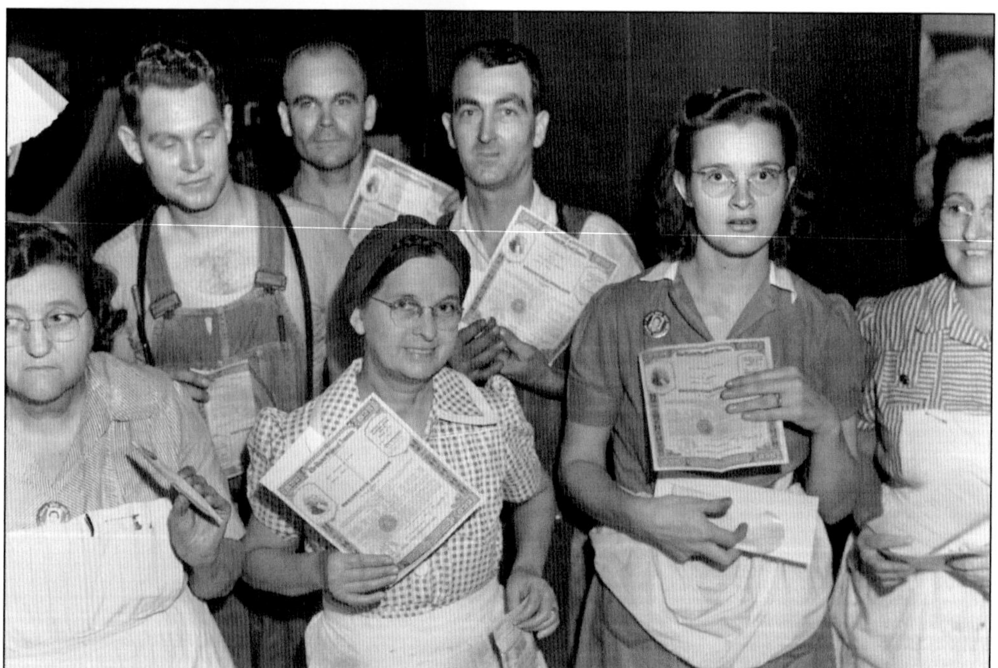

Bemis workers proudly display their War Bonds, purchased on payday. In the back row are, from left to right, Elco Hensley, B. Taylor, and Homer Hampton; the people in the first row are unidentified. (Courtesy Bemis Historical Society.)

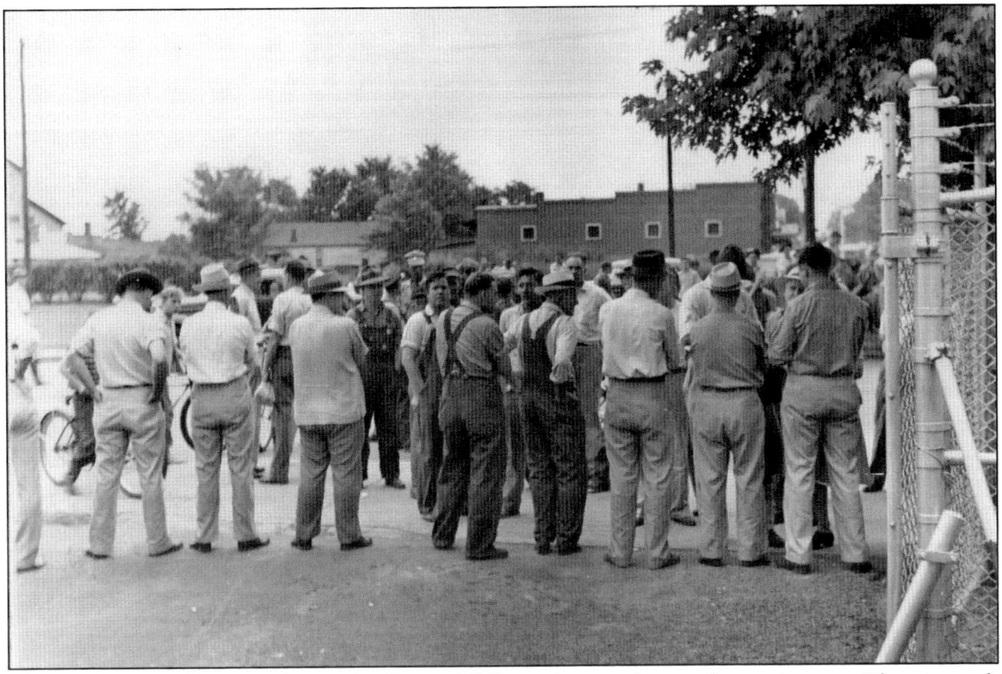

During the 1946 labor strike at the Bemis Mill, workers picket at the main gate. The six-week strike by the textile workers ended in a 10¢ raise. (Courtesy Bemis Historical Society.)

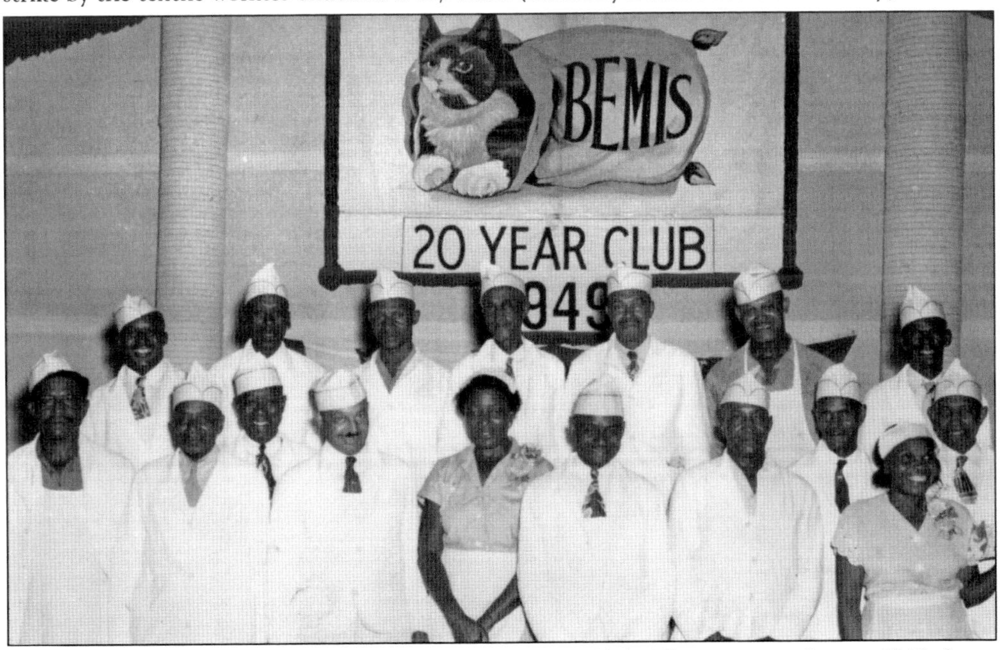

Loyal employees were recognized in the Bemis 20 Year Club. This picture taken in 1949 shows the existing segregation even in employee recognitions. From left to right are (first row) Joe Pope, Lewis Savage, Lee Spencer, George Swink, Viola Currie, Carnell Bell, Willie Butler, Ben Miller, Martha Williams, and Richard Butler; (second row) Ransom Hammond, Future Mercer, James Ivory, Henry Weddle, Wiley Currie, Jimmy Sandlin, and Joe Spann. (Courtesy Bemis Historical Society.)

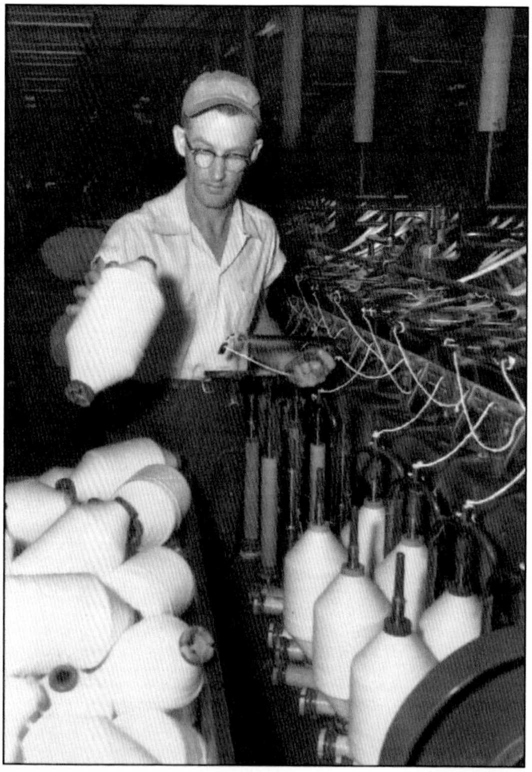

Gordon Cross sets spindles of thread in Bemis Cotton Mill in 1949. (Courtesy JMCL.)

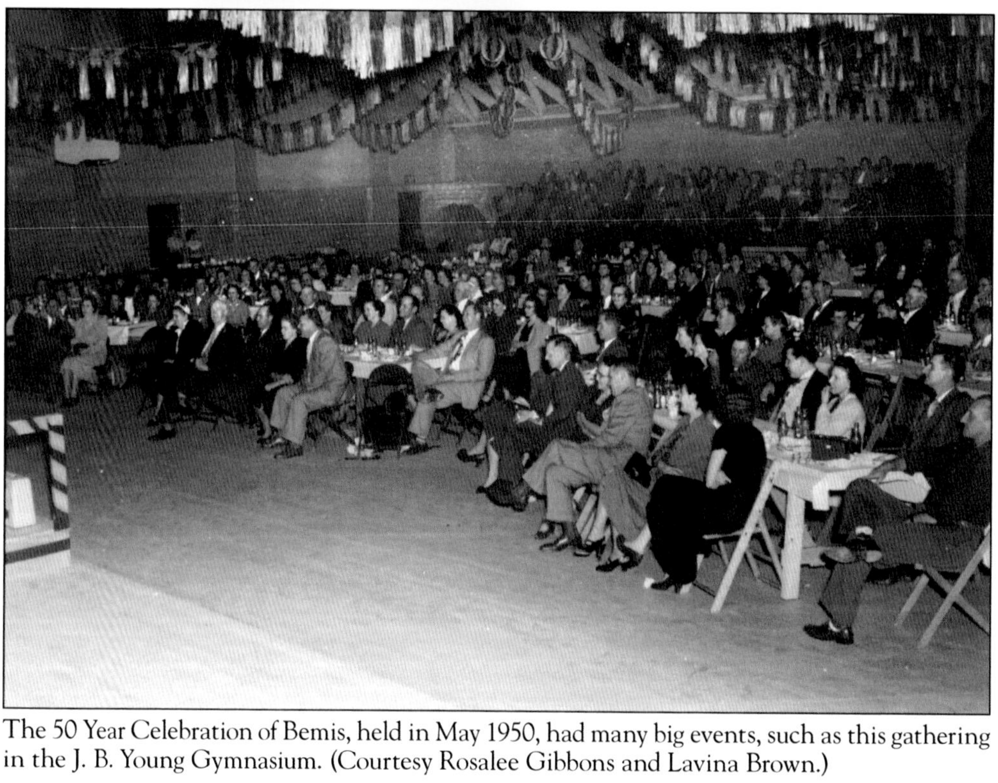

The 50 Year Celebration of Bemis, held in May 1950, had many big events, such as this gathering in the J. B. Young Gymnasium. (Courtesy Rosalee Gibbons and Lavina Brown.)

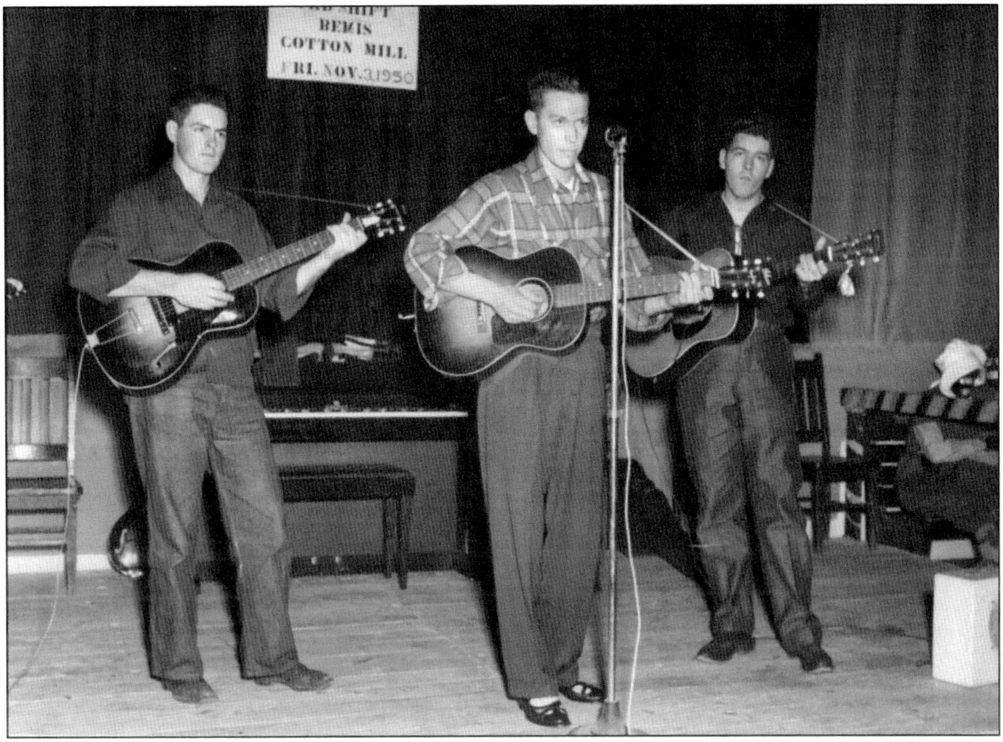

Part of the entertainment for the 1950 celebration was provided by, from left to right, Ed Cisco, W. A. Redden, and Dewayne Stewart. (Courtesy Rosalee Gibbons and Lavina Brown.)

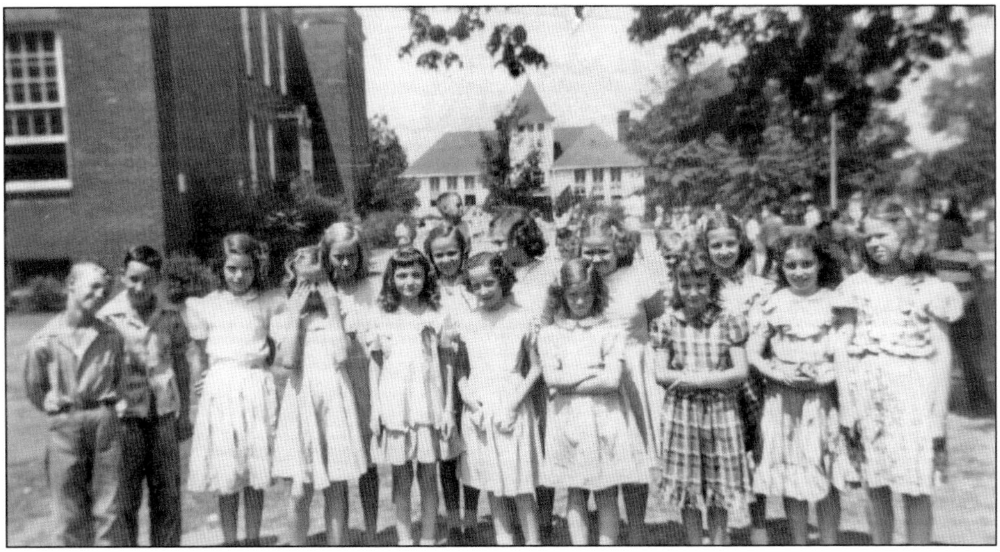

The white building was used as Bemis High School in the early 1930s. The brick building, built in 1925, was used as an elementary school until 1956. From left to right are (first row) Jodie Giddens, Darful Thomas, Carol Austin, Rebecca Fielding, Rosalee Jennings, Nancy Gaugh, Betty Lou Viers, Jenny Sue Bell, Jane Chester, and Barbara Warren: (second row) Sadie Lou Collins, Dixie Wyatt, Dorris Green, Jesslyn Brown, and Jeanett Black. (Courtesy Rosalee Gibbons.)

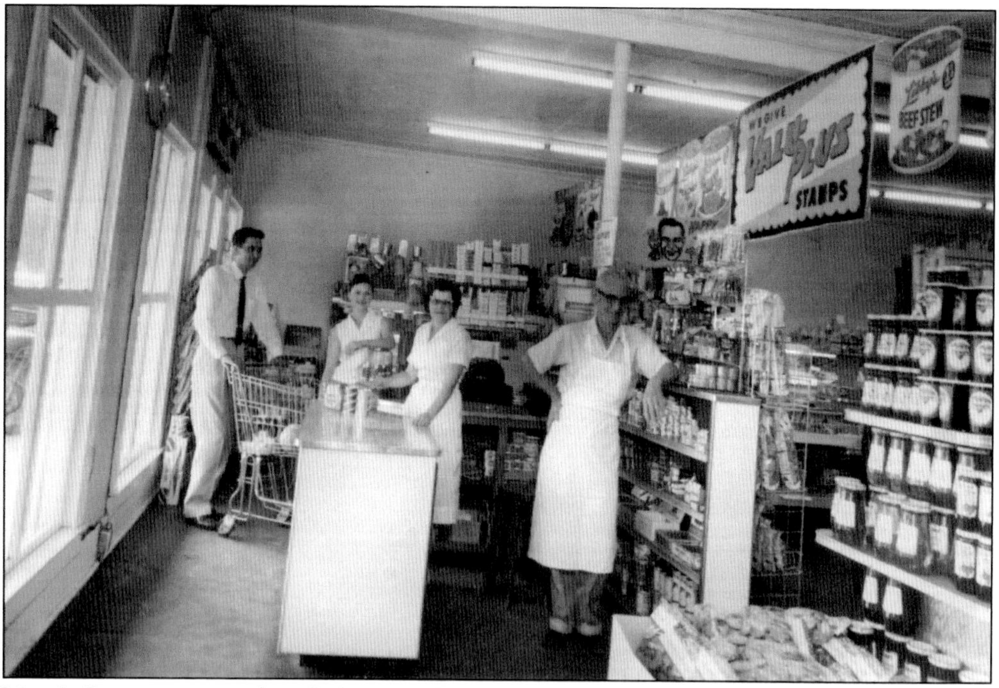

Mayo's Grocery operated on D Street in Bemis from 1938 to 1968. Pictured from left to right in the 1950s are Billy Mayo, Vickie Mayo, Olean Mayo, and Carl "Boots" Mayo. (Courtesy Billy Mayo.)

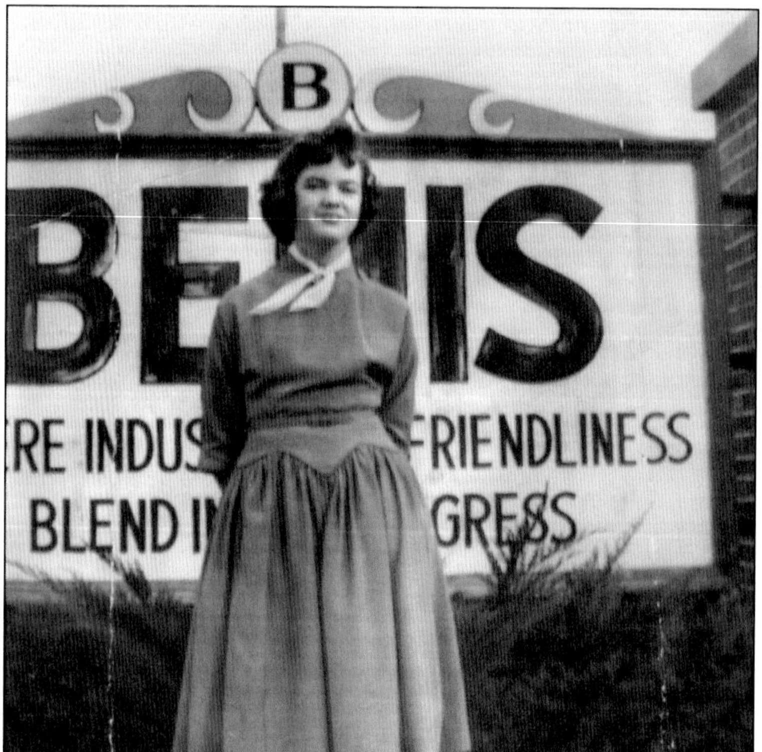

Margie England poses in front of the Bemis sign that says, "Bemis where industry and friendliness blend into progress." (Courtesy Carolyn Smith Callis.)

Three

Industrial and Business Growth

The resiliency of business and industry that began in 20th-century Madison County grew out of learning to meet customers' needs. For example, Frankland Carriage Company quit making carriages to sell auto parts and tires after they saw the importance of the automobile; then they began to sell furniture in their convenient downtown location, but with the movement of the retail trade out of downtown, they refurbished their building to store archival business records. That's just one example of a company that started in the early 1900s and adapted to the changing environment. Many others did the same in order to stay in business.

Limited industrial plants existed in Madison County until after World War II. An aluminum rolling plant was the first to start here in 1949–1950. Referred to as Aluminum Foil, the company was Consolidated Aluminum or Conalco. Rockwell International was the next large industry to open a plant in north Madison County in 1964–1965. Owens Corning, American Olean Tile, Quaker Oats, and Procter and Gamble followed in the late 1960s and early 1970s.

The early 1900s up to the 1960s produced retail and commercial development to serve the growing population, and most of these developments were in downtown Jackson. However, in the 1960s, commercial development started moving out of downtown. The opening of Old Hickory Mall provided a location for many of those retail establishments. Neighborhood development and strip malls soon took the place of retail trade in downtown Jackson. The completion of Interstate 40 across the northern portion of the county drew even more commercial development, as well as restaurants and tourist destinations.

When industrial growth provides jobs and commercial and retail development offers convenience, people will come. Madison County's population in the last three decades of the 20th century grew nearly 40 percent.

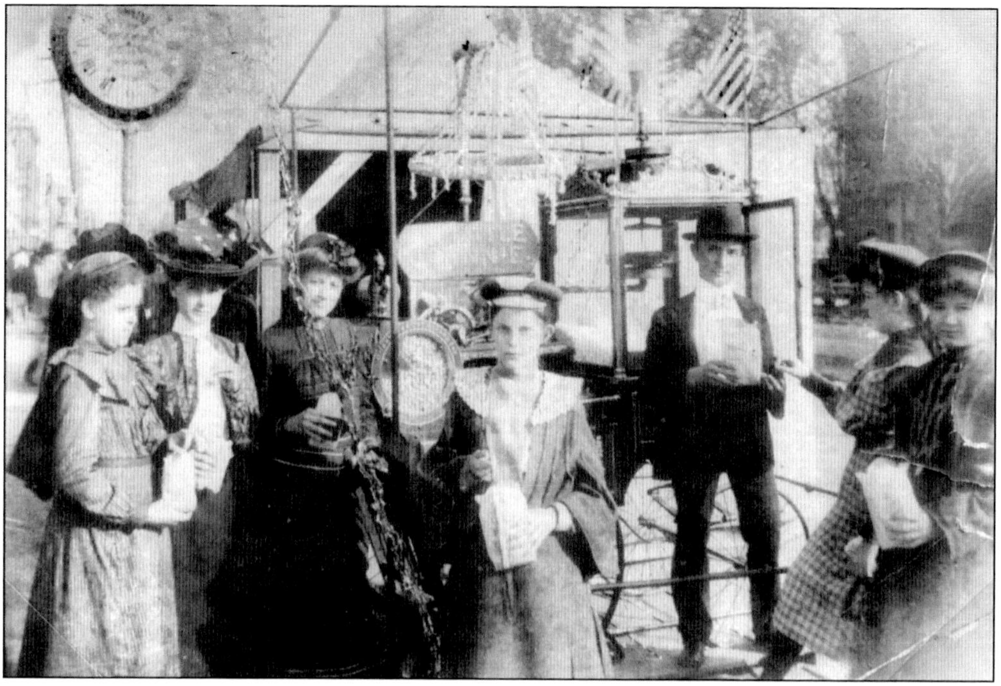

Johnny "Popcorn" Hudson operated first on Main Street. When he was told he couldn't operate on the streets any more, he moved to Lancaster Park off South Royal Street, where he and his family did business through the 1950s (below). Many families and individuals in the early 1900s walked to the park, ate Johnny's popcorn for 5¢ a bag, drank mineral water from the well, and rode home on a streetcar. The 1950s picture shows how even Johnny's Popcorn changed with the times by adding snow cones. (Above, courtesy JMCL; below, courtesy Ralph Barber and Dr. John Barber.)

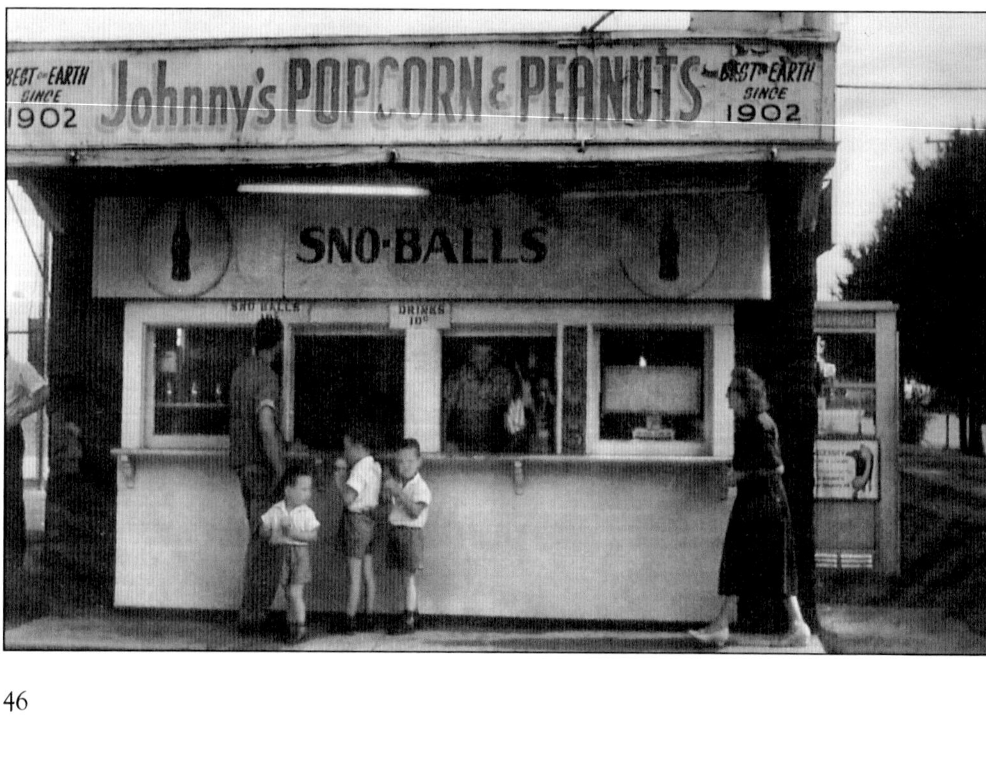

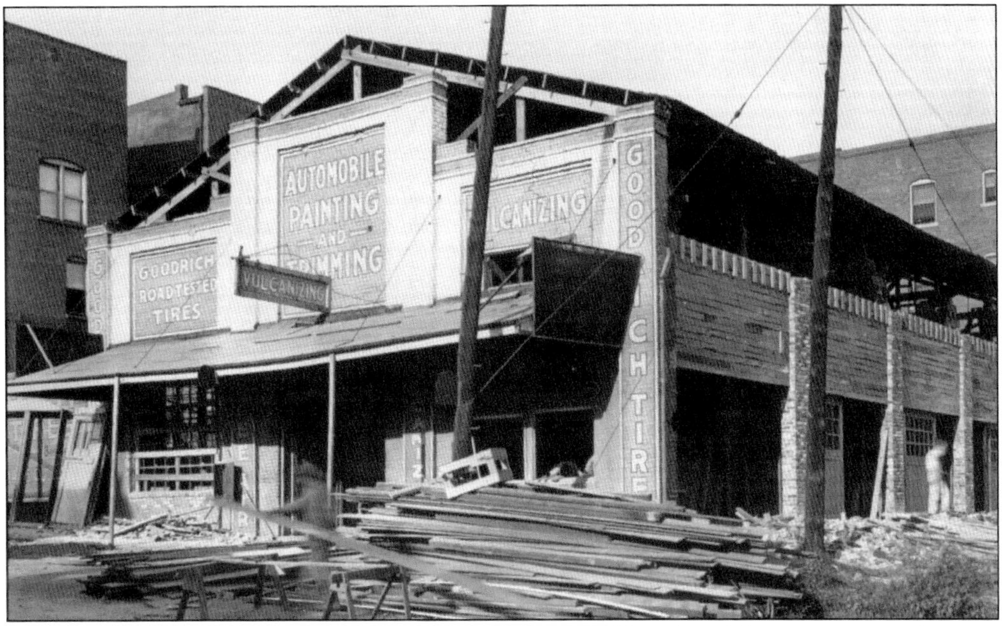

The Frankland Carriage Company started in Jackson in 1903 and made buggies, wagons, hearses, and phaetons. This picture shows how it looked about 1913, when Frank M. Frankland and his sons realized that the automobile would be the future of transportation, so they adjusted their business to selling tires and auto parts. Their shop was on the corner of Market (now Highland) and Chester Streets. (Courtesy JMCL.)

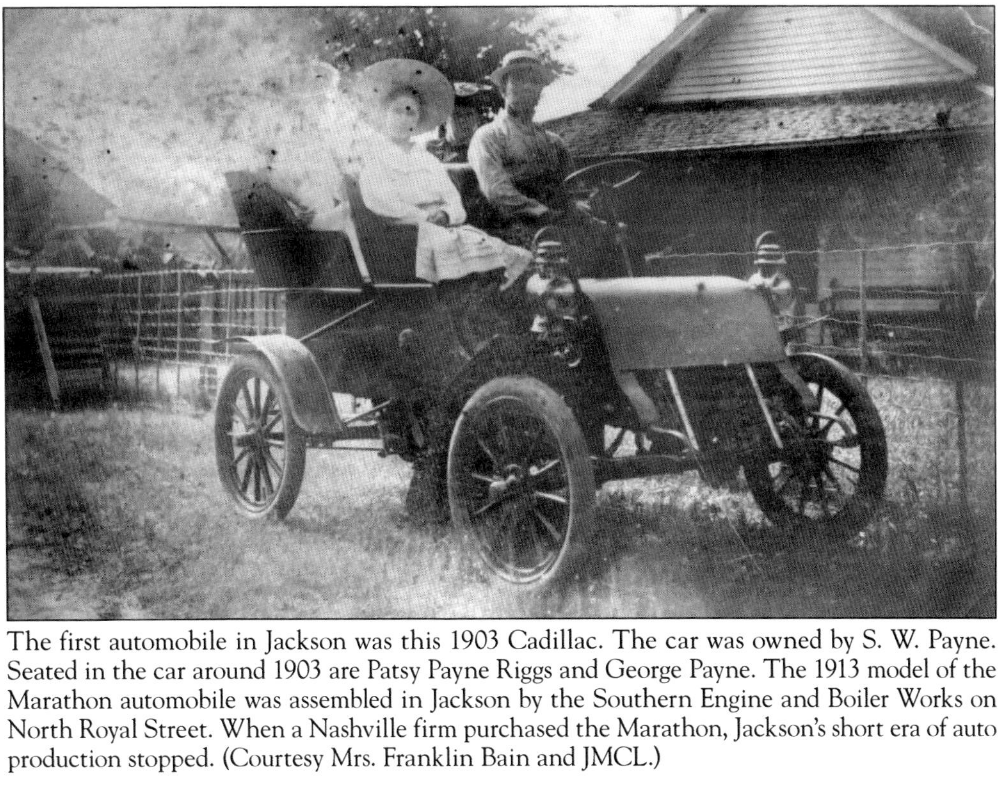

The first automobile in Jackson was this 1903 Cadillac. The car was owned by S. W. Payne. Seated in the car around 1903 are Patsy Payne Riggs and George Payne. The 1913 model of the Marathon automobile was assembled in Jackson by the Southern Engine and Boiler Works on North Royal Street. When a Nashville firm purchased the Marathon, Jackson's short era of auto production stopped. (Courtesy Mrs. Franklin Bain and JMCL.)

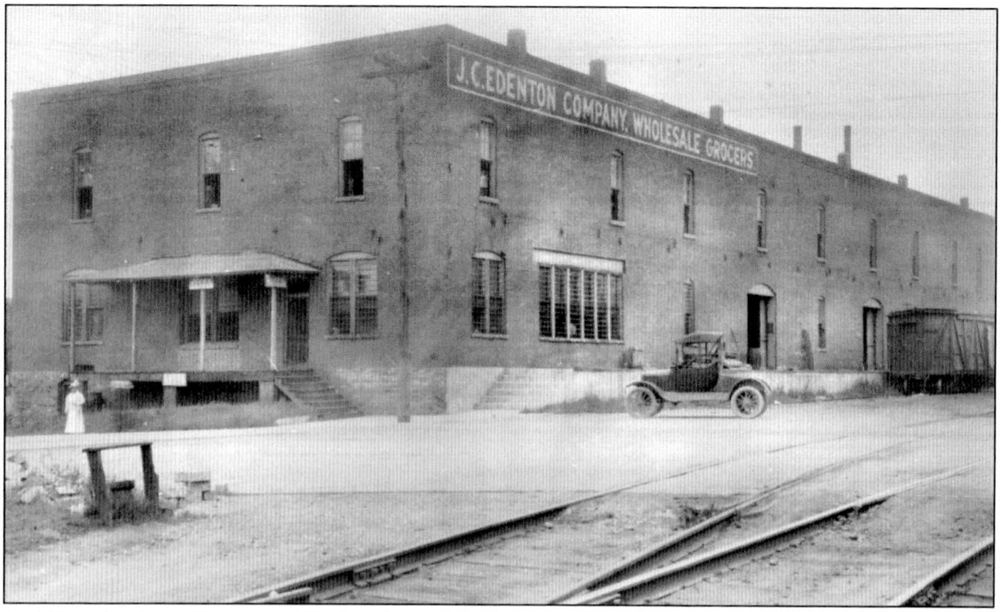

In 1904, the J. C. Edenton Wholesale Company moved into its new building on Main Street, seen here, where it was the first to give free delivery to retail customers. A 1904 edition of the *Sun* called it the "leading wholesale grocery house in the state." The firm had 11 branches outside Jackson by the late 1920s. (Courtesy Frank Procter.)

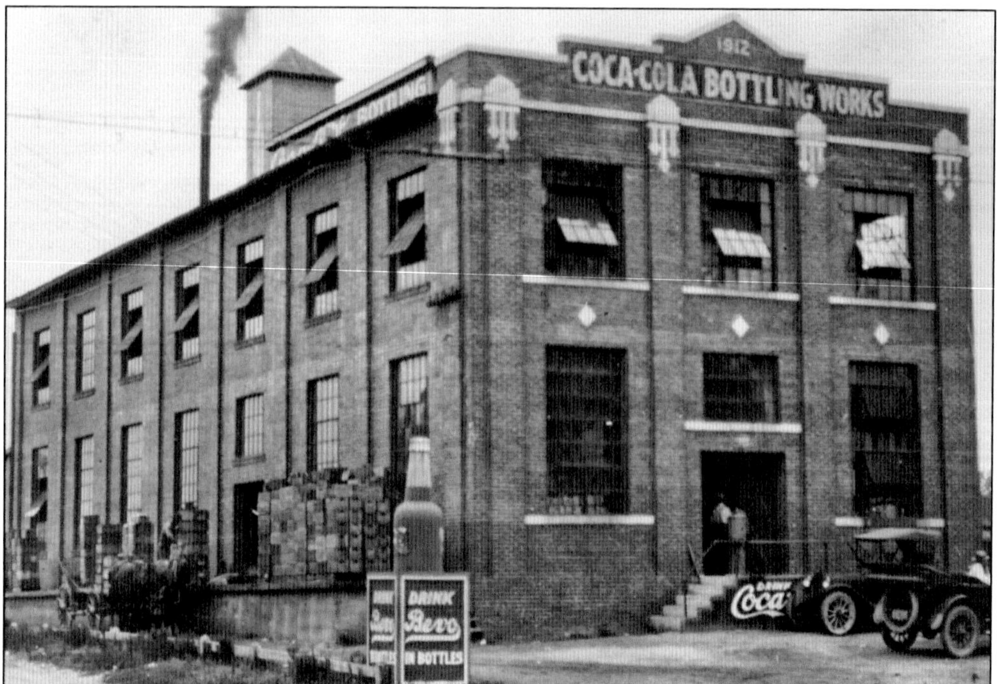

Coca-Cola was a new drink in 1905, when Paul Russell came to Jackson from Chattanooga, where he had been working for the Coca-Cola plant in that city. He rented a small building on North Royal and Orleans Streets and started a plant here. By 1912, he constructed a small building on Bolivar Street, which continued to operate until the early 1990s. (Courtesy Frank Procter.)

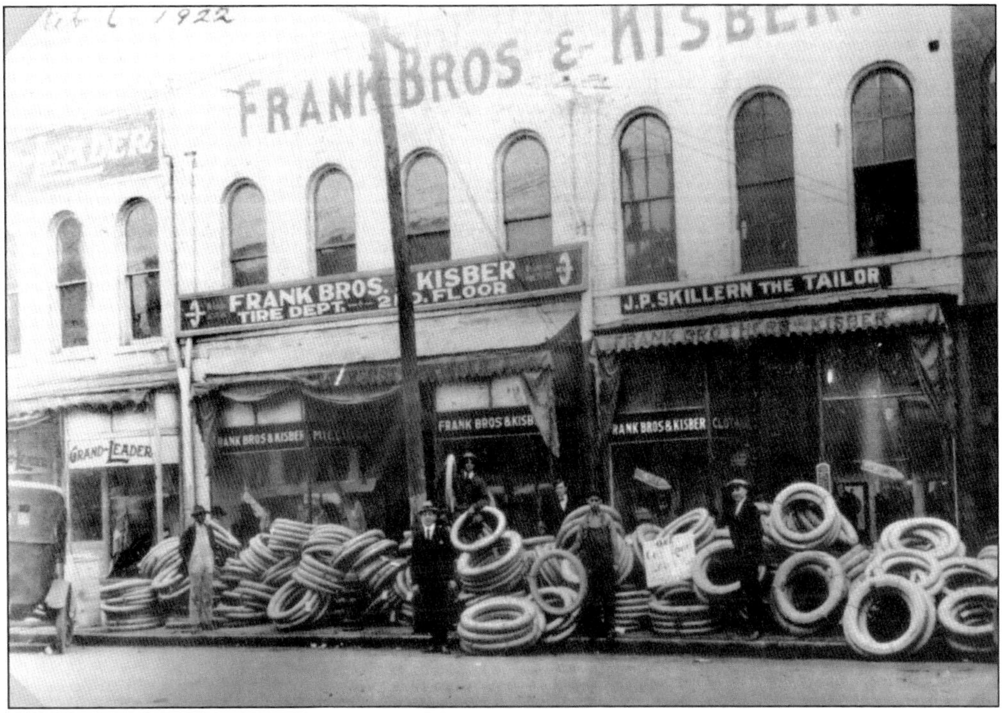

The Frank Brothers and Kisber Tire store in Jackson was established in 1905. (Courtesy the Kisber family.)

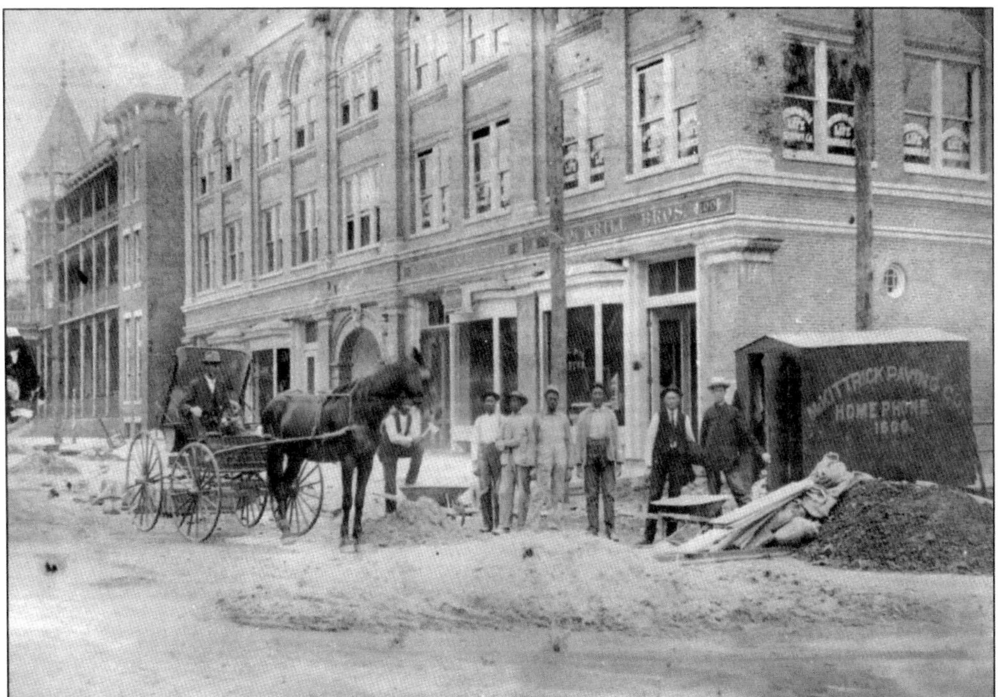

John Cockrill, of Cockrill Brothers Plumbing Company at 102 East Baltimore Street, is inspecting the paving being done in front of the Southern Hotel around 1906. (Courtesy JMCL.)

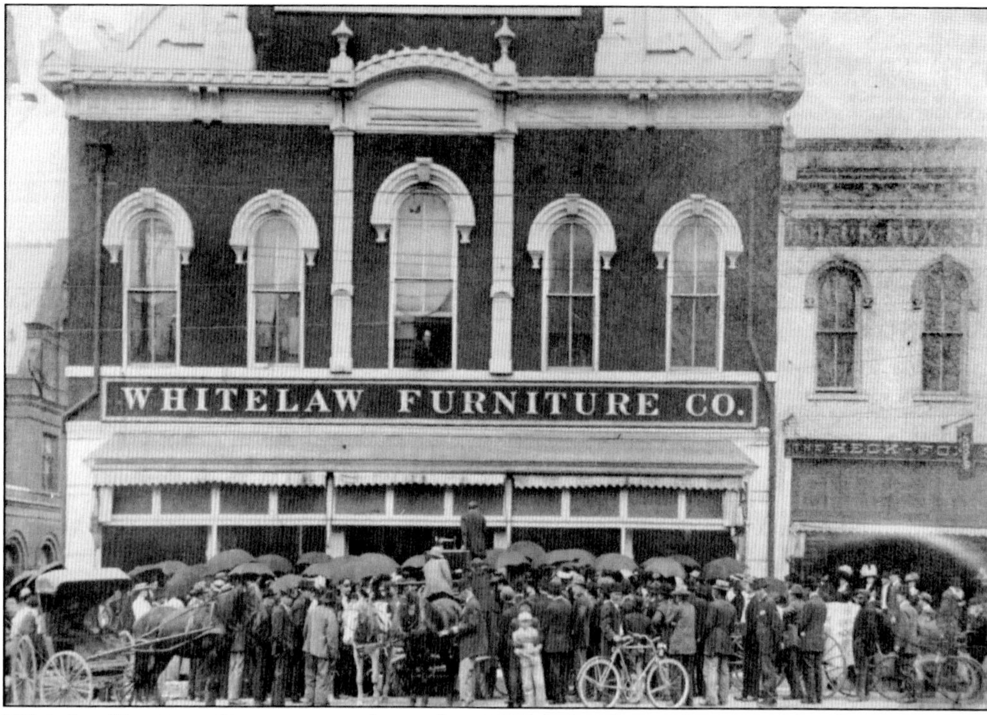

Whitelaw Furniture Company was located at 205 Market Street (now Highland) next to a red brick building used as the U.S. Post Office. (Courtesy JMCL.)

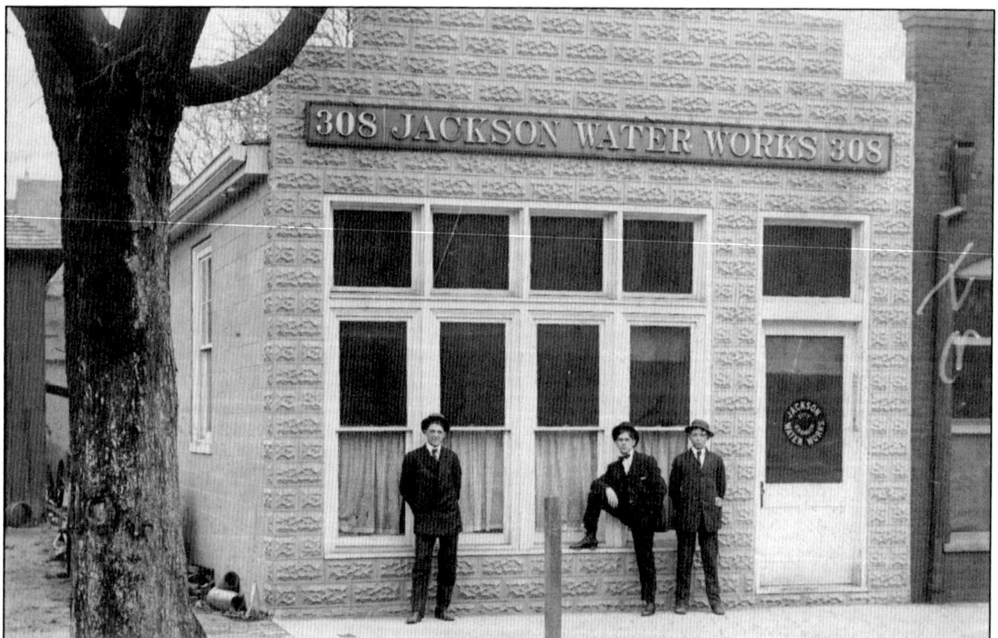

Thanks to W. F. Alexander and engineer Sam Lancaster, the City of Jackson developed a modern water system in the late 1800s. "There is no excuse for a man drinking any injurious beverages when Jackson is so well supplied with water," wrote the editor of the *Forked Deer Blade* on July 18, 1885. Shown here is the Jackson Water Works office in the early 1900s. (Courtesy JMCL.)

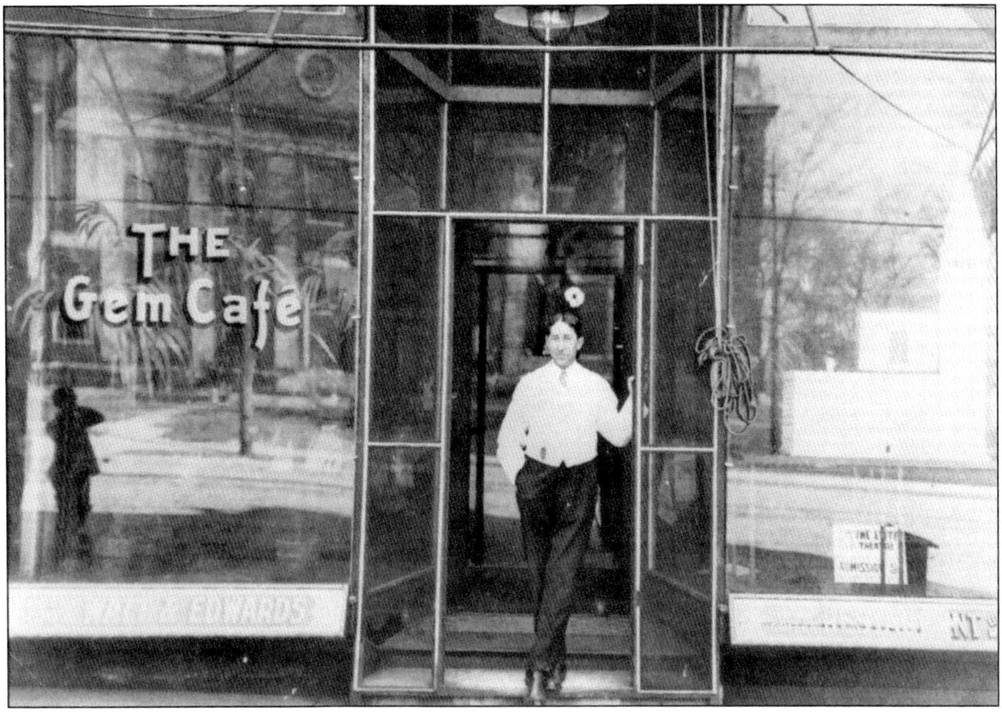

Gem Café was located at 112 Liberty Street. The proprietors were Watt and A. F. Edwards. (Courtesy JMCL.)

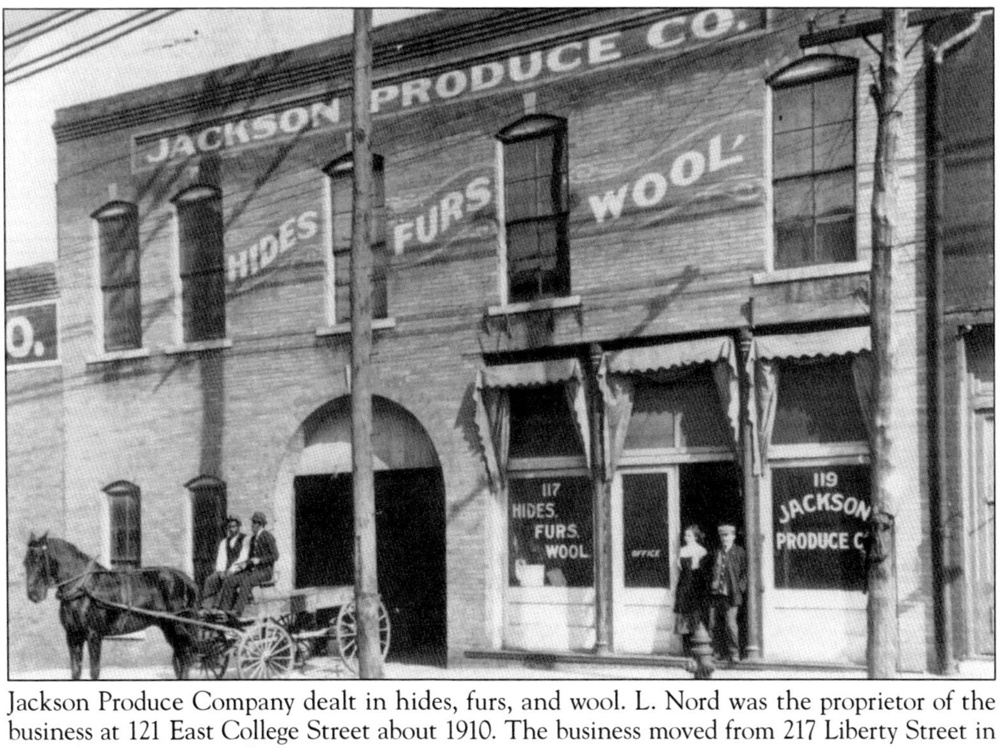

Jackson Produce Company dealt in hides, furs, and wool. L. Nord was the proprietor of the business at 121 East College Street about 1910. The business moved from 217 Liberty Street in 1906. (Courtesy JMCL.)

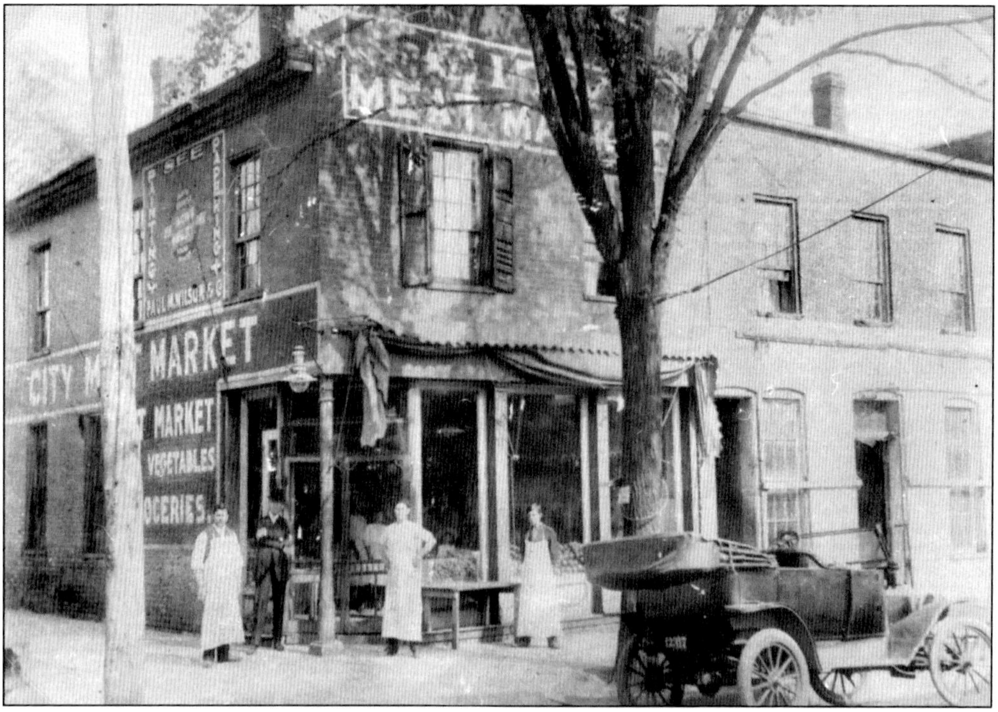

City Meat Market was located at 102-104 South Church Street, at the corner of Main and Church Streets, about 1912, and the manager was A. D. Barnes. (Courtesy JMCL.)

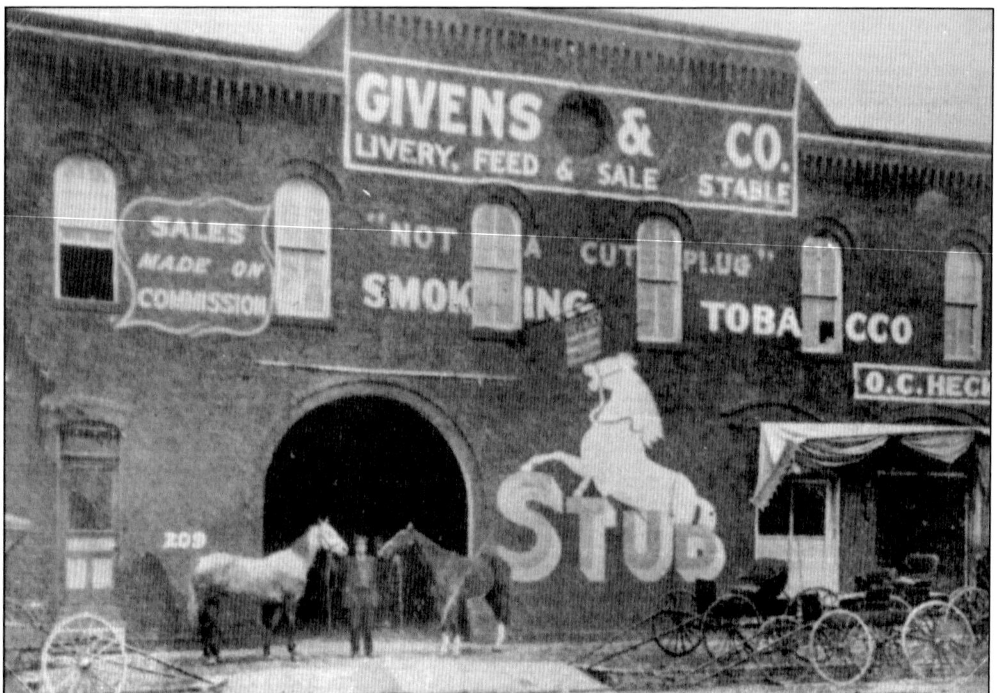

The E. L. Givens Company was at 209 West Main Street about 1912. To the right is the business of O. C. Heck at 205 West Main Street. (Courtesy JMCL.)

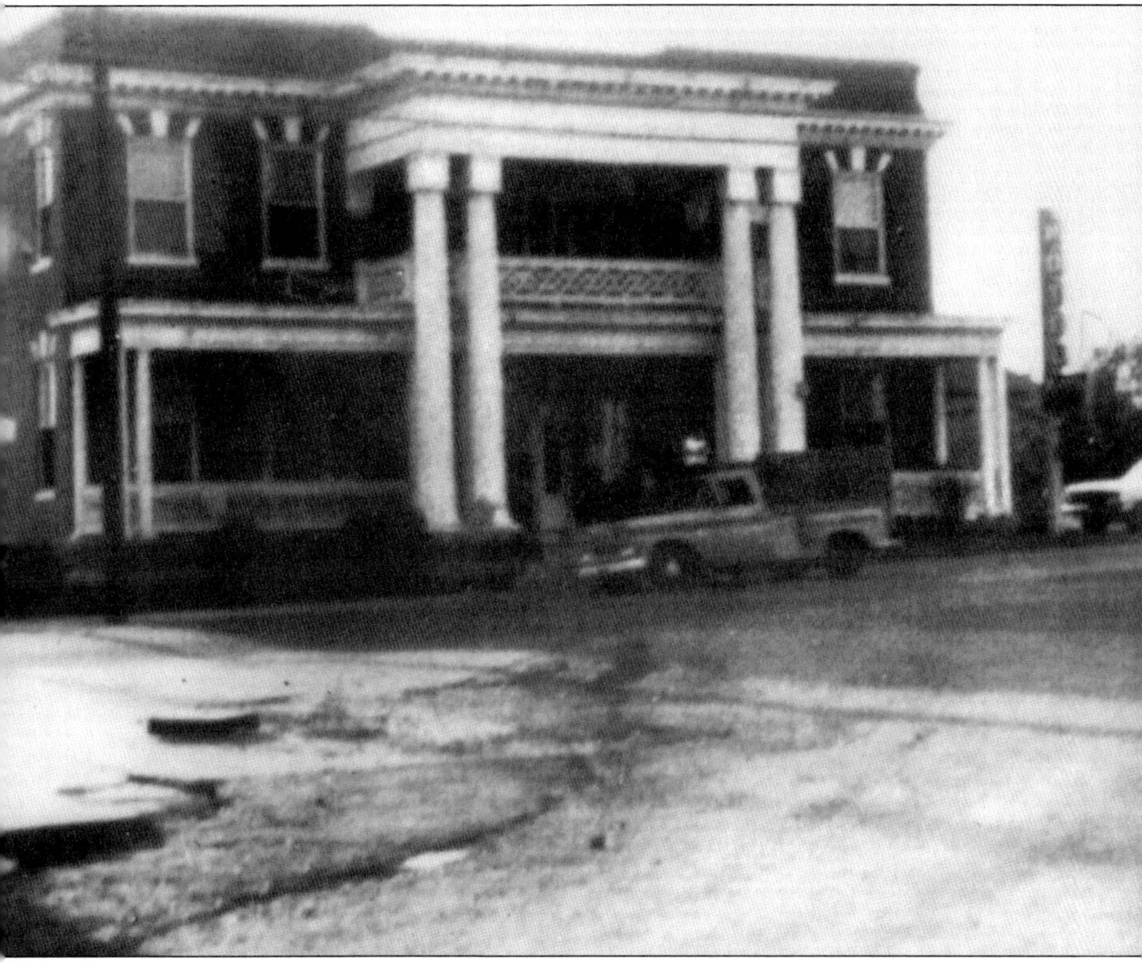

The Murphy Hotel/Neely House, pictured here, began as a boardinghouse and a railroad hotel. In 1907, the NC&StL Railroad constructed a new brick passenger depot on the east side of South Royal Street. When the Neely family obtained the deed and property at 575 South Royal Street about 1910, they decided to tear down the frame boardinghouse and construct a new brick two-story hotel. A magazine supplement to the *Jackson Sun* dated about 1912 describes it as the "new modern hotel building . . . modern in every detail, with hot and cold running water in every room." In 1946, Lillie Neely sold the hotel for $5,000 to Robert J. Murphy, and it operated as the Murphy Hotel until the City of Jackson purchased it in October 1987. In 1992, it was placed on the National Register of Historic Places. Following a 2003 tornado, the city sold the property to Hal Crocker, who restored the building. Today it is called the Neely House and houses an upscale restaurant, professional offices, and very unique shops. (Courtesy JMCL.)

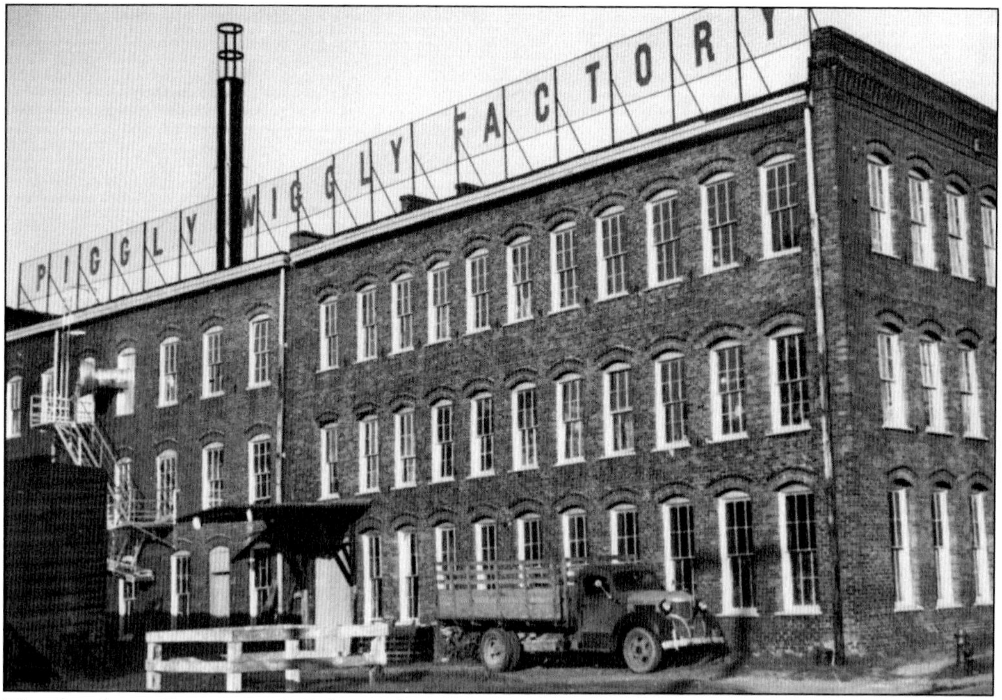

The Southern Seating and Cabinet Company was doing a large business in Jackson in 1895, when it ran a full-page advertisement boasting of being the "Largest and Oldest Concern of its kind in the South." They made church, hall, bank, and office fittings and fixtures. In 1917, Clarence Saunders bought the company and turned it into the Piggly-Wiggly plant on Preston Street. (Courtesy JMCL.)

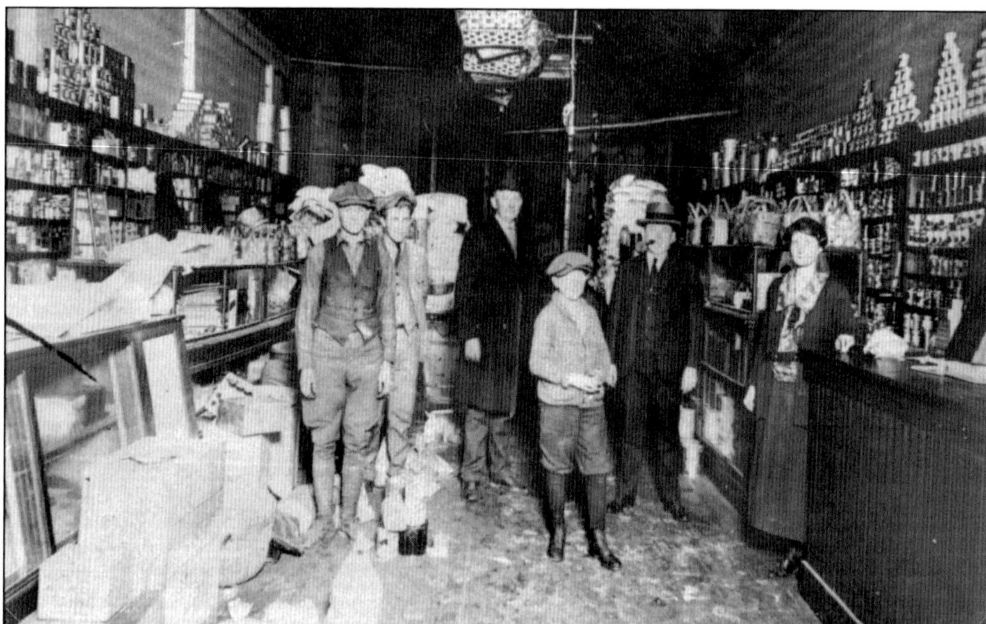

Duncan Demombreum, left, and Hassie Morrison, right, are shown here in Johnson's Groceries, Hardware, and Auto Supplies at 112-114 North Liberty Street about 1923. (Courtesy JMCL.)

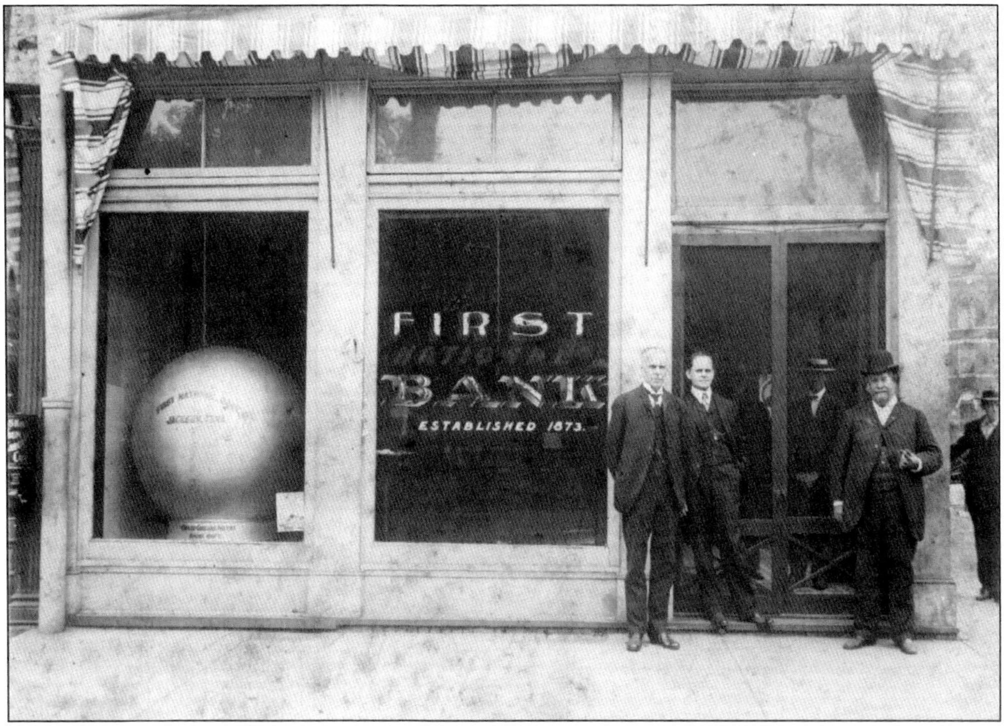

First National Bank, on the corner of Main and Liberty Streets, was established in 1874 and had been converted from the Jackson Savings Bank, chartered in 1873. In this 1890 picture are, from left to right, J. W. Vanden, Thomas Taylor, and John Wisdom. The First National Bank relocated to the eight-story building below on the corner of Main and Market (later Highland) in 1928, and that building served the citizens of Jackson and surrounding areas until 1995, when it was imploded to make room for the new city hall. (Both courtesy JMCL.)

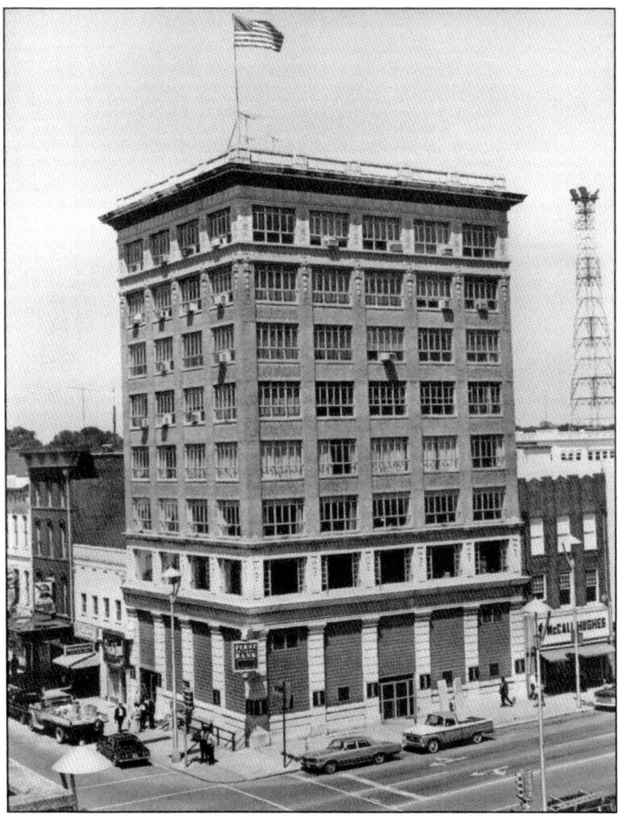

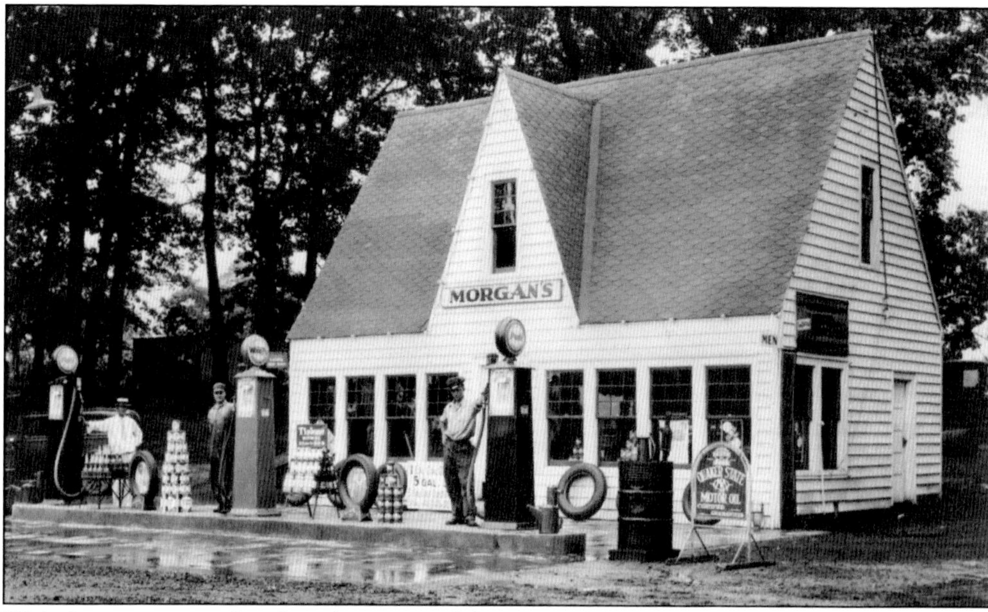

With the emergence of modern America and the automobile, gas stations became very important to the community. E. L. Morgan opened his first gas station in 1930. Morgan, pictured on the right, not only grew his service station business, but he also became a very powerful behind-the-scenes man in state politics in the 1940s, 1950s, and 1960s. (Courtesy JMCL.)

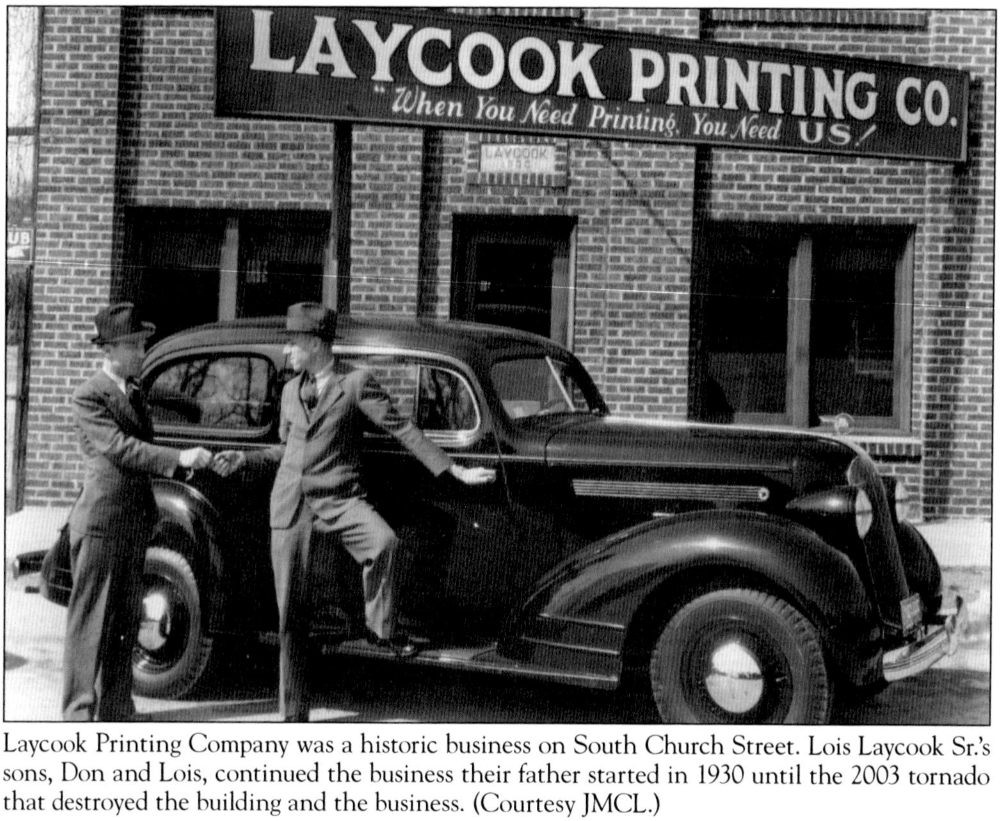

Laycook Printing Company was a historic business on South Church Street. Lois Laycook Sr.'s sons, Don and Lois, continued the business their father started in 1930 until the 2003 tornado that destroyed the building and the business. (Courtesy JMCL.)

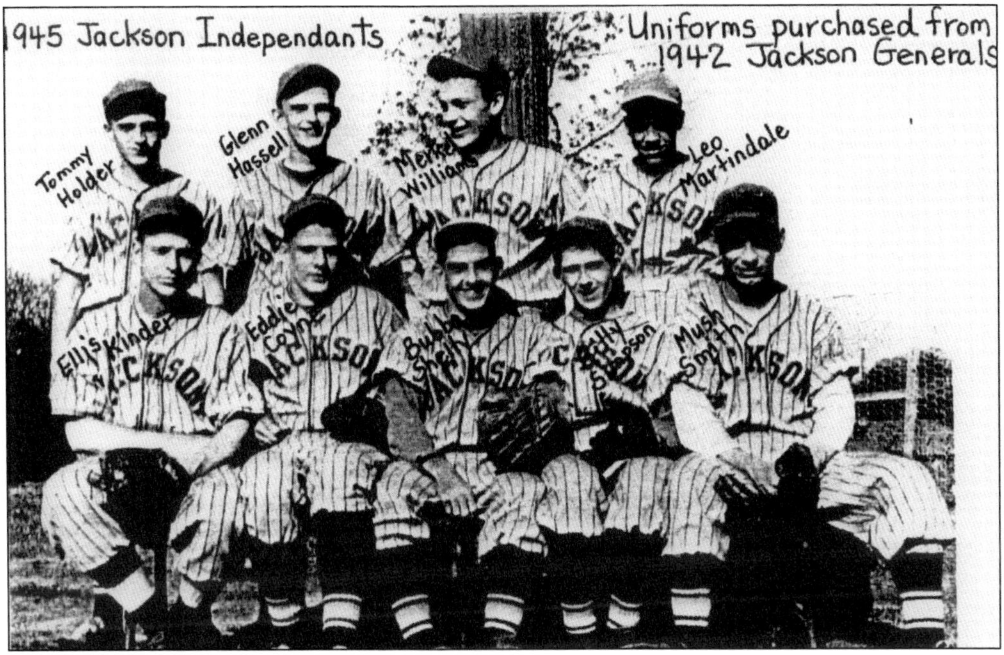

Hartle Gilland's businesses included professional baseball teams. The 1945 Jackson Independents (formerly the Jackson Generals of the 1930s) are, from left to right, (first row) Ellis Kinder, later with the Boston Red Sox and in the Red Sox's hall of fame; Eddie Coyner, Bubba Shelly, Billy Simpson, and Mush Smith; (second row) Tommy Holder, Glenn Hassell, Merrel Williams, and Leo Martindale, later a Jackson city councilman. (Courtesy E. Maurice Stansell Sr.)

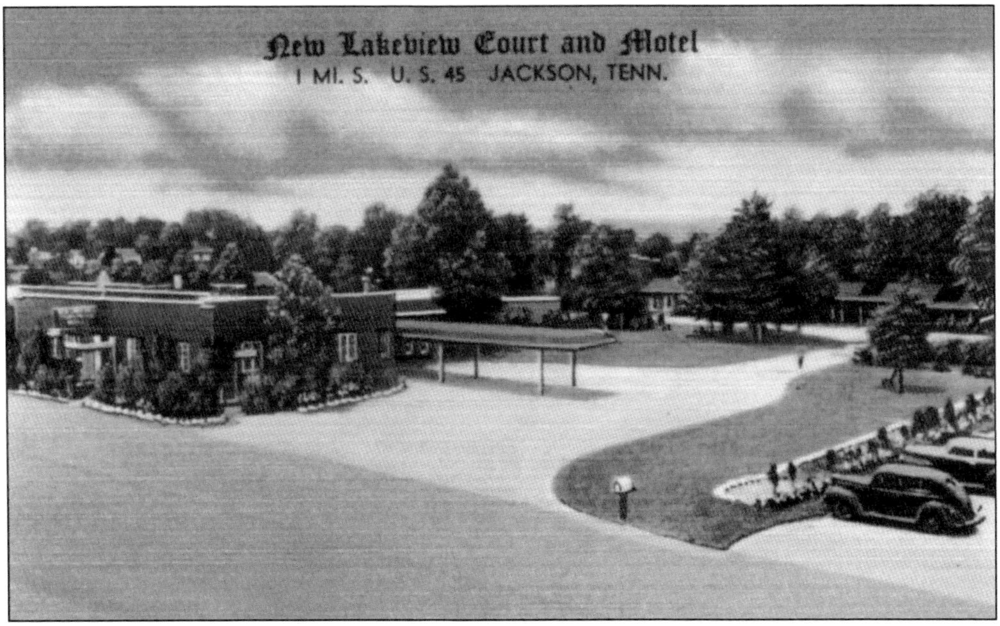

Hartle Gilland built one of the first motels in Madison County, the Lakeview, after U.S. Highway 45 was constructed south of Jackson in the early 1930s. Gilland brought Chester County barbecue to Madison County and served it at the Pit. He also owned the Eagles Club, which was later converted into the Steak House. (Courtesy E. Maurice Stansell Sr.)

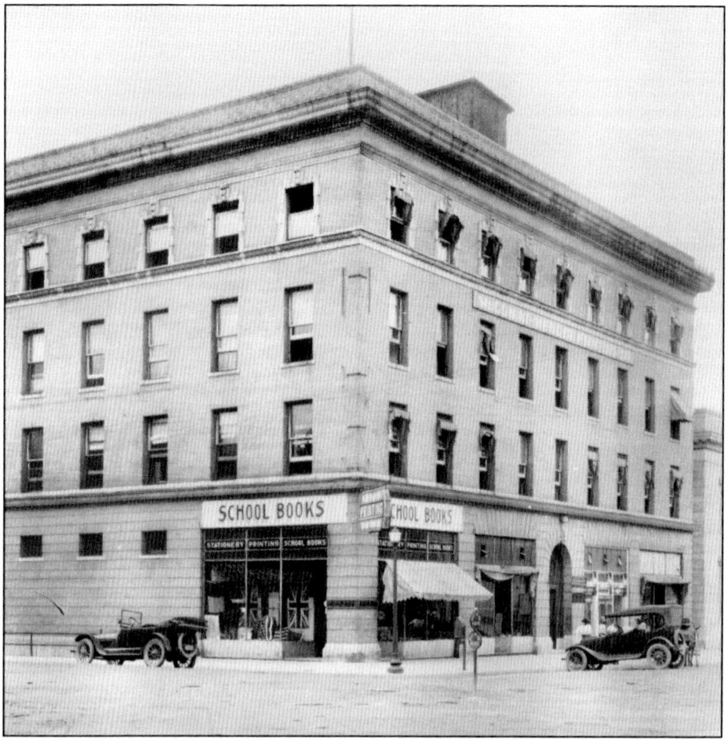

McCowat-Mercer, the oldest family-operated business in Madison County, started in 1873 and continues today. Specializing now in custom packaging for many industries, this oldest printing company in Jackson produced many of the early city directories and published several history books. This picture shows the company at the corner of Church and Lafayette Streets, but it has been on Riverside Drive for over 50 years. (Courtesy JMCL.)

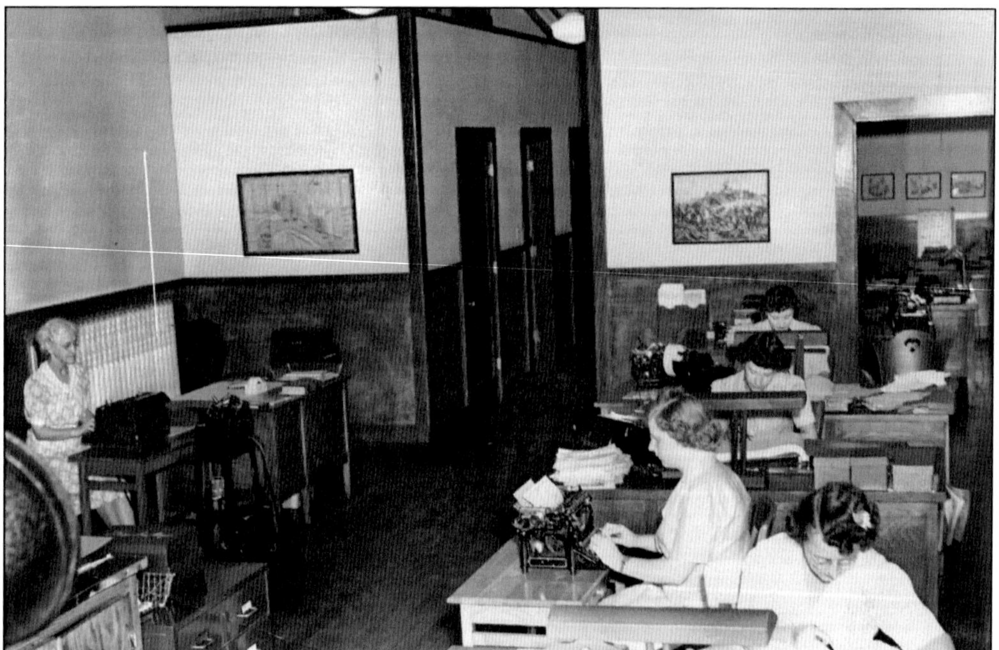

This photograph shows the old McCowat-Mercer office in 1942. At left is Gertrude Green, and at right, from back to front, are M. Bredenback, Snooks Scott, Frances Smith, and Clyde Lawrence. This office was in the McCowat-Mercer building on Church Street. (Courtesy JMCL Seale Johnson Collection.)

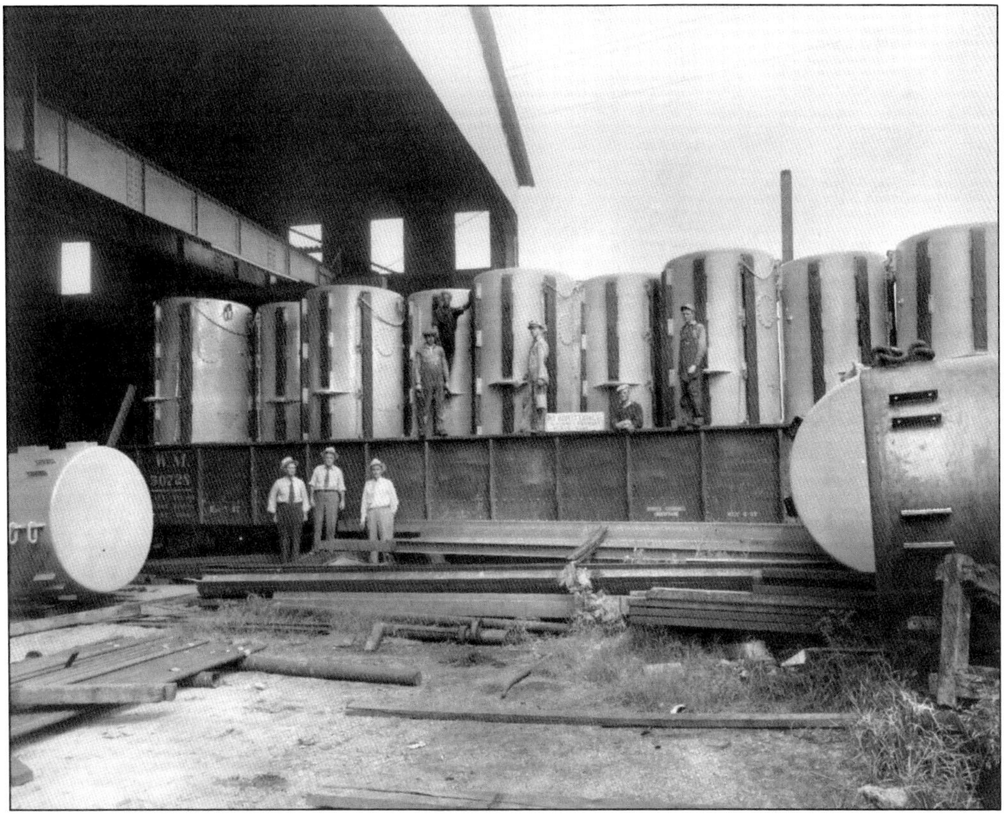

The Williams Steel Company, formerly Kirby-William Steel, delivered large shipments of pontoons, like those seen here, for World War II. John Williams is the man in the center on the ground. John Williams, the head of Williams Steel, was also a farmer and inventor. (Courtesy Elsie Williams.)

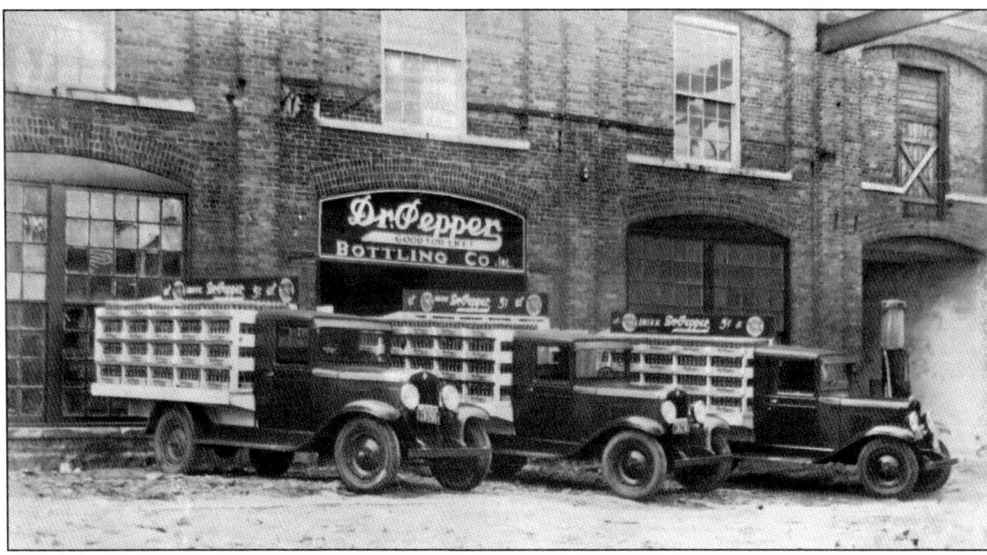

Pictured here is the Dr. Pepper Bottling Company around 1930. The first location was on North Royal Street. (Courtesy Joe and Suzanne Patty.)

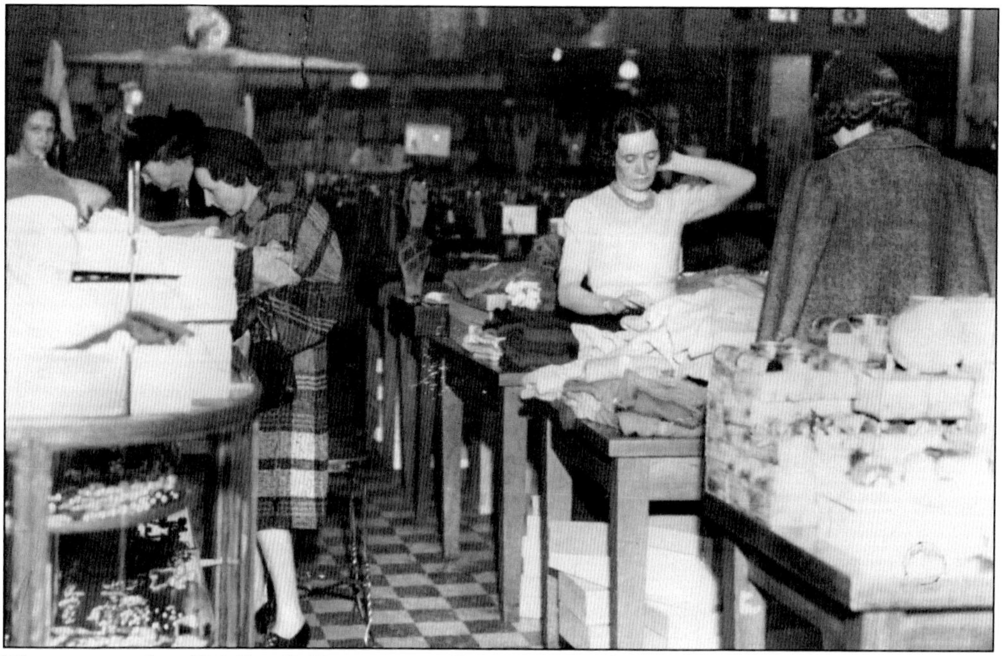

The main aisle of Holland's Department Store, pictured in 1939, was always full of people. From left to right are Helen Schulz, Frances Fite, Johnnie Cockeil Webb, and unidentified. (Courtesy William Holland Jr.)

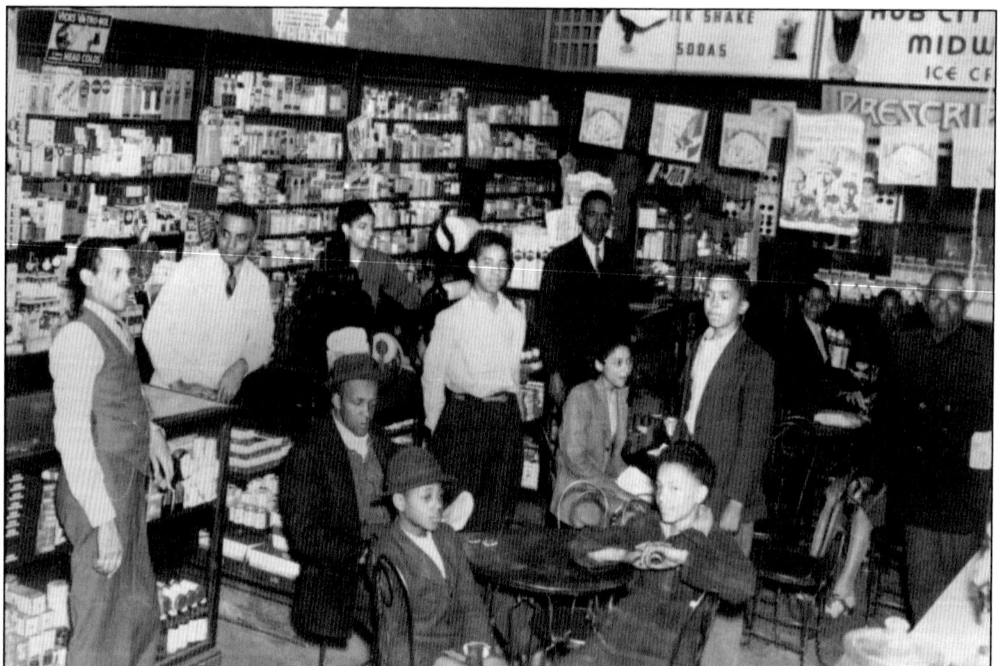

The Hub City Drug Store on West Lafayette Street, shown here in 1942, was established in late 1890s by Tom Davis. Three other pharmacists served as proprietors during its 80-year history: Dr. James Hightower, Dr. A. Z. Maney (second from left), and Dr. John Frierson. It continued to serve the African American population well into the 1970s. (Courtesy JMCL.)

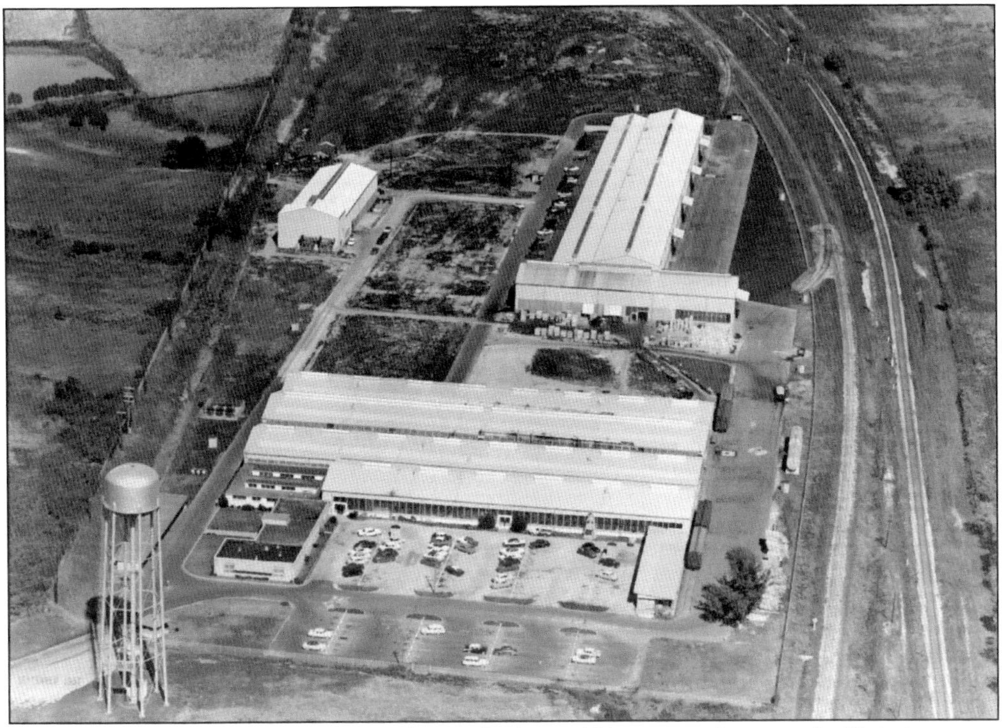

In 1949, construction began on this plant, which would begin production of rolled aluminum sheets in 1950. Aluminum Foils, Inc., was the first major manufacturing facility to locate in Jackson after World War II. By 1964, the plant was known as Consolidated Aluminum Company, then Conalco, and in the 1990s, it would be called Ormet. Today it is J. W. Aluminum Company. (Courtesy Fulton Mullis.)

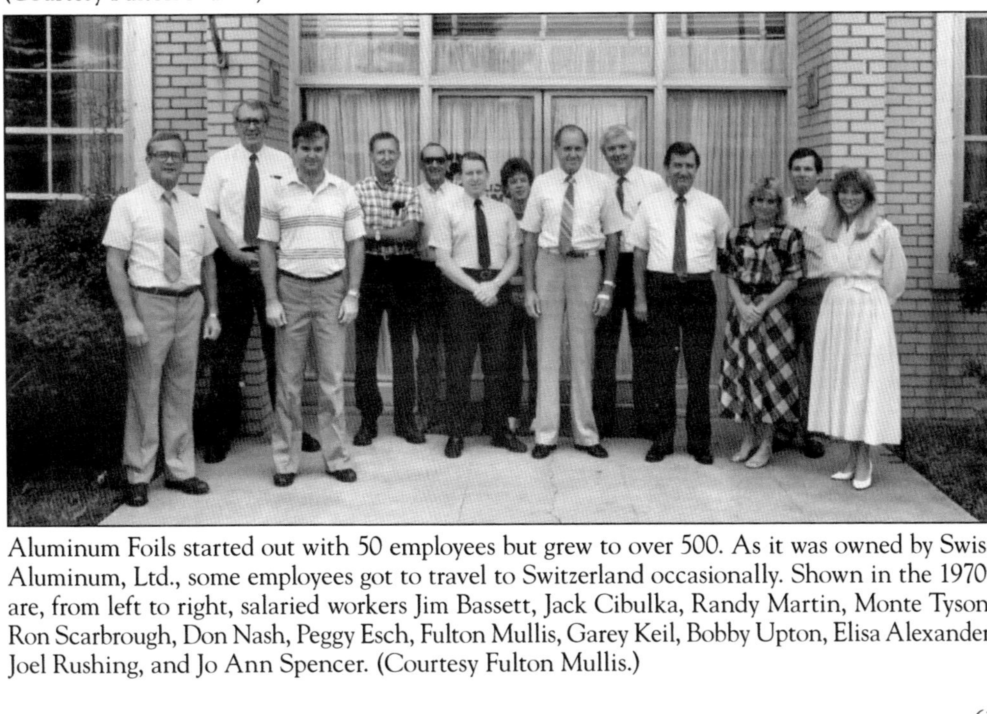

Aluminum Foils started out with 50 employees but grew to over 500. As it was owned by Swiss Aluminum, Ltd., some employees got to travel to Switzerland occasionally. Shown in the 1970s are, from left to right, salaried workers Jim Bassett, Jack Cibulka, Randy Martin, Monte Tyson, Ron Scarbrough, Don Nash, Peggy Esch, Fulton Mullis, Garey Keil, Bobby Upton, Elisa Alexander, Joel Rushing, and Jo Ann Spencer. (Courtesy Fulton Mullis.)

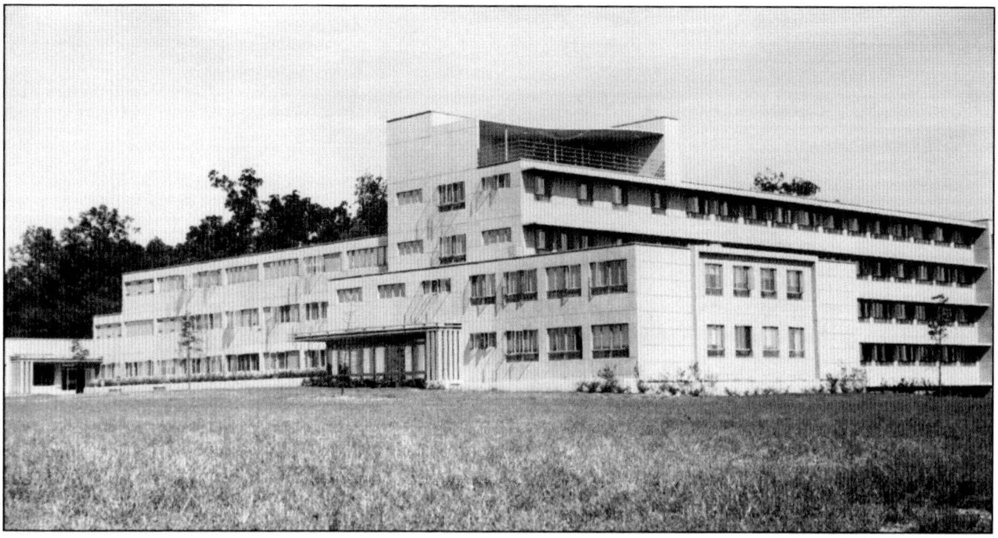

Jackson–Madison County General Hospital opened on August 11, 1950, after a number of prominent doctors and community leaders sought to open a government-sponsored facility through the Hill-Burton Act. During the first year, 5,005 patients were admitted, 930 babies were delivered, and 2,470 operations were preformed by a staff of 35 doctors. Today the Jackson facility is run by West Tennessee Health Care and has 635 beds. (Courtesy JMCL.)

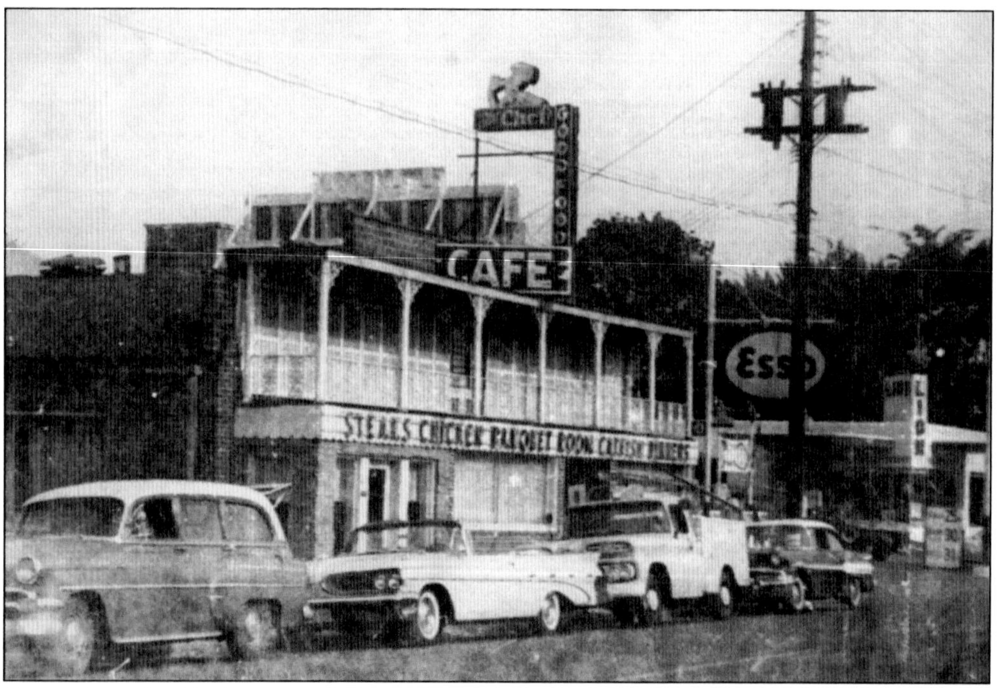

Shown here the Chef restaurant, formerly located at 212 South Royal Street, advertises steaks, chicken, a banquet room, and catfish dinners. It is pictured next door to the Estes Esso station and a Lion gas station, where regular gas is 29¢ a gallon. The picture was taken about 1958. (Courtesy JMCL.)

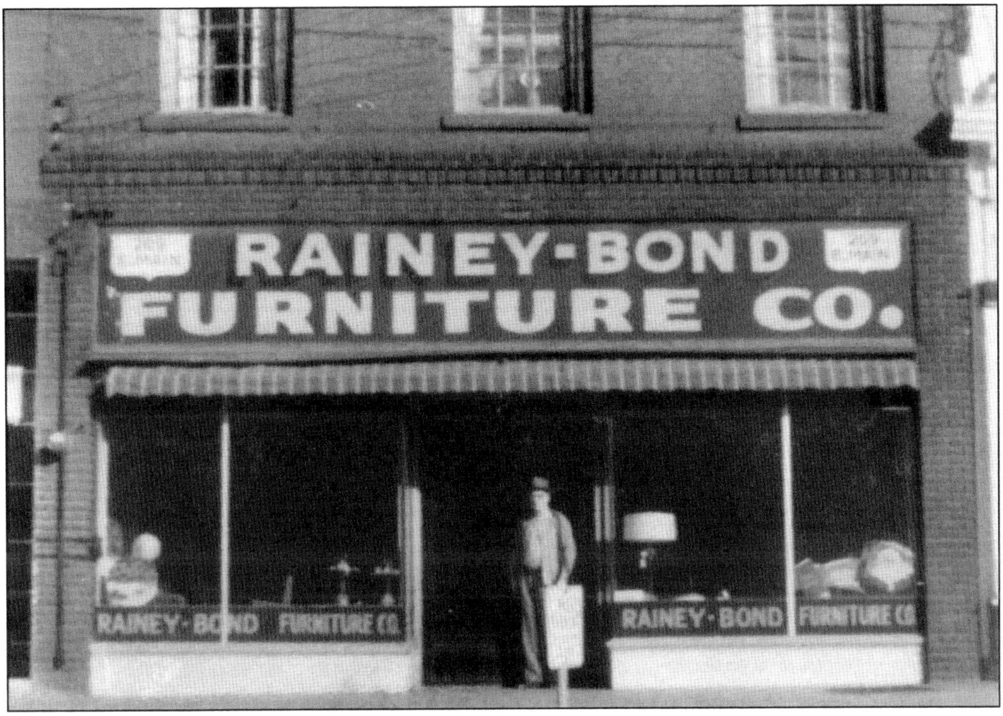

Retail businesses flourished in downtown Jackson in the 1950s, especially furniture stores. In the photograph above, Frank Rainey stands in the doorway of his furniture store in 1953. Below, in another 1953 photograph, are, from left to right, George Moore, Prentyce Utley (brother of Maudie Utley Rainey), Frank Rainey, and Maudie Rainey standing ready to serve their furniture customers. (Both courtesy Jackie Utley and Geraldine Rainey.)

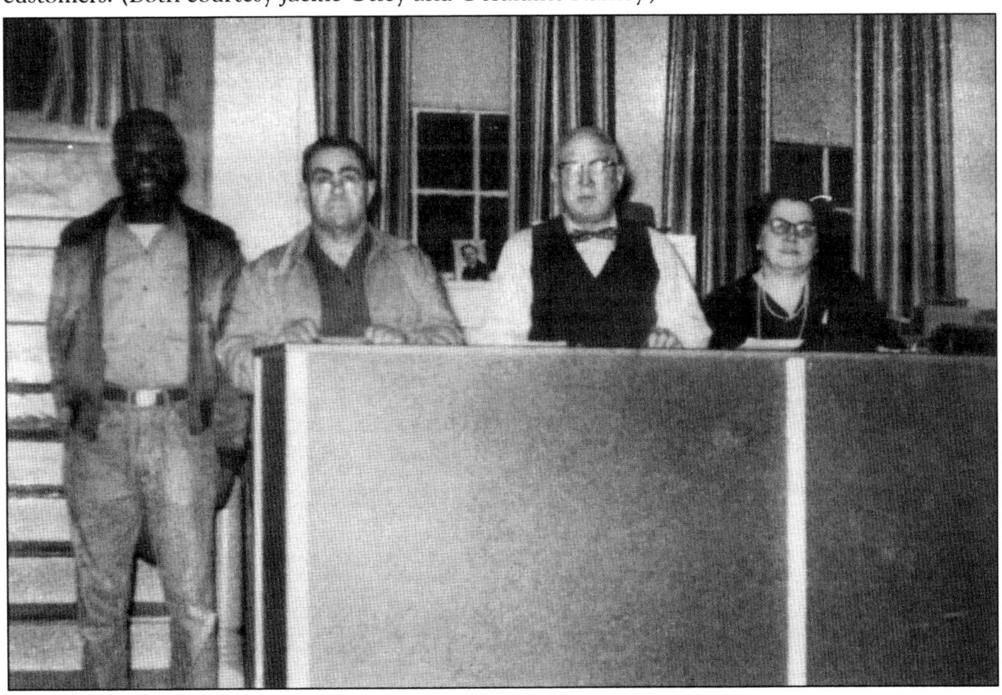

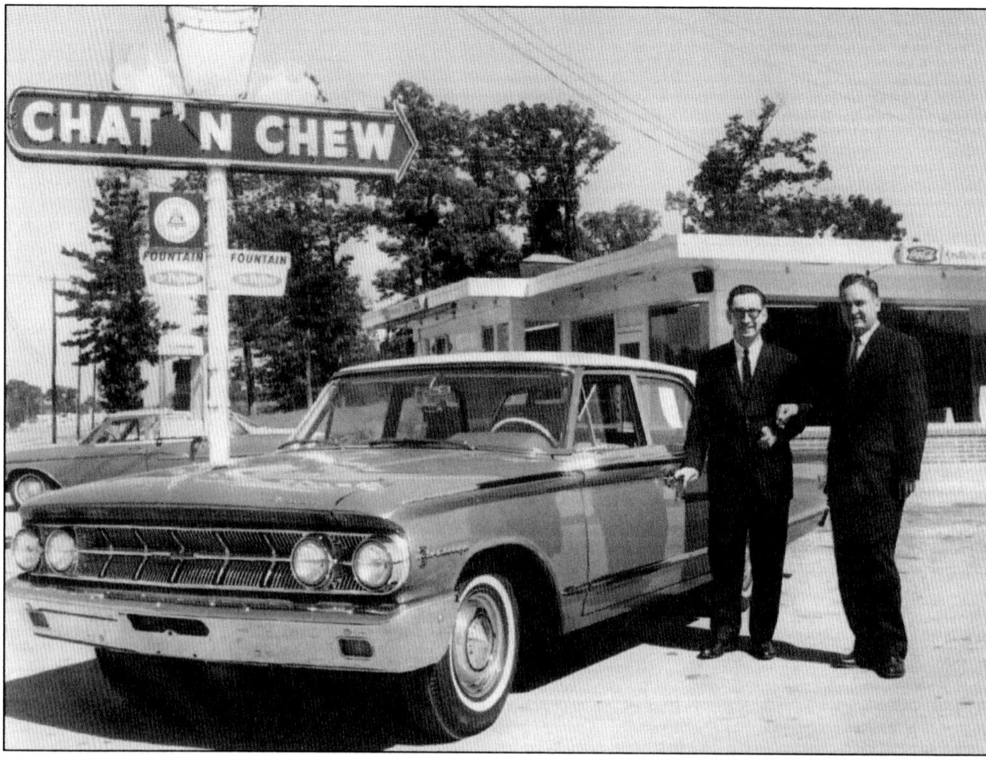

Murray Cook gives O. D. Holifield the keys to a new car at the Chat 'n Chew in the 1950s. Sandra Morgan named the Chat 'n Chew in the 1950s, and it became a popular hangout for South Side students. (Courtesy Betty Holifield.)

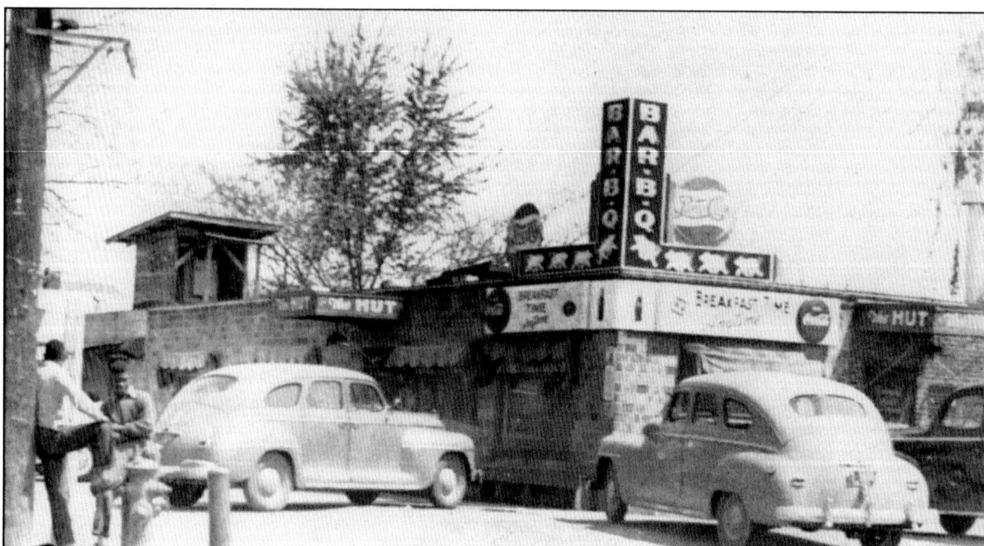

Most customers at the Hut sat in their cars where they ate their "pig" sandwiches and drank their cokes. J. T. Hamilton purchased the Hut from Mike Tucker in 1950 and kept it until 1980, when it was sold several times over. The location of the Hut is now a Walgreens at Highland and Campbell Streets. (Courtesy JMCL.)

John Burton Tigrett, Isaac B. Tigrett's nephew, came to live with his uncle in Jackson in the early 1930s. After World War II, John was in business in Chicago, and by 1950, he had returned to Jackson and started Tigrett Enterprises, a factory that made novelty toys and items such as the Pitch Back, shown in this April 1960 photograph. Tigrett used famous sports figures in marketing. (Courtesy Jimmy Gibbons.)

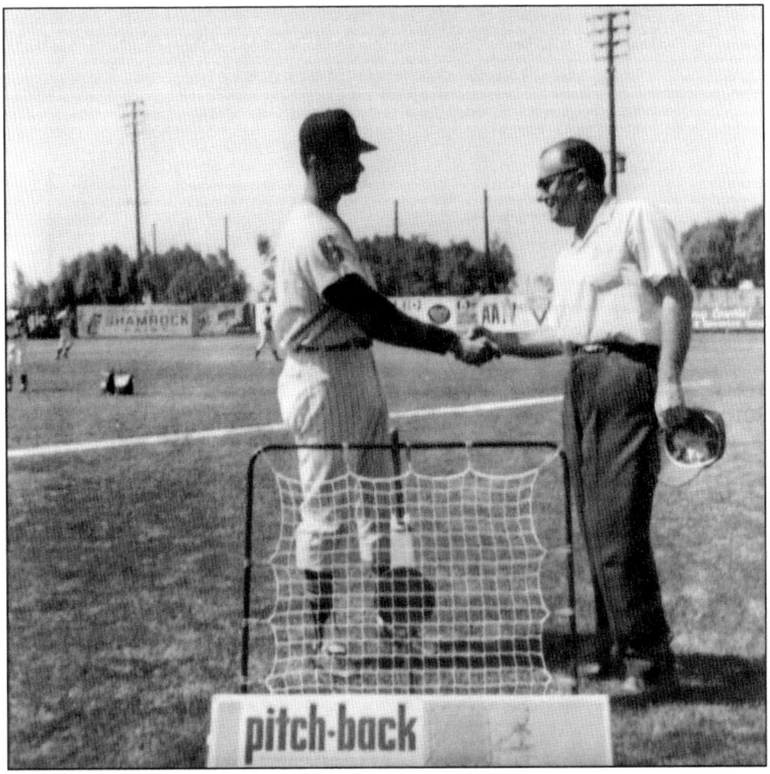

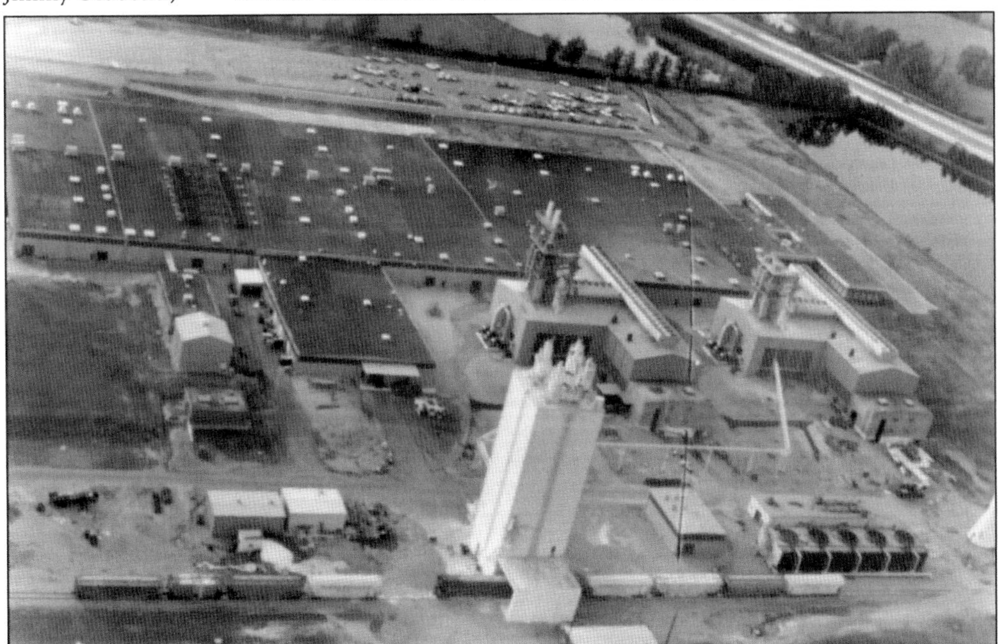

Owens Corning, a manufacturer of fiberglass insulation, built its plant in west Madison County in the late 1960s and began operations on January 10, 1969. In November 1976, a strike occurred, with the Teamsters Local 667 picketing. After periodic layoffs, the company closed the plant in 1986 but reopened it in 1994 with a much smaller force. (Courtesy Richard Higgins.)

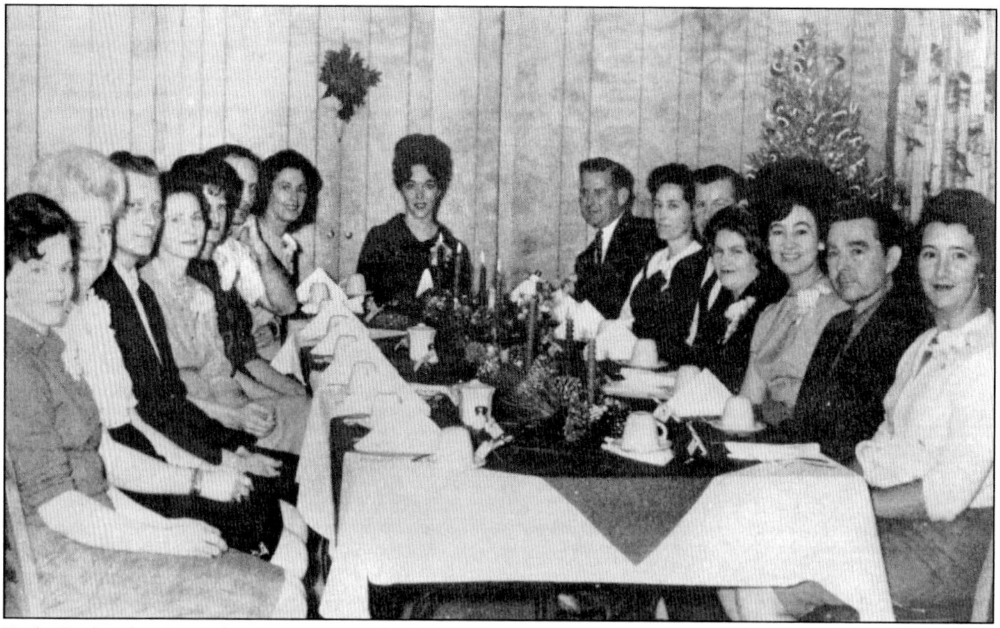

Dale Dole, the first plant manager of Rockwell Manufacturing, hosts a Christmas luncheon for employees in 1964. From left to right are Dot Erwin, Betty Little, George Lorentsen, Katie Reasons, Ruth Stewart, Frank Davis, Ann Johnson, Carolyn Henderson, John Ulmer, Barbara Davenport, Dale Dole, Patsy Nichols, Alice Blankenship, Jim Sanders, and Mary Young. (Photograph by Gerald Hicks, courtesy John Ulmer.)

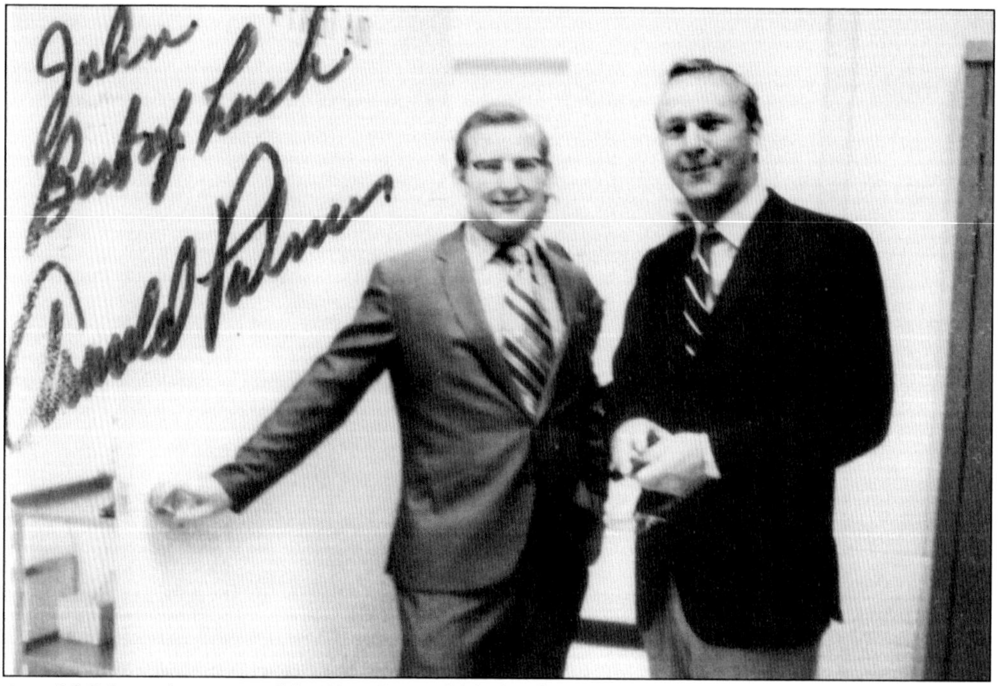

Arnold Palmer, known as "the King" in golf, helped to market Rockwell power tools that were painted green by saying, "Go for the Green." Palmer is shown with longtime human resource director John Ulmer in the 1970s, when Palmer visited the Jackson plant. (Courtesy John Ulmer.)

Rockwell International, a power tool manufacturing operation, first came to the area in 1964 and had its plant built and in operation in 1966. In 1981, Porter Cable purchased the plant, and it is currently owned by Black and Decker. Two buildings and a distribution center are located on 177 acres at the intersection of Highway 45 North and Passmore Lane with 700 employees. (Courtesy John Ulmer.)

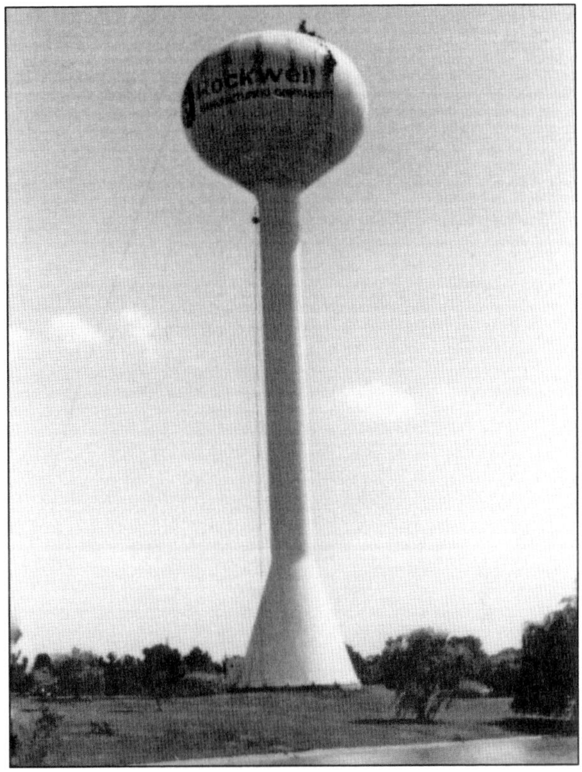

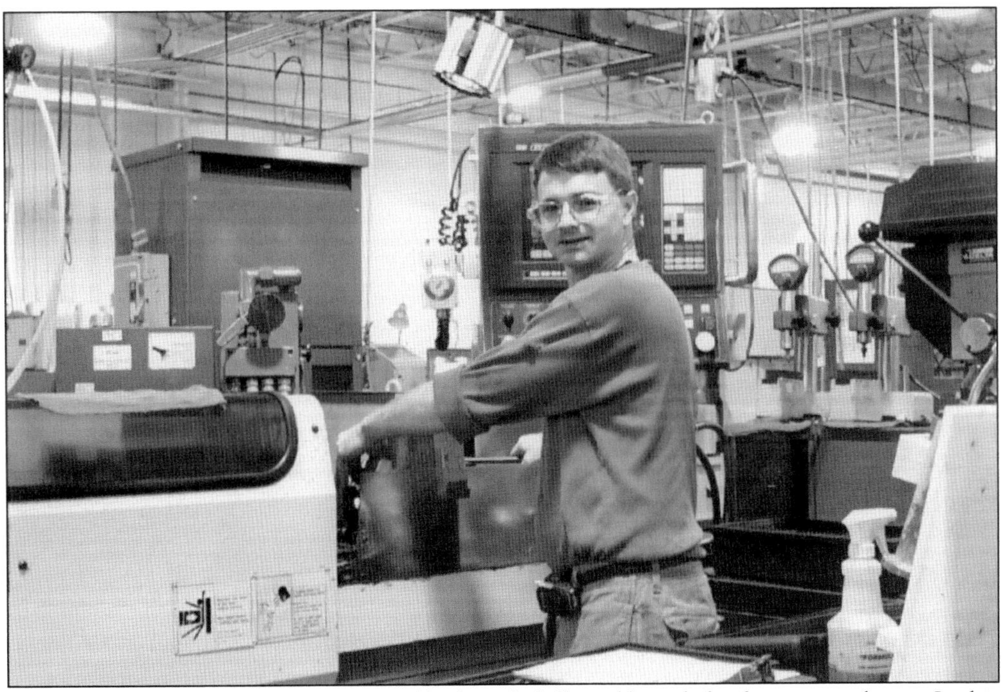

Porter Cable (Black and Decker) required high-tech skills and knowledge from its employees. In this photograph, Joel Gibbons, after programming his machines, is running two CNC (Computerized Numerical Control) grinders. (Courtesy Rosalee Gibbons.)

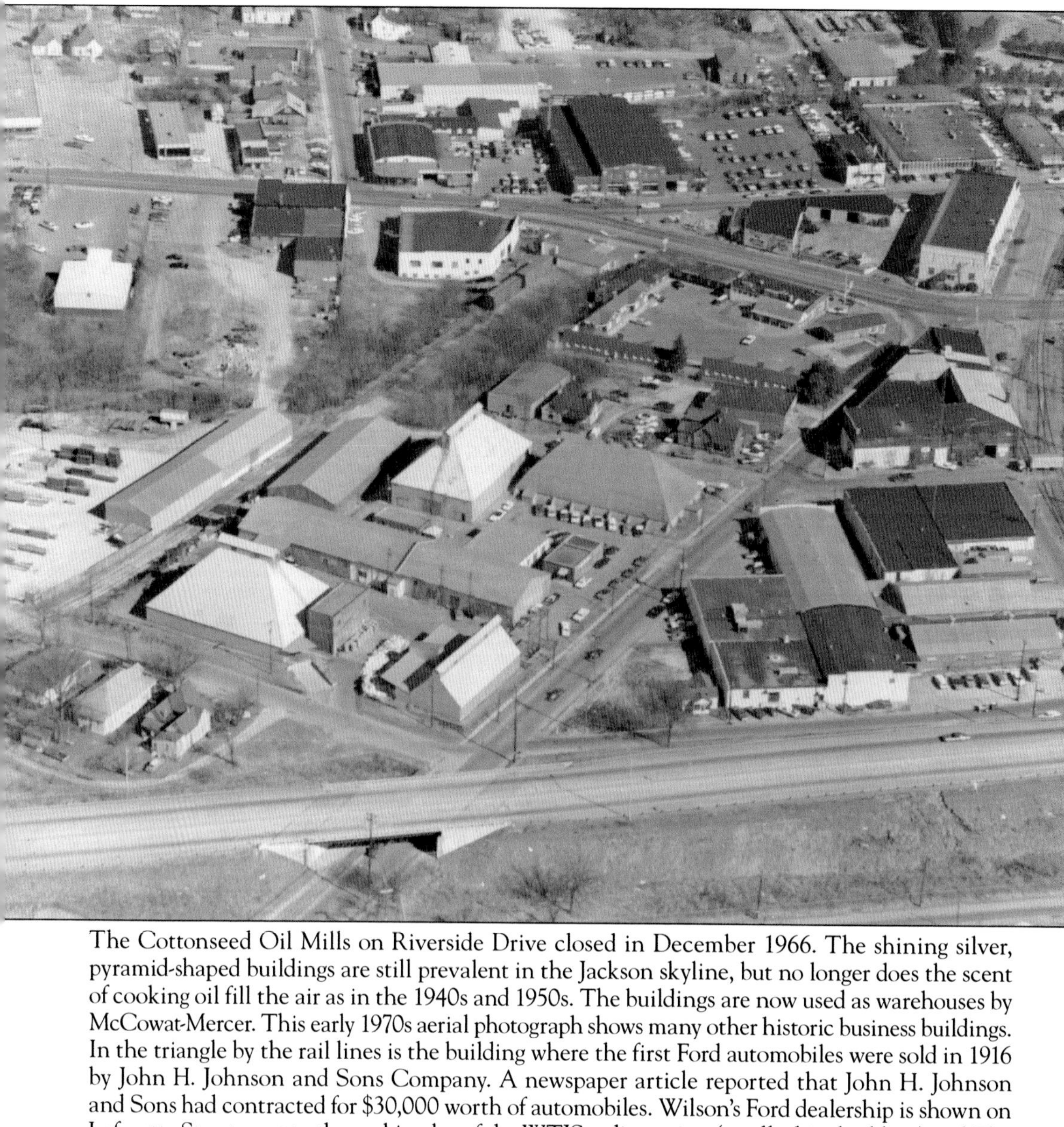

The Cottonseed Oil Mills on Riverside Drive closed in December 1966. The shining silver, pyramid-shaped buildings are still prevalent in the Jackson skyline, but no longer does the scent of cooking oil fill the air as in the 1940s and 1950s. The buildings are now used as warehouses by McCowat-Mercer. This early 1970s aerial photograph shows many other historic business buildings. In the triangle by the rail lines is the building where the first Ford automobiles were sold in 1916 by John H. Johnson and Sons Company. A newspaper article reported that John H. Johnson and Sons had contracted for $30,000 worth of automobiles. Wilson's Ford dealership is shown on Lafayette Street next to the parking lot of the WTJS radio station (small white building) and The Jackson Sun plant, built in the late 1950s. The Oldsmobile dealership is west of Wilson Ford at the corner of Lafayette and Johnson Streets. This photograph shows the new bypass built from the center of downtown west to connect to I-40. (Courtesy McCowat-Mercer.)

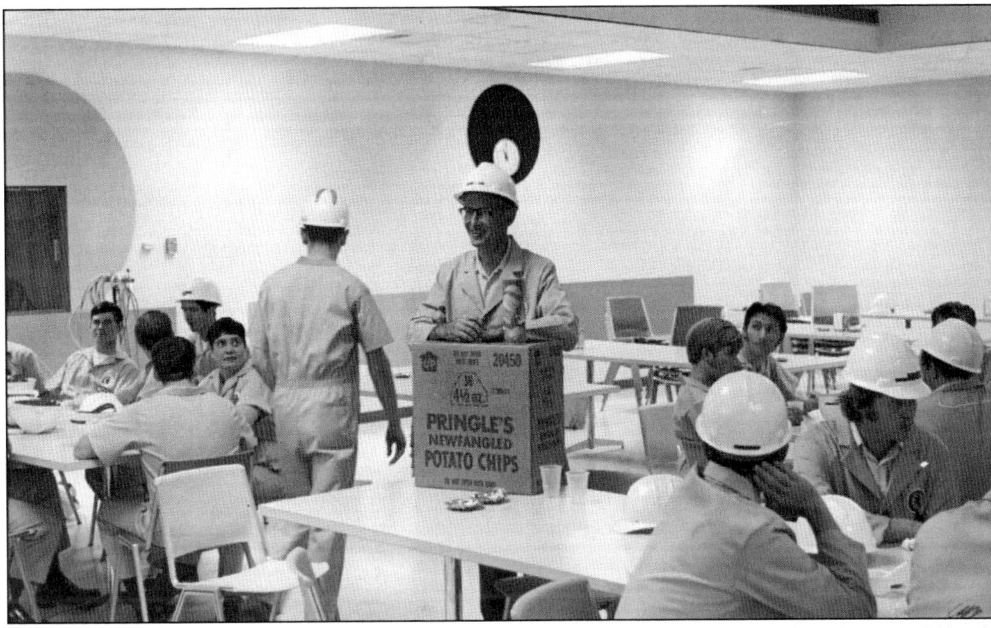

Procter and Gamble Manufacturing Company announced in October 1969 that they would build a food plant in Jackson, Tennessee. The construction of the plant was ongoing in 1970. By 1971, the first case of Pringles was shipped (above). Today the plant is 37 acres under roof on a 170-acre site at the eastern boundary of Jackson on a railroad line with its own spur. The 2003 tornado that ravaged Madison County from west to east did significant damage to the plant, but no one was injured. Some 1,220 people from Madison County and surrounding counties are employed by Procter and Gamble. (Both courtesy Randy Kennedy of Procter and Gamble.)

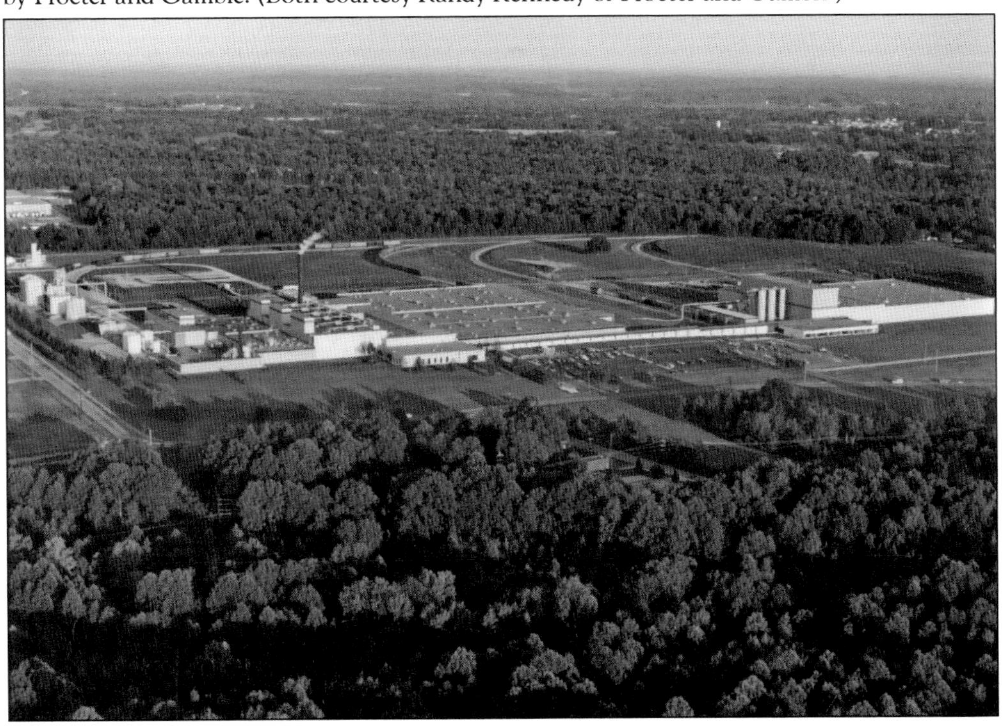

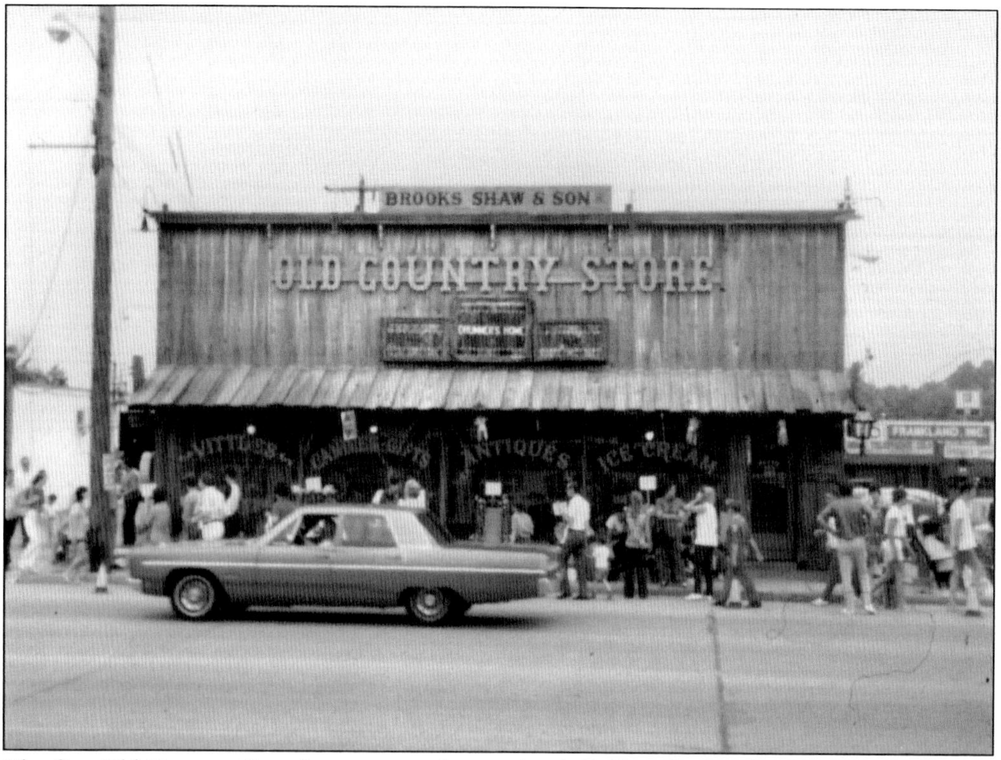

The first Old Country Store became a reality in April 1965 in the hands of Brooks Shaw, who started out collecting antiques as a reprieve from his stressful corporate job. Beginning as a museum, it soon became a fully operational store, ice cream parlor, and restaurant on Airways Boulevard with Norwood and Joyce Jones as storekeepers. (Courtesy Norwood Jones.)

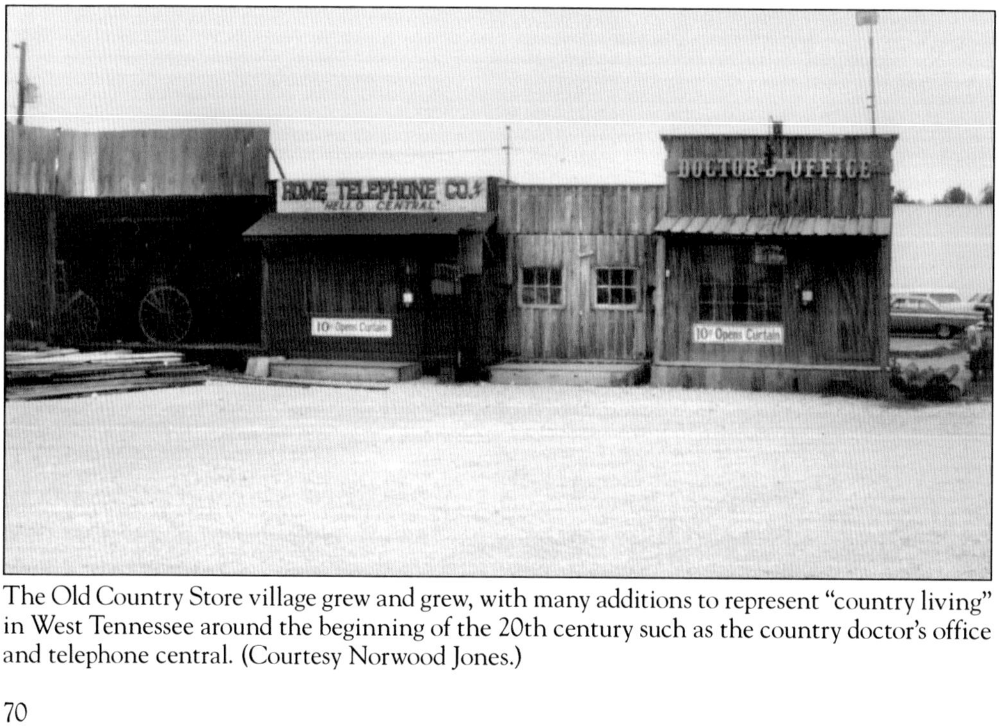

The Old Country Store village grew and grew, with many additions to represent "country living" in West Tennessee around the beginning of the 20th century such as the country doctor's office and telephone central. (Courtesy Norwood Jones.)

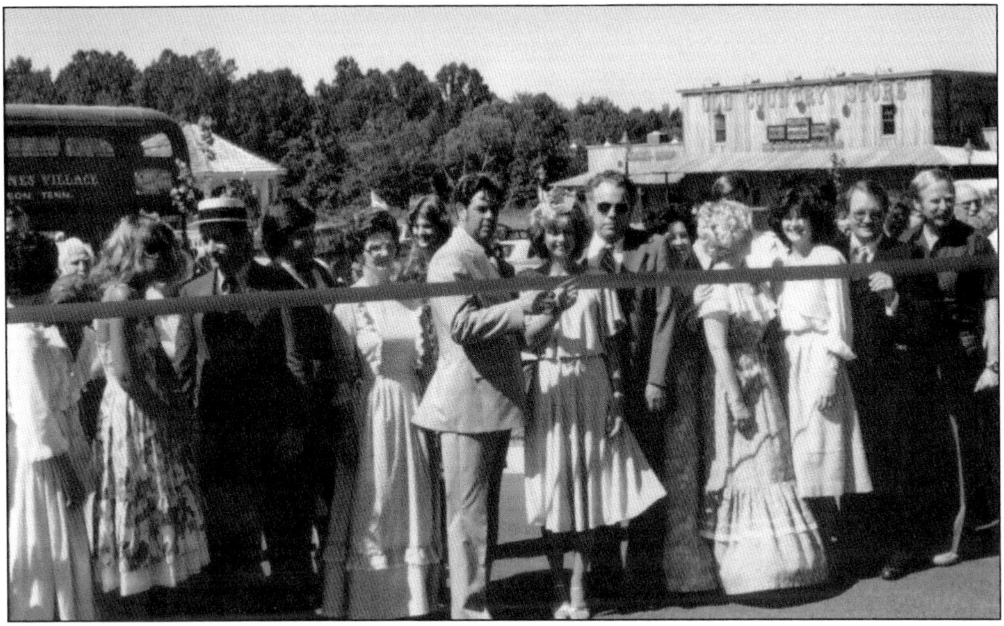

Jackson mayor Bob Conger cut the ribbon for the opening of the Old Country Store and the Casey Jones Village in 1978 at its new location next to I-40. Joining him are, from left to right, Norwood Jones in his straw hat, Clark Shaw, Ann Shaw, Conger, Miss Tennessee Jill Beshears, and county executive Walter Baker Harris. Others are unidentified. (Courtesy Old Country Store and Norwood Jones.)

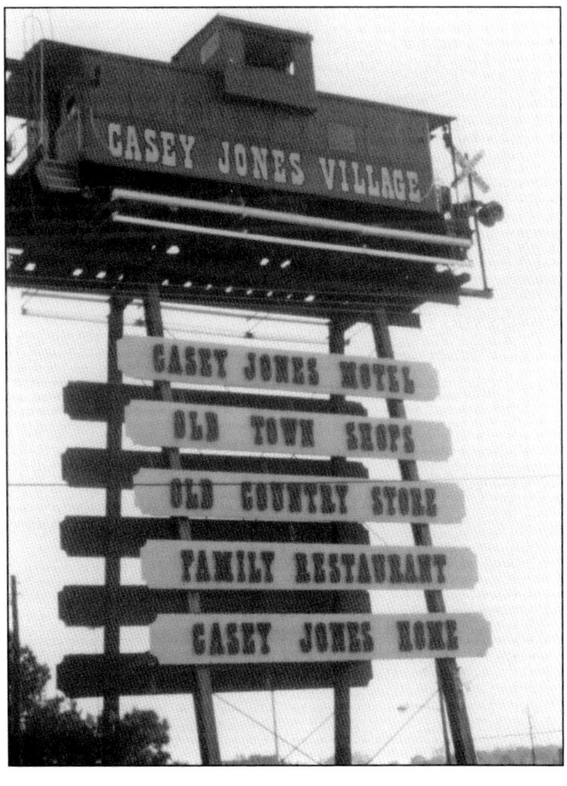

The familiar "Caboose in the Sky" sign attracted the attention of interstate travelers to the Casey Jones Village, the hotel, shops, the Old Country Store, the restaurant, and the Casey Jones home and museum. (Courtesy Old Country Store and Norwood Jones.)

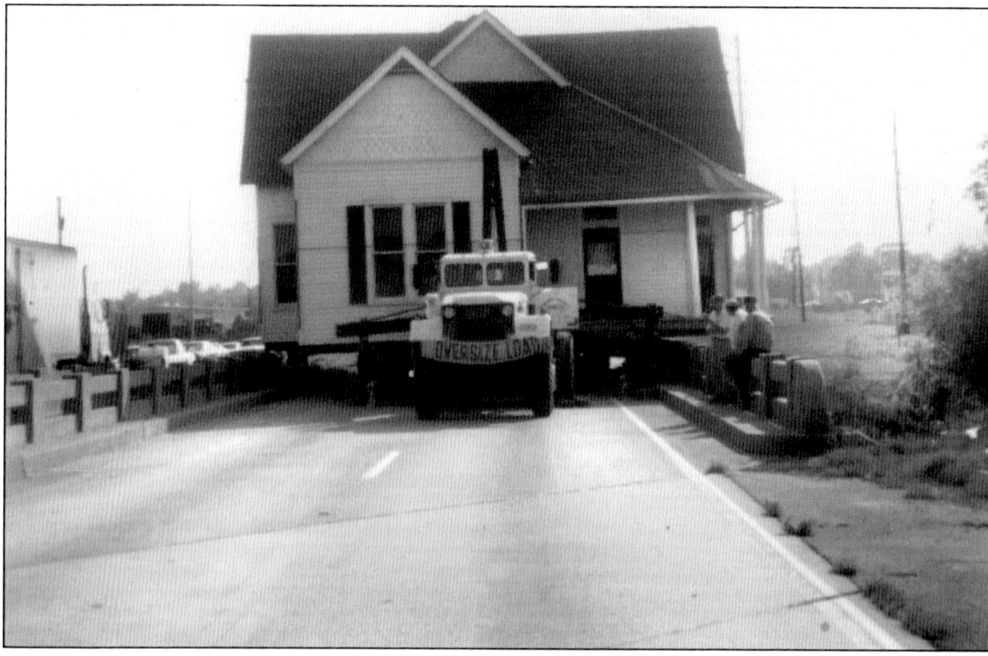

The Casey Jones House was moved from downtown Jackson on Chester Street to the Casey Jones Village in 1980. The new owners, the Old Country Store, planned to establish a railroad museum in the new location next to I-40 that would bring more tourists to the historic home. In the process of moving it, the house got stuck on the Highway 45 Bypass, but movers were able to jack it up and keep it in one piece. Engine 383, which was similar to the one Casey Jones was driving when he had his famous accident, was also moved from the downtown location to the village. (Both courtesy Old Country Store and Norwood Jones.)

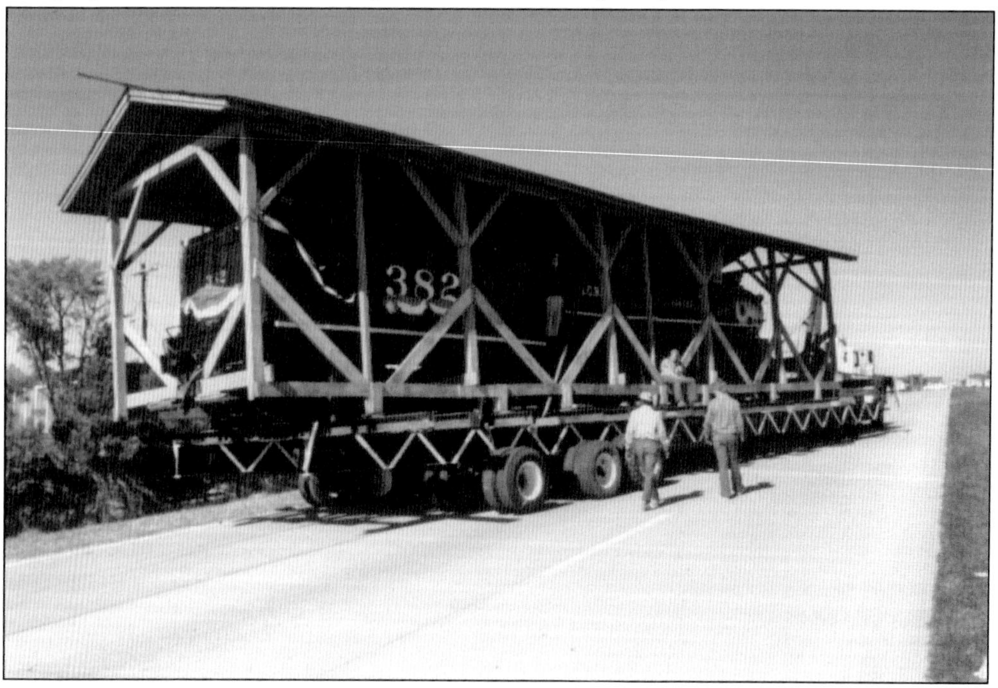

Joan Tomlin (left) and Frances Tigrett (right) were very excited to turn the first shovel of dirt for Sears, the first building at the Old Hickory Mall, in 1965. The Sears store and the First National Bank building were completed and open by October 1965. Joan's husband, Hewitt P. Tomlin Jr., and his sister, Frances, were co-owners of the mall. The man in the center is unidentified. (Courtesy Joan Tomlin.)

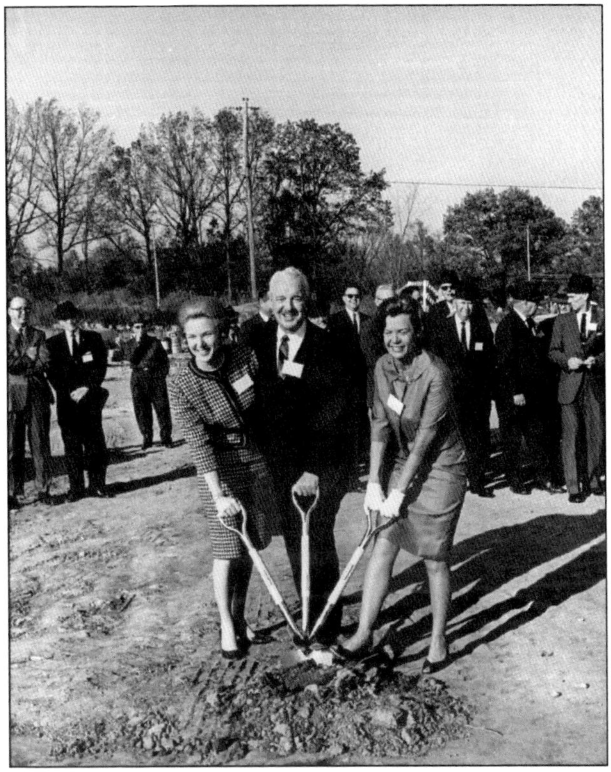

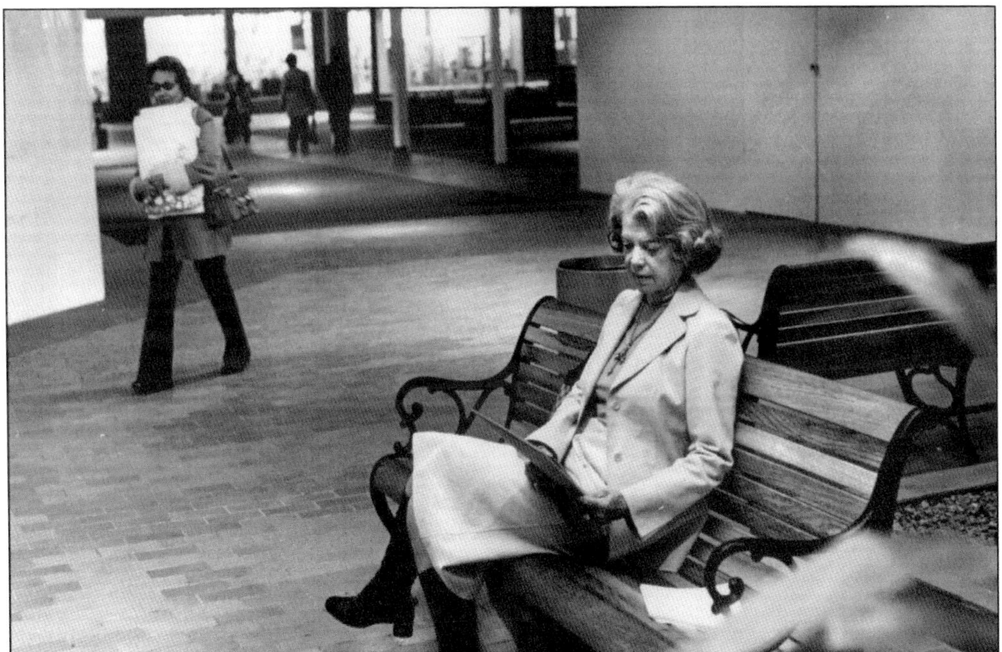

A modern-day enclosed mall was a dream come true for developer Frances Tomlin Tigrett, pictured enjoying her solitude on a bench in the Old Hickory Mall on January 25, 1979. The mall's grand opening was held in July 1967. (Courtesy the *Jackson Sun*.)

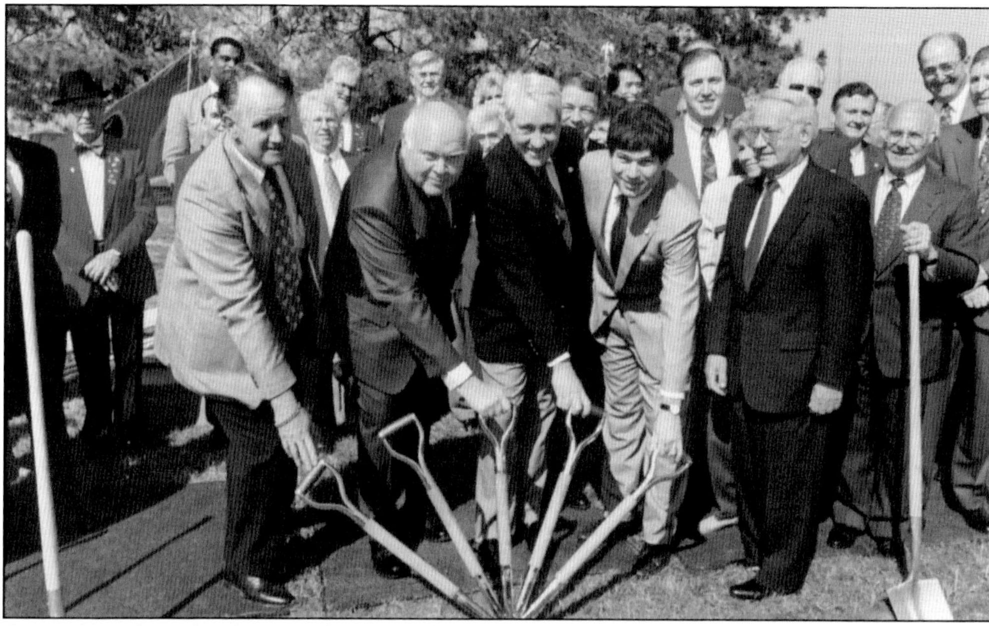

Ground-breaking for the McWherter Technology Center at Jackson State Community College took place on March 25, 1994, with, from left to right, Pres. Walter Nelms, Gov. Ned R. Wherter, state senator Joe Nip McKnight, and state representative Matt Kisber turning the first shovel of dirt. Many other dignitaries and chamber of commerce "Red Coats" surround the action. (Courtesy JSCC.)

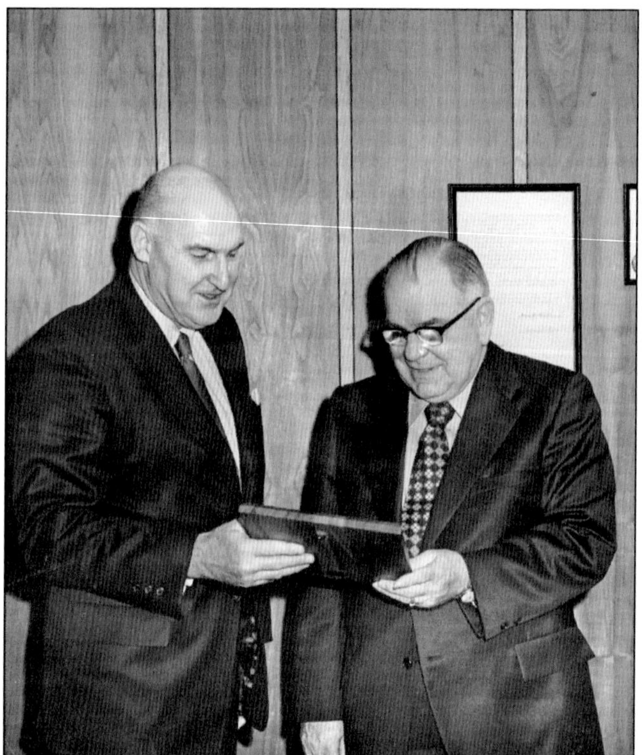

Jackson State Community College's first president, Dr. F. E. Wright, recognizes Dr. Jack Thompson, administrator of the Jackson–Madison County General Hospital, for helping the college establish allied health academic programs, which helped to train needed medical personnel for the area. (Courtesy JSCC.)

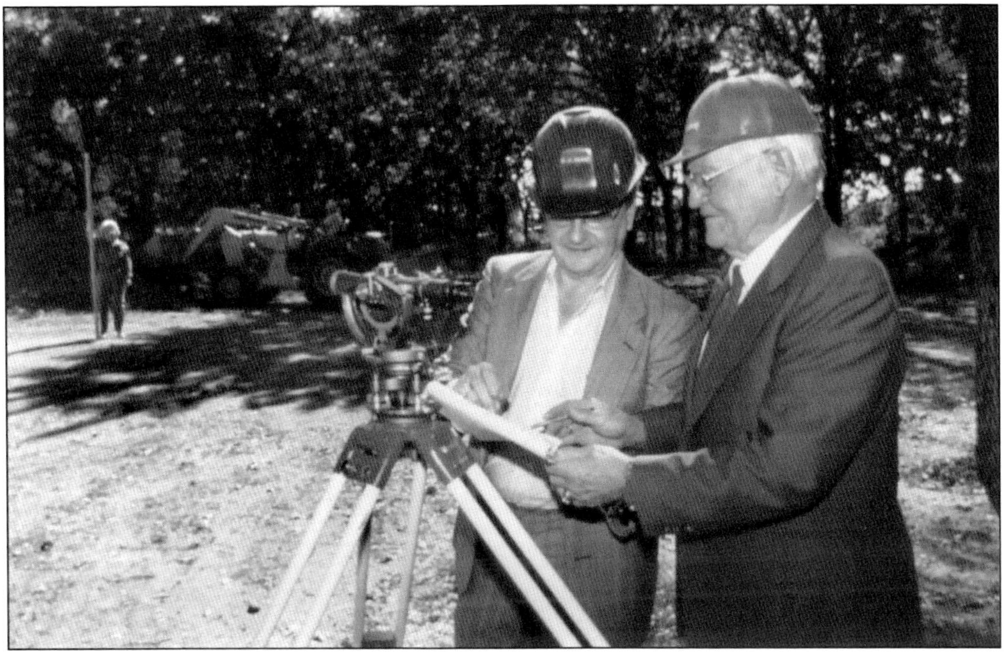

A new manufacturing endeavor was brought to Madison County by Bill Ranne, shown here with his father, B. H. Ranne, as construction of Reliable Coatings plant was underway in Madison East Industrial Park in 1986. They moved into their building in 1988 and began applying unique powder coatings to manufactured items. (Courtesy Bill and Judy Ranne.)

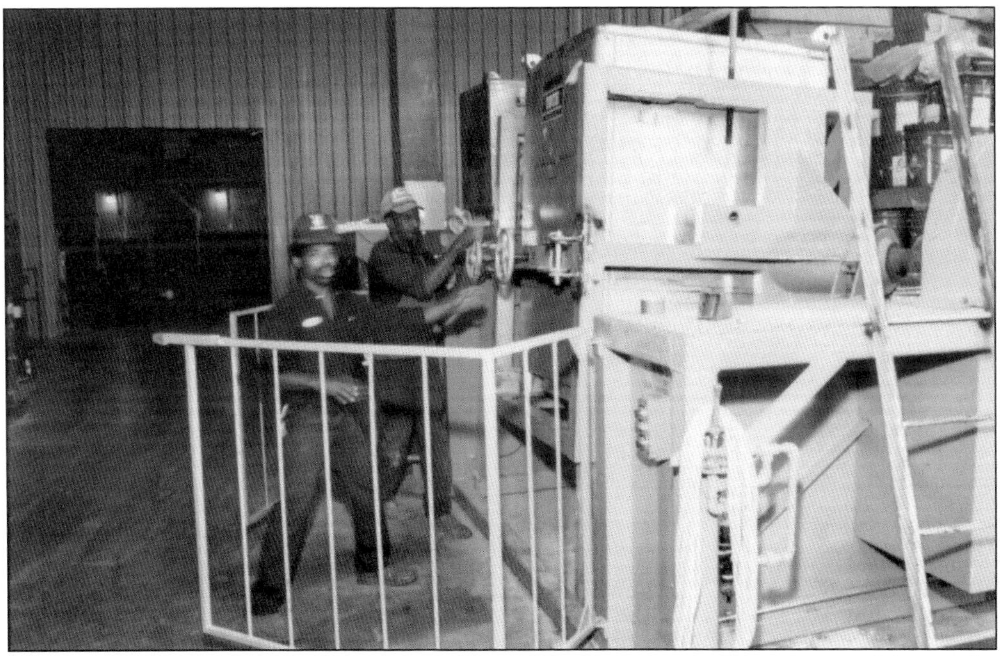

B. H. Ranne, formerly the chief engineer with Mary Kay Cosmetics in Texas, invented the powder tumbler shown here. His son, Bill, installed the process in his Reliable Coatings plant in Jackson, Tennessee, and also had a plant in Texas. Reliable Coatings in Jackson employed 106. (Courtesy Bill and Judy Ranne.)

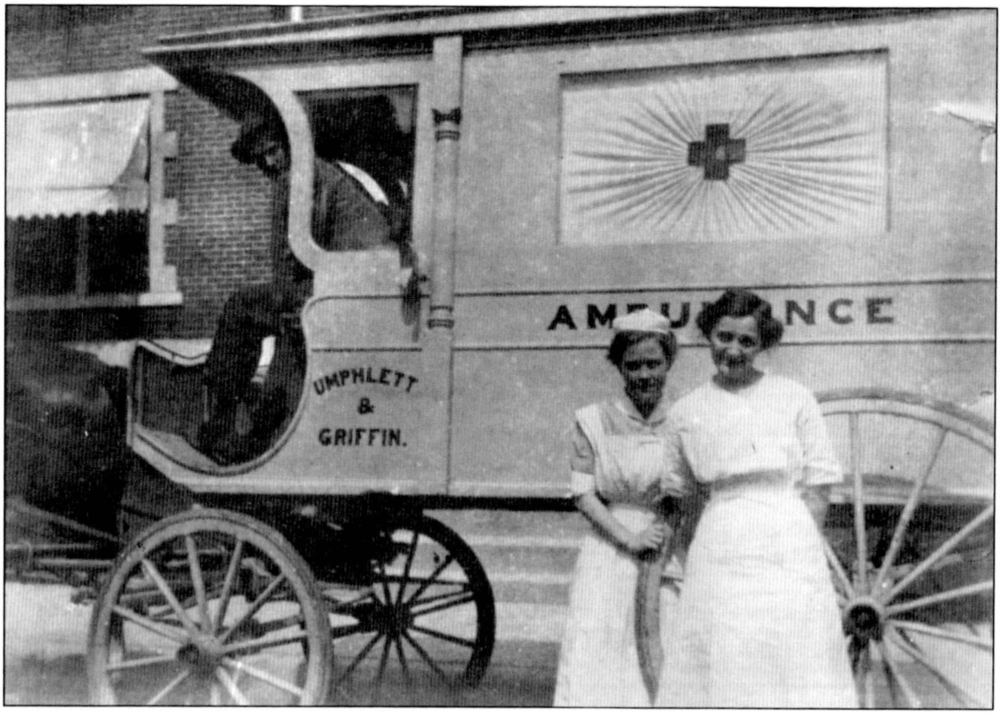

Umphlett and Griffin Funeral Home, established in 1852, used this horse-drawn ambulance around 1910. (Courtesy Griffin Funeral Home.)

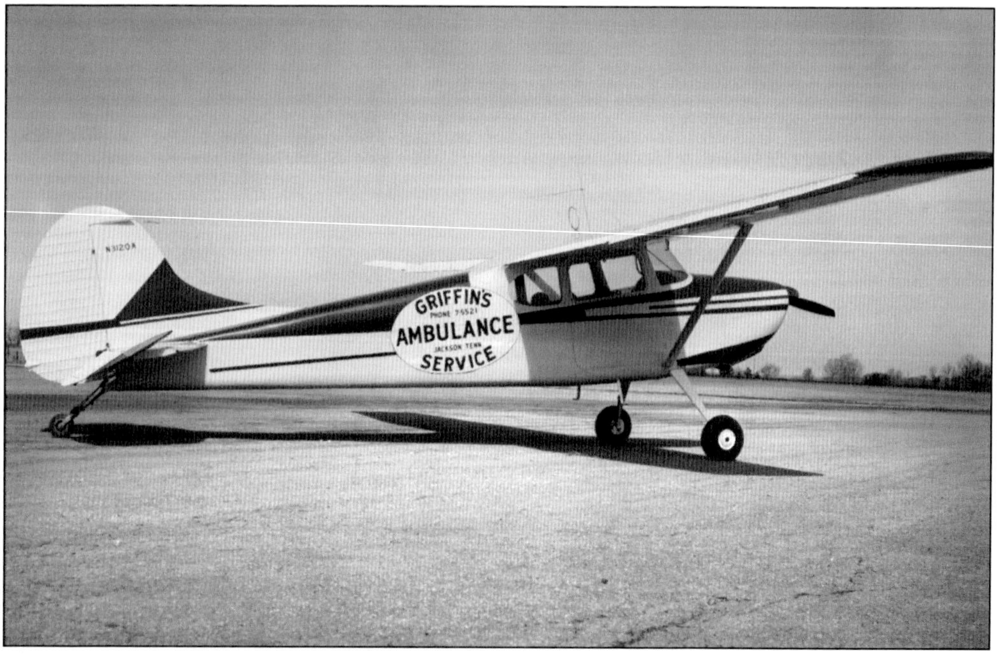

This 1959 picture of Griffin Funeral Home's Airplane Ambulance illustrates the resiliency of local businesses. The funeral home's ambulance business went from horse and buggy in early 1900s to air transportation by mid-century. The Jackson airport terminal was built by 1958. (Courtesy JMCL.)

Four

Outstanding Women in Business

Women in Madison County early in the 20th century were no different from other females in this country at that time. Their roles were primarily those of wives and mothers, homemakers, and housekeepers. But times were changing. Education became important for women as well as men. Voting rights for women were being pursued with much passion by many women, including some in Madison County. Sue Shelton White, born in neighboring Chester County, joined the woman suffrage movement in 1912 and moved to Washington, D.C., to help pass the 19th Amendment. After ratification, she obtained her law degree and practiced in Jackson from 1926 to 1930 but soon returned to D.C. to work in the Roosevelt administration. Another Jacksonian, Pauline LaFon, who would become mother of Vice Pres. Al Gore, waited on tables to pay her way through Union University and in 1936 became the 10th woman to obtain a degree from Vanderbilt University Law School. She never returned to Jackson to live, but her mother, brother Judge Whit LaFon, and other family members continued to live here.

Other opportunities were also opening up for women. Lucia Glynn Michaelis began a cosmetology school in 1926 and helped train many women to operate their own beauty shop businesses.

Early in the 1900s, educational opportunities were brought to the farm and rural women through the Home Demonstration Club and 4-H. Girl Scout troops in urban settings helped to build young women full of self-esteem and confidence.

Industrial employment for women was limited in the area, but after the Bemis Cotton Mill opened, many women with small hands were needed to operate the looms. After the 1930s, automation eliminated much of the need for the small female hands, but women continued to be employed at the cotton mill even as employment for males grew.

Women have always been servers and cooks, but as public employment opened up, female servers in restaurants could make a decent wage, and women cooks became restaurant owners.

Jackson has been lucky to have top females in real estate, marketing, banking, insurance, allied health fields, and many other strategic positions.

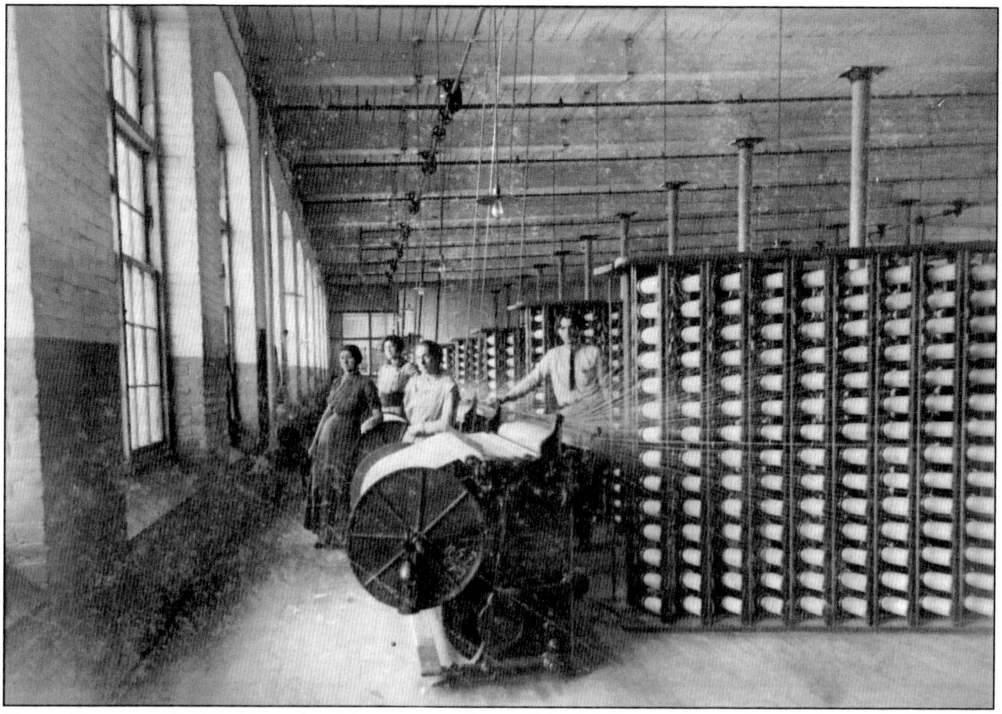

Bemis historian Joel Jackson, based on stories from older people and pictures such as the two here, guessed that all spinners in the Bemis Cotton Mill from 1901 until the 1930s were women with a male boss. George Reeves, at right, is the foreman. (Both courtesy Bemis Historical Society and Betsy Reeves Babb.)

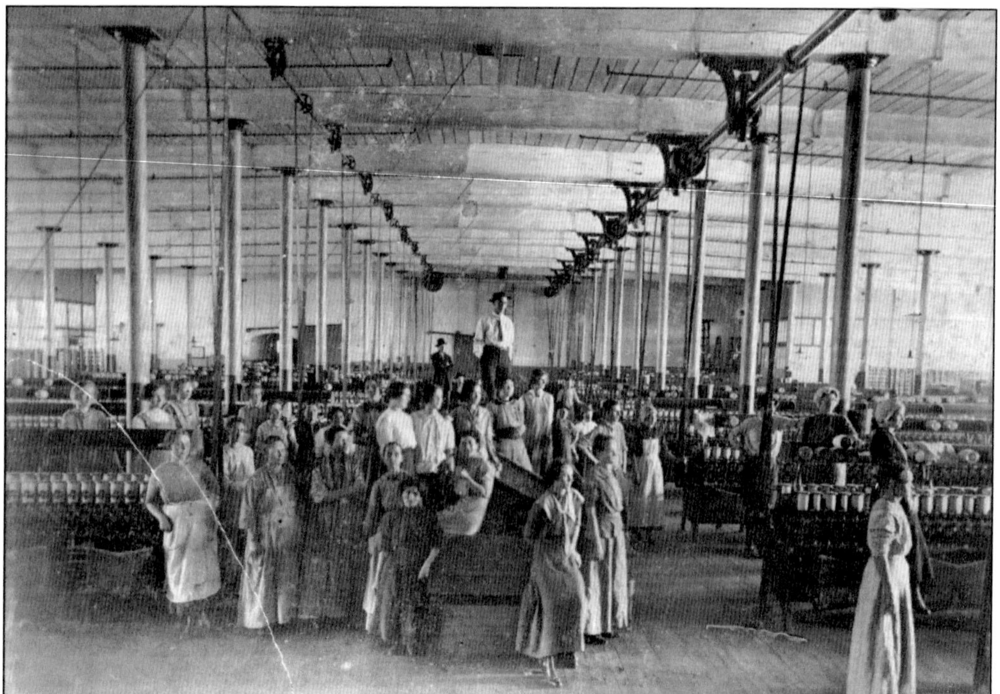

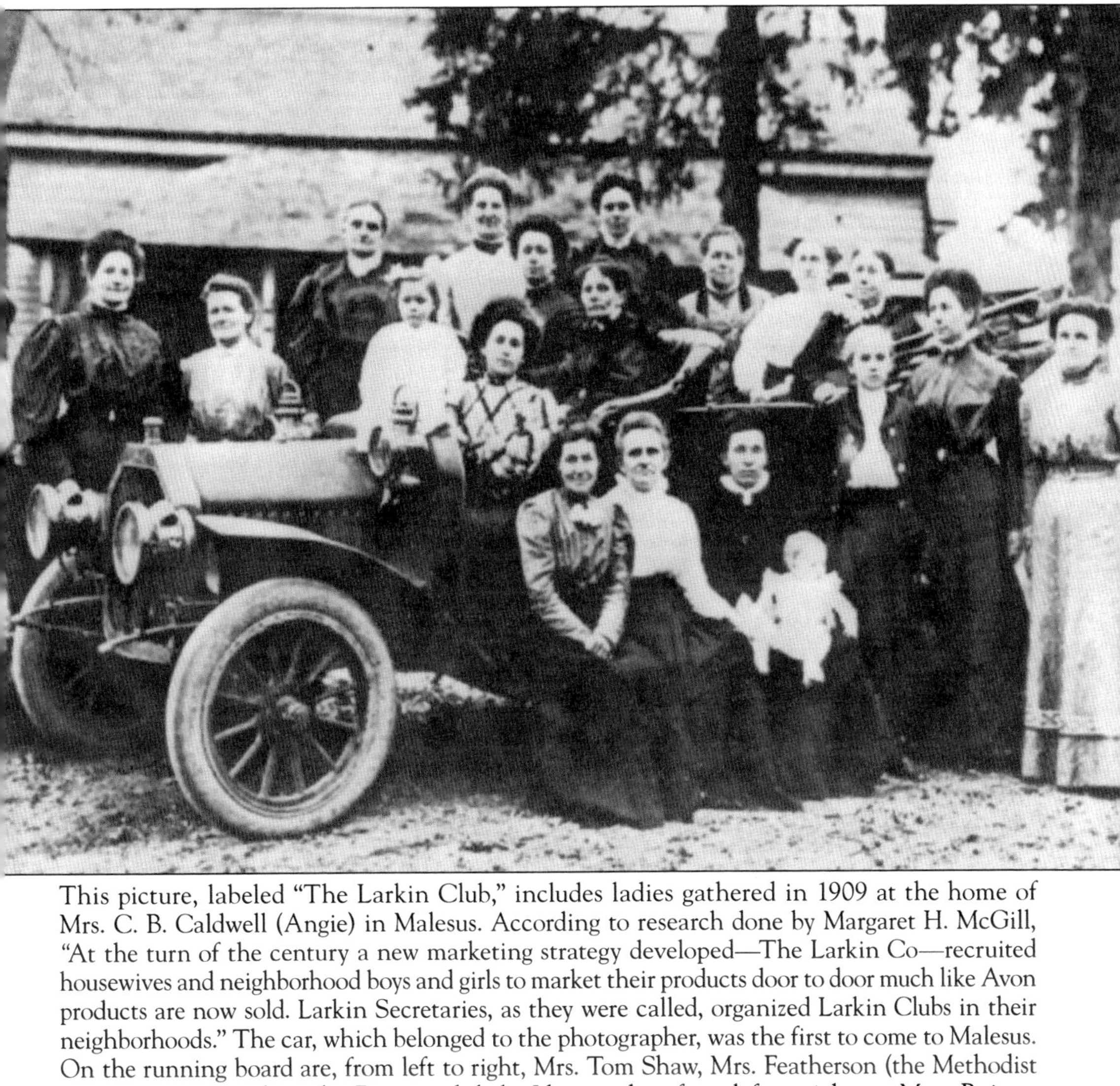

This picture, labeled "The Larkin Club," includes ladies gathered in 1909 at the home of Mrs. C. B. Caldwell (Angie) in Malesus. According to research done by Margaret H. McGill, "At the turn of the century a new marketing strategy developed—The Larkin Co—recruited housewives and neighborhood boys and girls to market their products door to door much like Avon products are now sold. Larkin Secretaries, as they were called, organized Larkin Clubs in their neighborhoods." The car, which belonged to the photographer, was the first to come to Malesus. On the running board are, from left to right, Mrs. Tom Shaw, Mrs. Featherson (the Methodist minister's wife), and Bertha Davis with baby Ida; standing from left to right are Mary Raines, Eula Taylor (principal of Malesus School), and Mrs. J. A. Freeling; sitting in front seat are, from left to right, Angie Caldwell with baby Mamie, Mrs. Joe Hudson, and Kate Dubois; from left to right in the backseat are Mrs. Dubois, Mrs. Ida Raines, and a visitor; standing in back row from left to right are Stella Parr with niece Louise Mainord, Mrs. Rutherford, Mary E. Hammond, Lucy Harton, Mrs. Mary Lake, and Mrs. W. L. Mott. (Courtesy of Margaret H. McGill.)

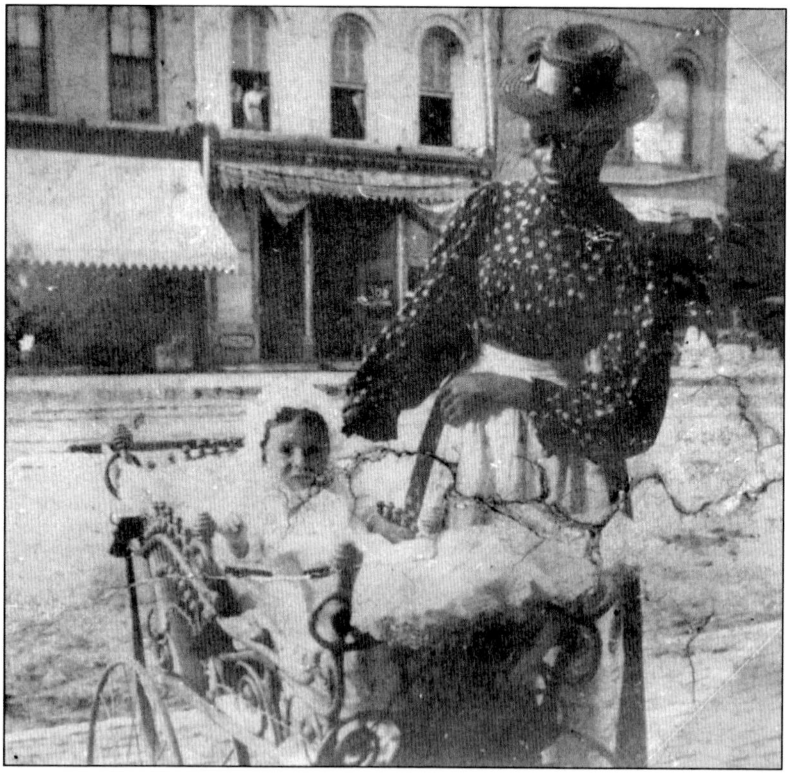

Some women in the early 1900s worked as domestics, and some took care of other people's children. This picture depicts baby girl Baum in a carriage on East Main Street with an unidentified attendant. (Courtesy JMCL.)

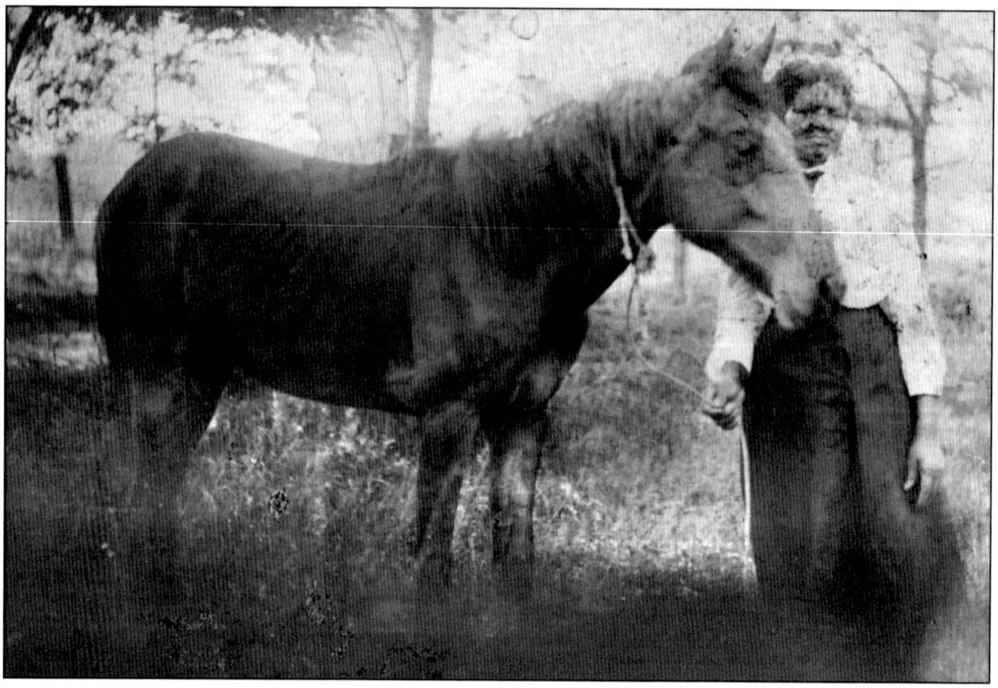

Anne Eliza Hurt and her husband, Rufus Hurt, established Hurt's store in 1912 on the corner of Lane Avenue and Pine Street. At the time, that part of Jackson was undeveloped, and the Hurts raised horses, cows, chickens, cotton, and a large vegetable garden. (Courtesy Ruby Hurt Booth.)

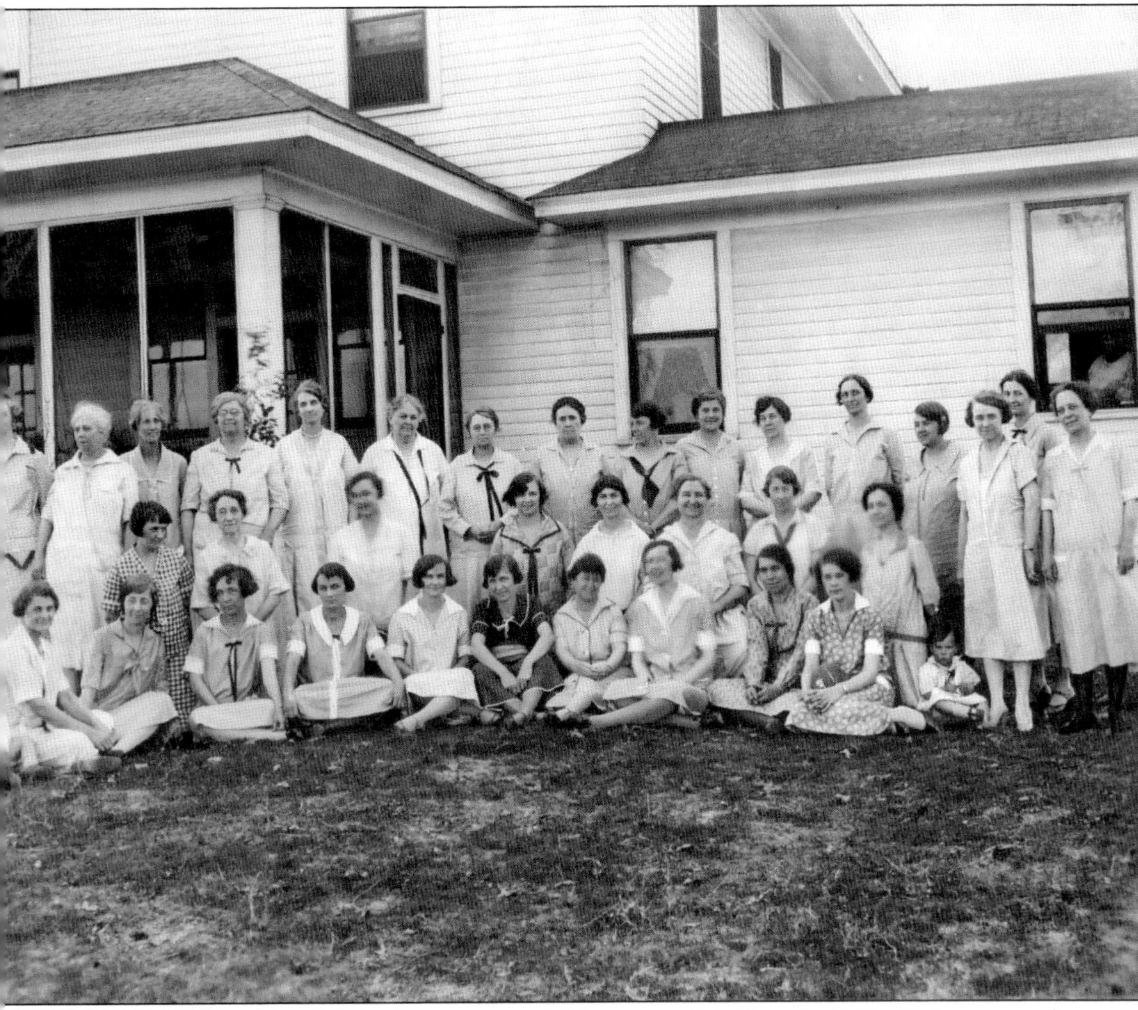

Ethel Bond Baker recorded the following in a 1986 history of Madison Hall: "In 1914, a group of women met in Anderson Presbyterian Church for an all day quilting and made plans to organize a Home Demonstration Club. Mrs. Lansden, our county agent, and Miss McKenzie from the Extension Department at Knoxville, met with this group. This topic was discussed over and over as it was the first of its kind in Madison County and also in West Tennessee. The next meeting was held in the home of Mrs. A. S. Johnson [above] and the club was fully organized. Mrs. A. S. Johnson was elected president with Mrs. C. E. Campbell the secretary. This was a very important afternoon in the history of Madison County as it was the first home demonstration club organized." (Courtesy Madison County Agricultural Extension office and Billie H. Jennings.)

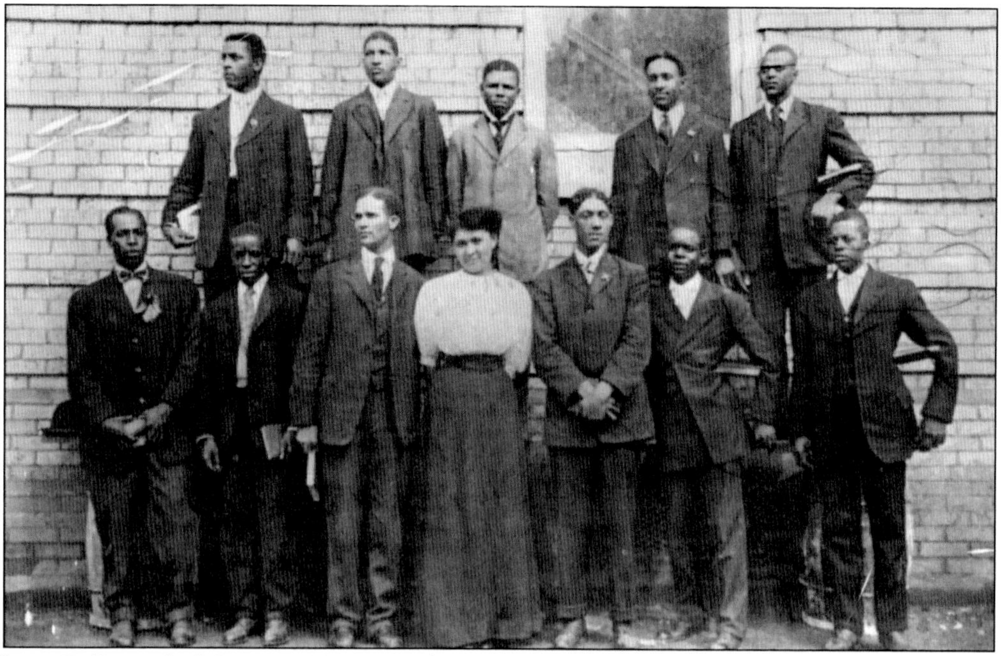

Lane College, which began in 1882 in Madison County as a high school for black students, started its college courses in 1896 and was then known as Lane College. In 1908, a women's residence hall was constructed, and on May 28, 1913, the first female graduated. Her name was Ernestine Ginerva Anderson. (Courtesy Lane College Library.)

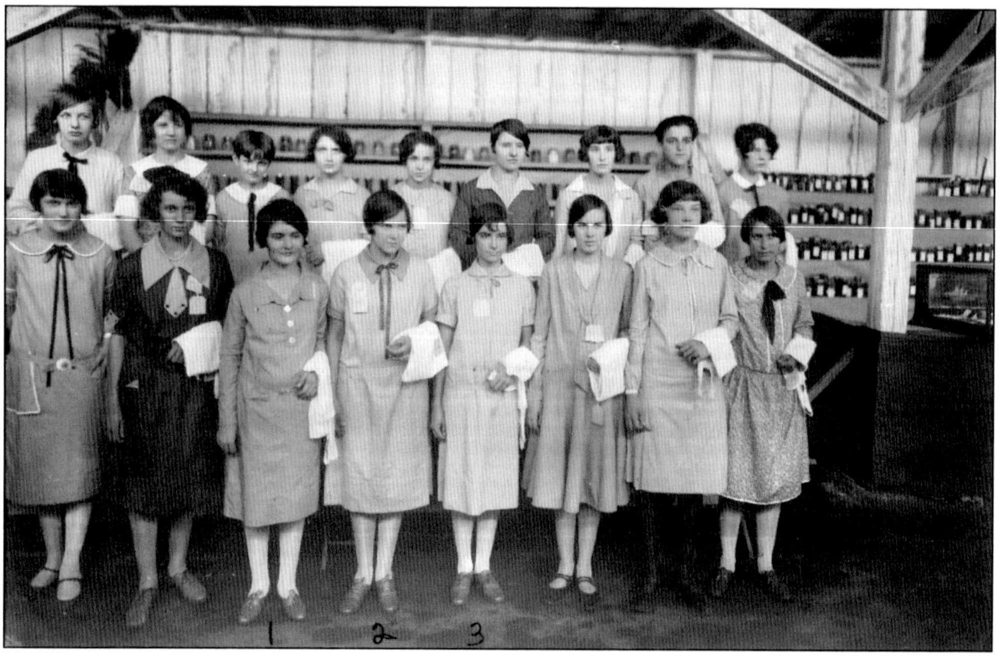

Members of 4-H who entered items in the West Tennessee Fair are ready to participate in cooking demonstrations with their white aprons in the 1920s. Number 1 is Louise Lassiter (Boone); number 2 is Lacy Lassiter (Kincannon); and number 3 is Ruth Boone (Shaver). (Courtesy Madison County Agricultural Extension office and Billie H. Jennings.)

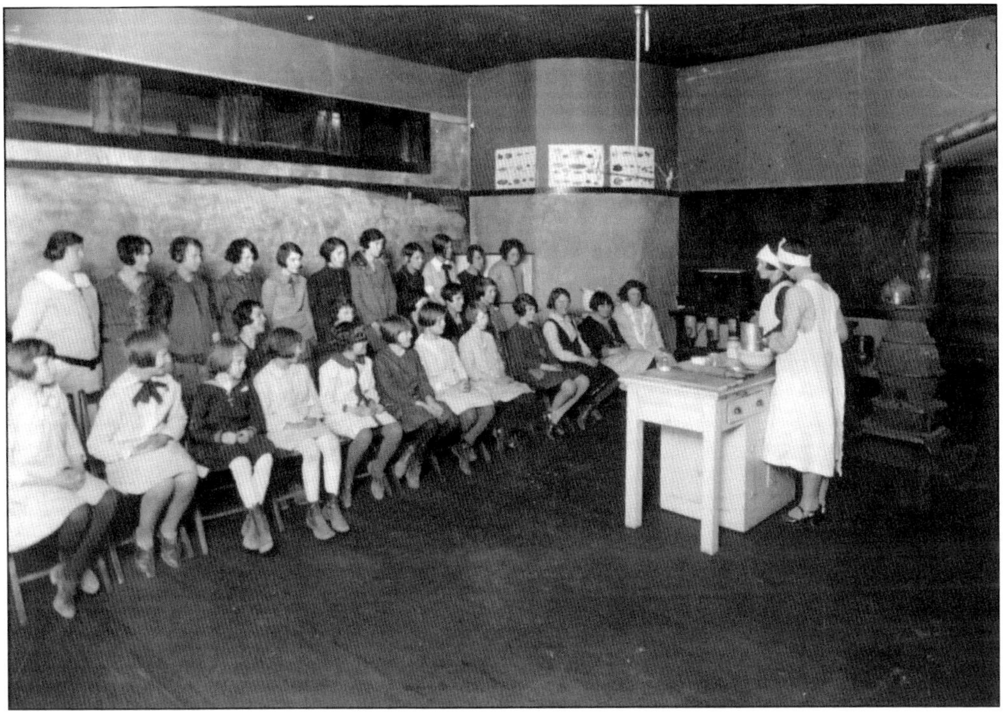

Young 4-H members watch a cooking demonstration by older 4-H members in the 1920s. (Courtesy Madison County Agricultural Extension office and Billie H. Jennings.)

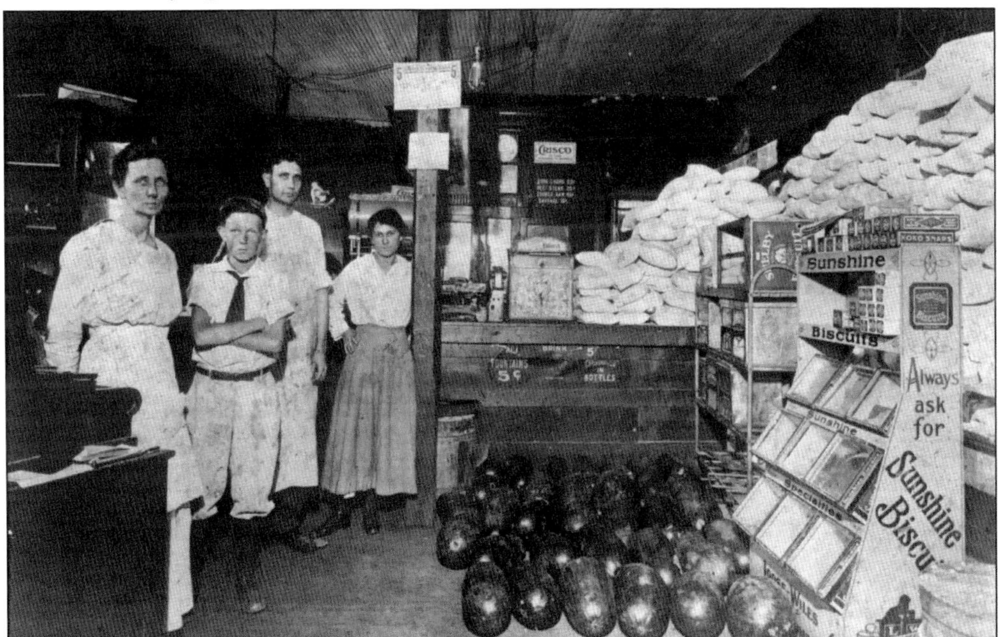

Early in the 20th century, grocery stores were operated by women while their husbands worked on the farm or in another type of employment. Shown here in 1916 is Robert's Grocery, run by Mary Roberts (left). Others shown are from left to right, Noel, James McNatt, and Hattie McNatt. (Courtesy Mary Roberts.)

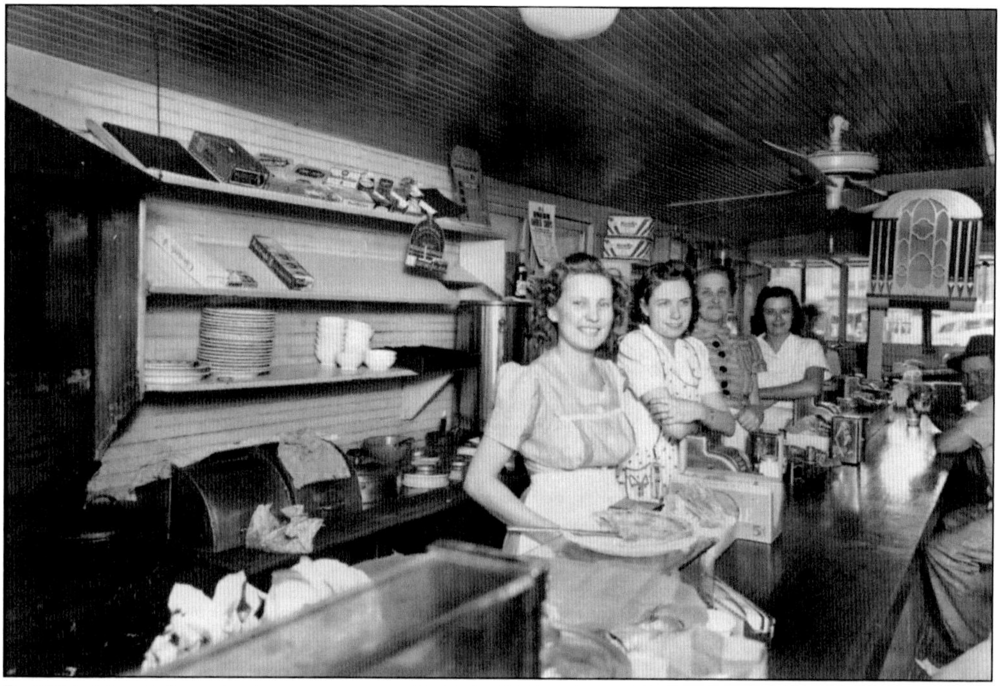

By 1935, Mrs. Roberts had a restaurant called Mrs. Robert's Eat Shoppe on West Main Street. In the 20th century, wait staff in restaurants were usually women. From left to right are Mary McDonald, Mary Etta Day, May Britt, unidentified, and a customer. (Courtesy Mrs. Mary Roberts.)

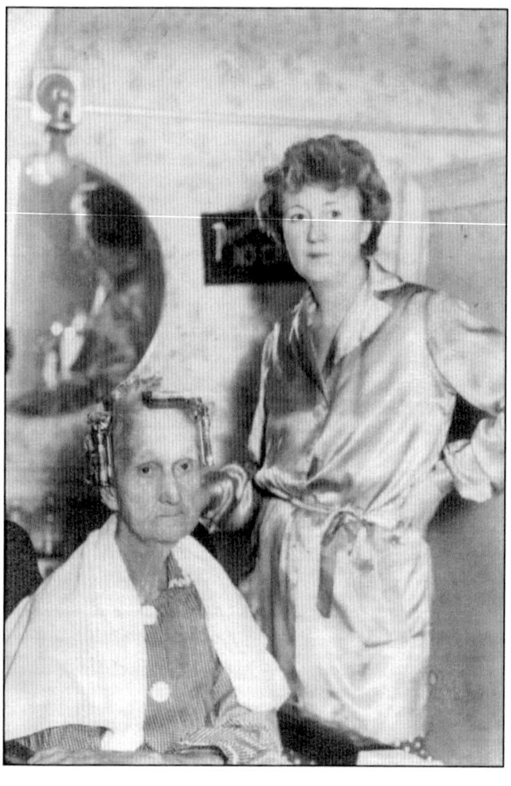

Lucia D. Glynn Michaelis (standing) operated one of the first beauty salons and was the first proprietor of a school for cosmeticians in Jackson, dating from 1926. She graduated from the Marinello School of Chicago, Illinois, in 1924 and did postgraduate work at the Marinello School in New York. The patron in this picture is unidentified. (Courtesy Linda J. Higgins.)

In a brochure explaining her Michaelis School of Cosmeticians at 210 North Church Street, she encourages prospective students, "Arrange now to get started on the road to independence and earn an assured income in Beauty Culture, the fastest growing profession for women." (Courtesy Linda J. Higgins.)

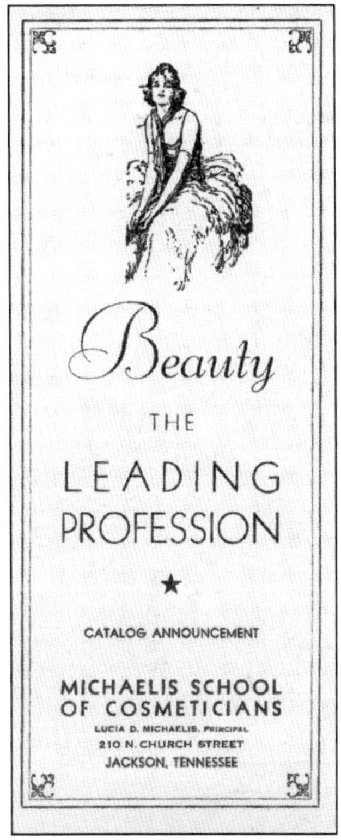

Beauty

THE

LEADING
PROFESSION

★

CATALOG ANNOUNCEMENT

MICHAELIS SCHOOL
OF COSMETICIANS
LUCIA D. MICHAELIS, PRINCIPAL
210 N. CHURCH STREET
JACKSON, TENNESSEE

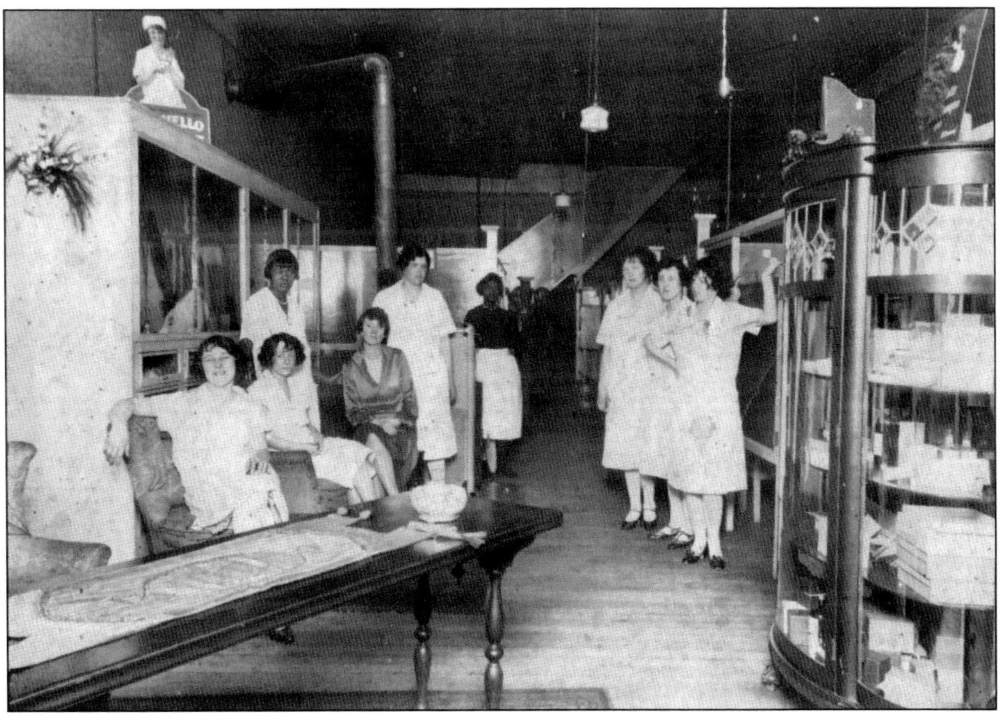

Many, many cosmetologists in Jackson said they studied under Lucia Michaelis and got their start at her school. (Courtesy Linda J. Higgins.)

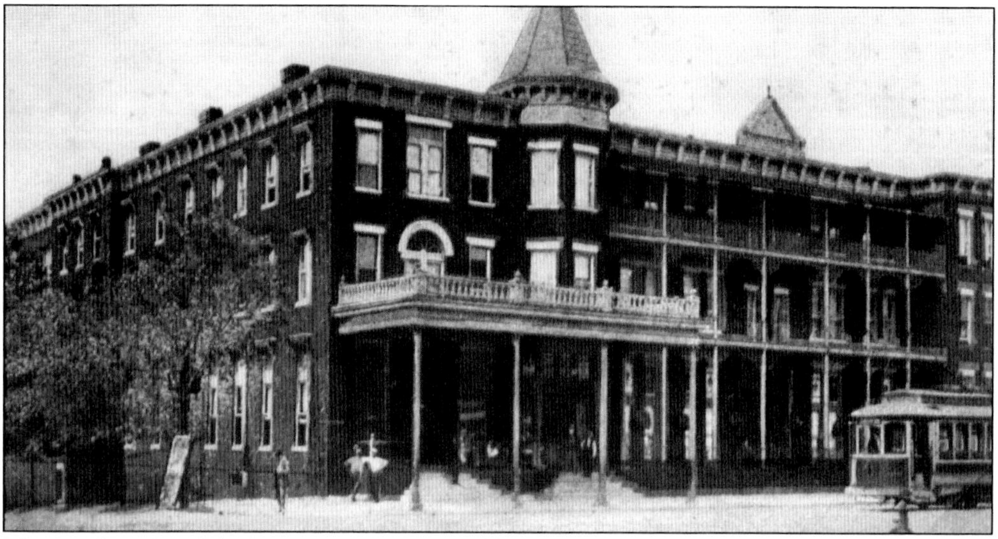

The Southern Hotel, built in 1890, was managed by Mrs. J. A. Day, who brought many conventions to the city. In 1924, the old Southern Hotel was purchased by Albert Noe and his son, Albert Jr., who tore down all but a south wing and erected an eight-story building. The Italian-style exterior and the lavish interior, which included a mezzanine and the elegant Gold Room, provided the site for conventions, luncheons, dinner parties, school banquets, and other memorable events in the lives of Jacksonians. In 1980, it was turned into a high-rise for the elderly and was successfully managed by Connie Crocker. After the 2003 tornado, which hit Jackson, did significant damage to the structure, Hal Crocker restored the building, including the lobby, the mezzanine, and the rental rooms. (Both courtesy JMCL.)

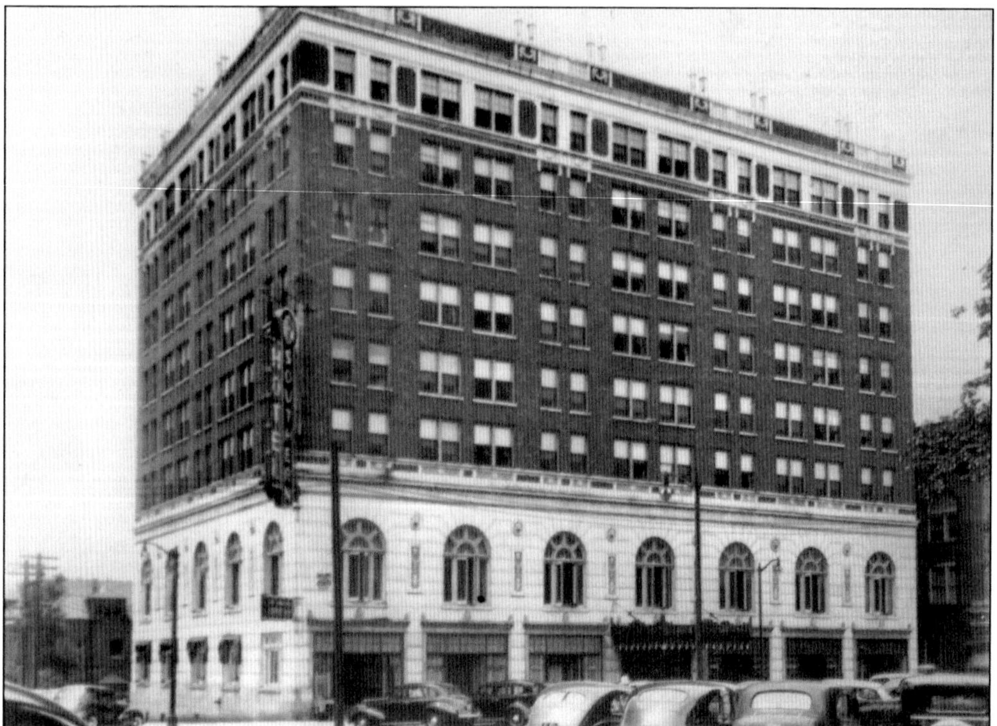

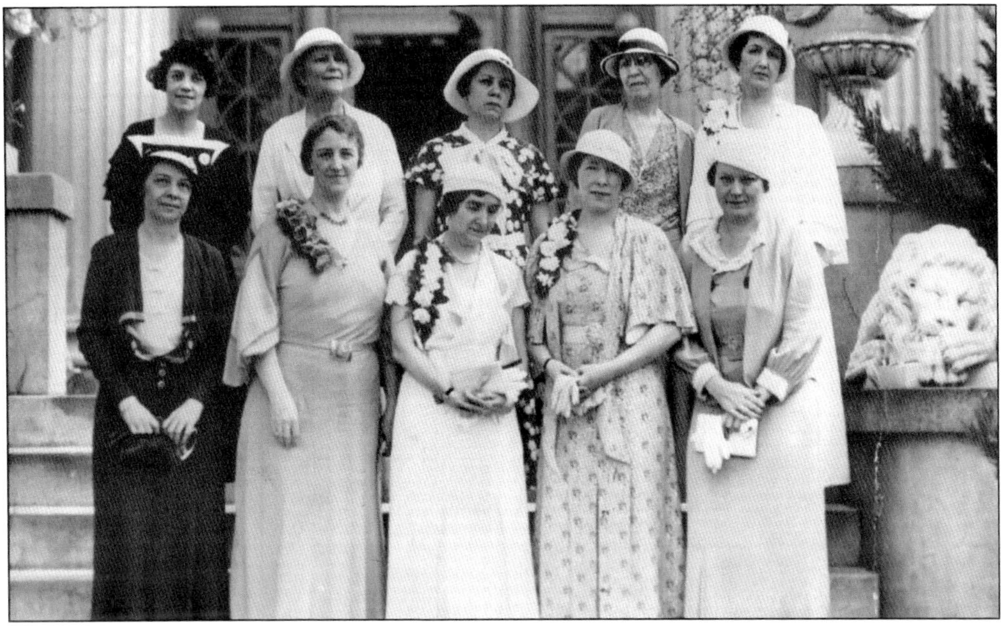

Sally Pigford entertained luncheon guests at her home, Chevy Chase. From left to right, are (first row) Irma Tomlin, Mrs. Pigford, Mrs. McAllister (the wife of Gov. Hill McAllister), an unidentified friend of Mrs. McAllister's, and Nelle Edenton; (second row) Sarah Stone, Annie Dabney, Bessie Brown, Norma Edenton, and Mamie Lee McKinnie. Note the corsages and hats worn in the 1930s. (Courtesy Joan Cook Tomlin.)

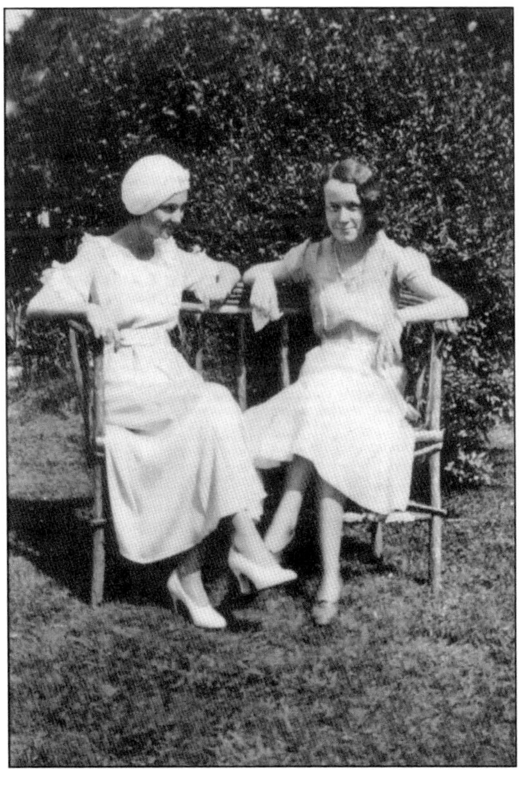

A beautiful young woman named Sadie Lou Matthews (right), pictured with Evelyn Reeves in the 1930s, was the only girl in a family of five. Her brothers thought so highly of her that they named their service station and grocery store for her. Even though Sadie was never involved in her brothers' businesses, her name will live on as "the Sadie Lou." (Courtesy Bemis Historical Society and Betsy Babb.)

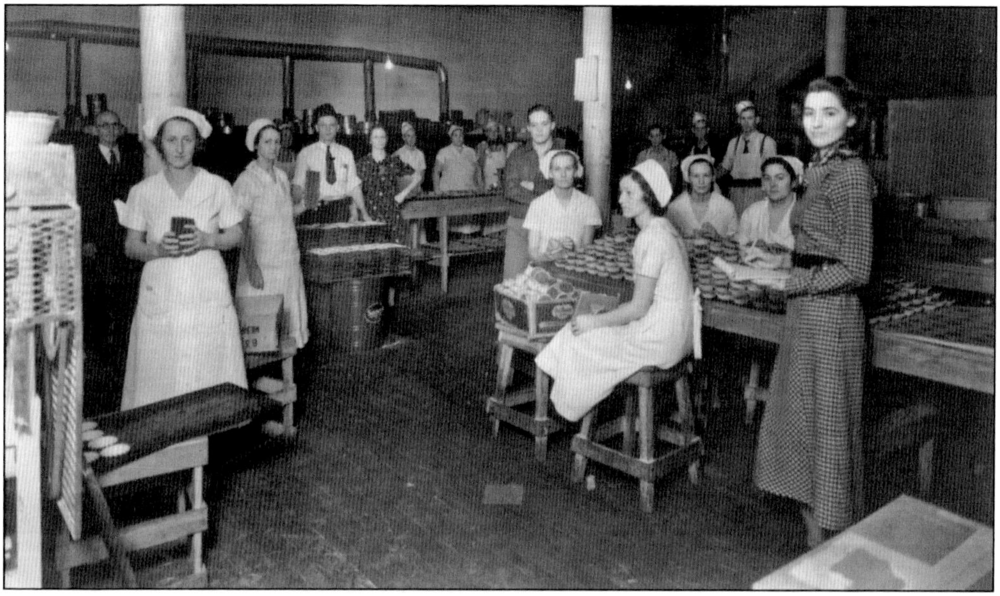

In 1934, Mrs. Earl Sullivan (Ruby Vick) began cooking pecan pies for a local businessman to sell on his snack route. Beginning in her home's kitchen, she produced 38 pies at a time in a small gas oven. In a couple of years, she enclosed her back porch and had a commercial oven installed. The business grew and expanded into a plant. In the 1960s, she moved the business to its present location on Preston Street. Mrs. Sullivan's Pies are sold throughout the United States. (Courtesy Victor Sullivan.)

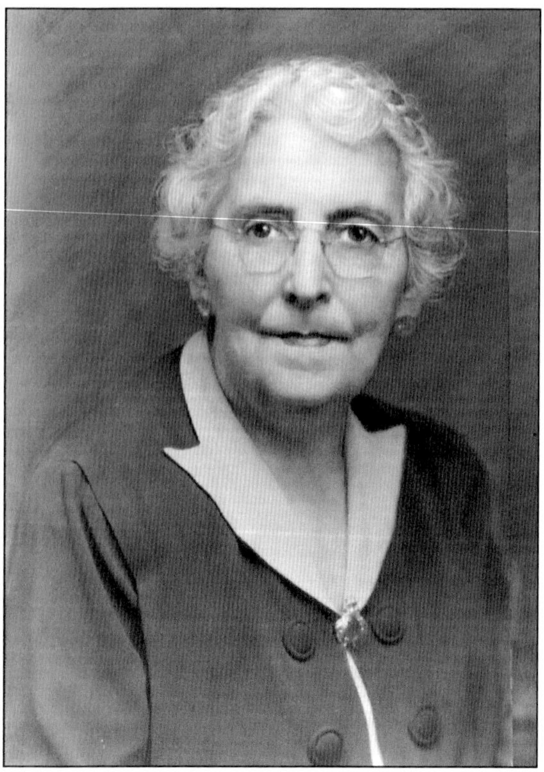

Alice Drake, who became librarian at the newly constructed Carnegie library in Jackson in 1905 and served in that post for almost five decades, was a charter member and the first president of the Jackson Business and Professional Women, which was organized in April 1919 at the library. (Courtesy JMCL.)

Emma Inman Williams authored *Historic Madison*, a detailed county history from the early 1800s through World War I. The first edition was published in 1946 and reprinted in 1972. She coauthored *Jackson and Madison County: A Pictorial History* in 1988. She served many years as director of the Tennessee Room, a genealogical reference room at the Jackson–Madison County Library, after teaching history at Jackson High School for 43 years. (Courtesy JMCL.)

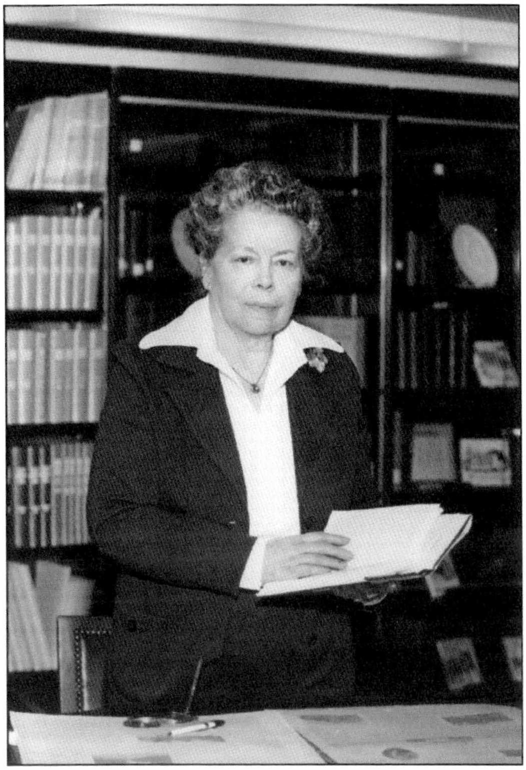

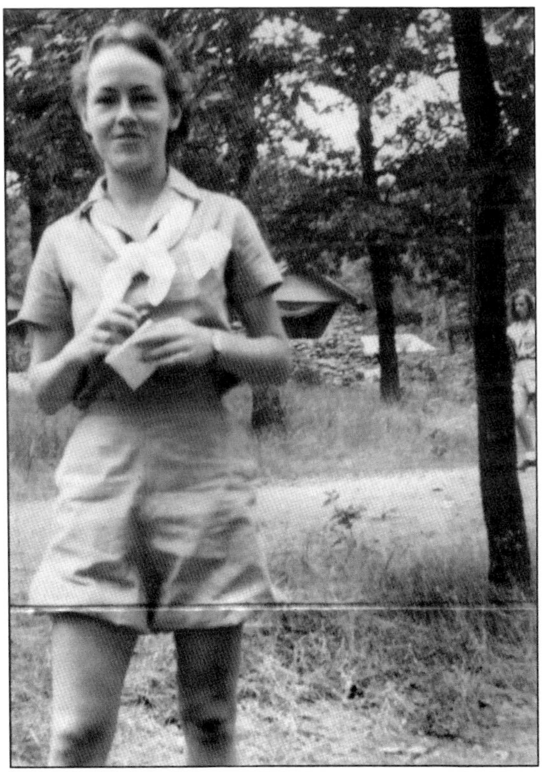

Virginia Carey Smith, shown here in 1940 as camp director at Camp Kiwani, helped establish Girl Scouting in 1941 in Madison County and then in 1959 the Reelfoot Girl Scout Council, covering 18 counties in West Tennessee. Camp Hazlewood opened in 1959 and served thousands of girls until sold in 2008. Virginia served as executive director of the council for 18 years, until her death in 1981. (Courtesy J. Phillip Smith.)

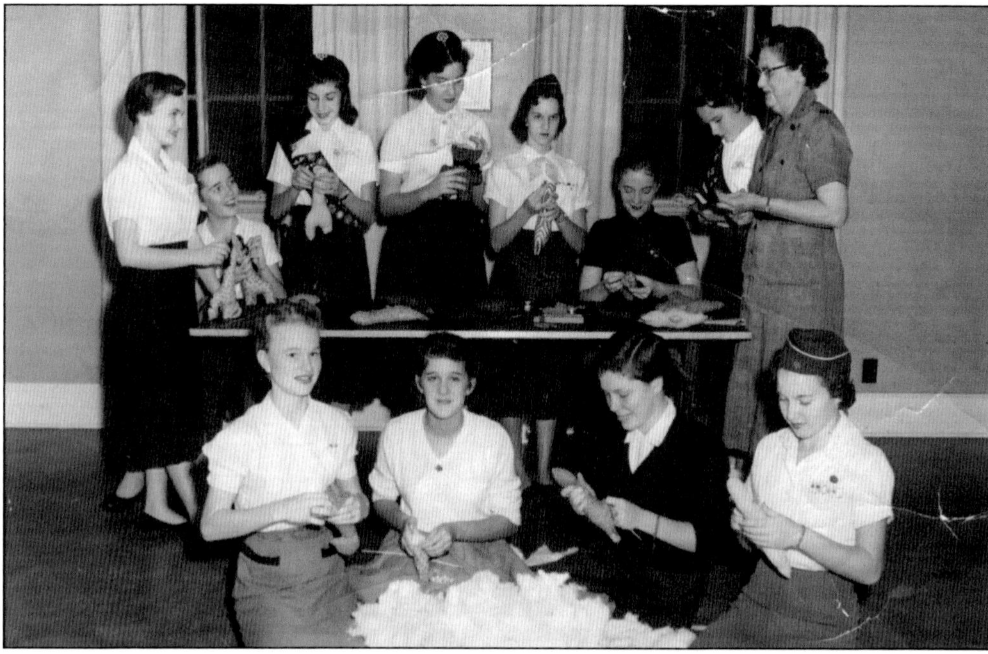

A senior Girl Scout troop meets upstairs at the Bemis Y. From left to right in front of the table are Barbara Vinson, Mary Helen Helton, Evelyn Eddleman, and Carolyn Ward. From left to right at the table are Frank Ann Naef, Kathy Pirtle, Helen Fry, Carolyn Smith, Gracie Nell Pirtle, Dee Brasher, Sherry Mills, and their leader, Rebecca Pogue. (Courtesy Carolyn Smith Callis.)

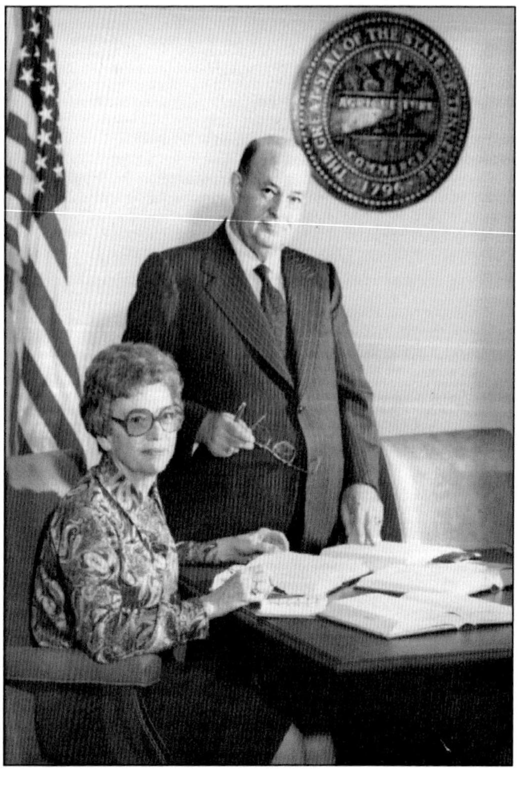

Anne Harris Schneider, a Cumberland Law School graduate, was the first female lawyer to practice for many years in Jackson and was a member of the county, the state, and the American Bar Associations, plus the Tennessee Women's Bar Association. The Jackson–Madison County Lawyers' Association Women's Chapter bears her name. She and her husband, Vic, had a law firm in Jackson from 1947 to 1983. (Courtesy Dr. Vicki Schneider Lake.)

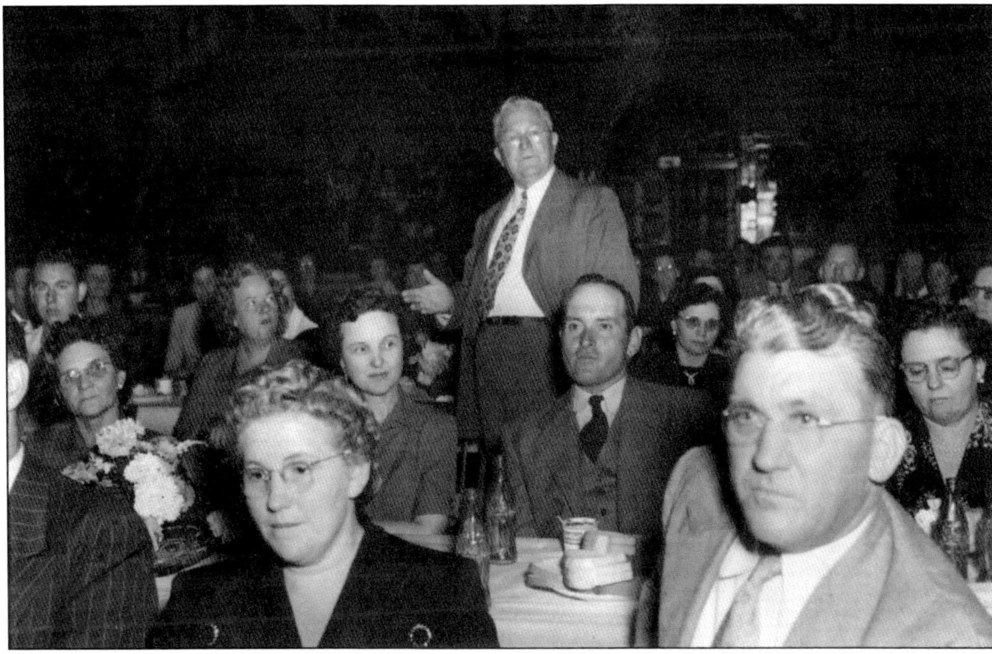

Fred Young, the second general manager of Bemis and son of J. B. Young, the first manager, is recognized at the 1950 celebration, and Byrnes Butler is looking up at him. Byrnes, the personnel director at Bemis for many years, became a person many individuals looked up to and respected. In front are Margaret and Milton Diggs. (Courtesy Rosalee Gibbons and Lavina Brown.)

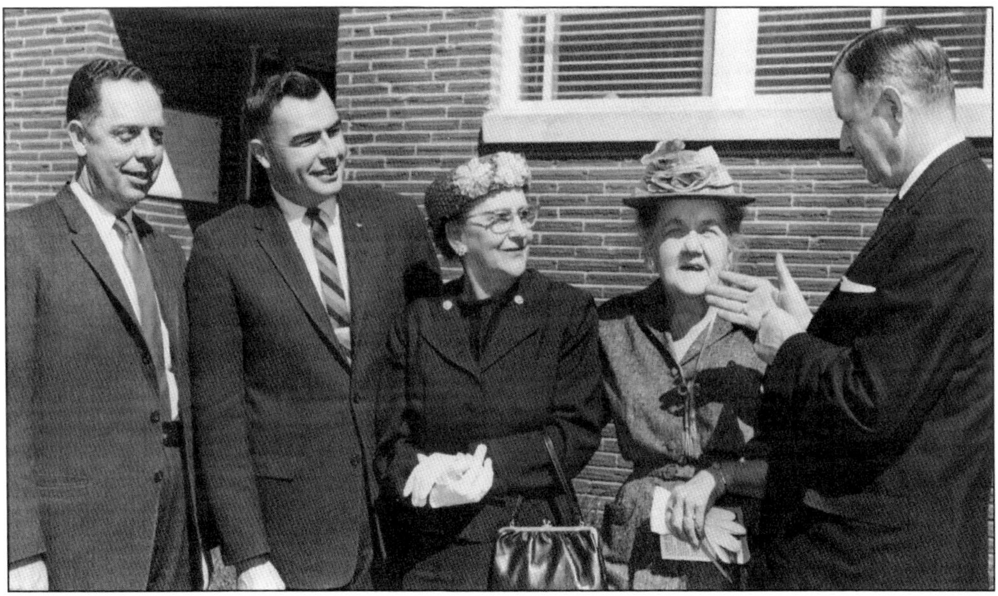

Ethel D. Bond (second from right) pioneered the Tennessee Farm Bureau women's organization and was the first woman inducted into the Tennessee Agriculture Hall of Fame in 1998. She cofounded the Home and County Department of the Tennessee Farm Bureau and served as chairperson from 1924 to 1967. Other Tennessee Farm Bureau members pictured in the 1950s are, from left to right, Clyde York, Murray Miles, Mrs. Jasper Taylor, Mrs. Bond, and Tom Hitch. (Courtesy the *Jackson Sun*.)

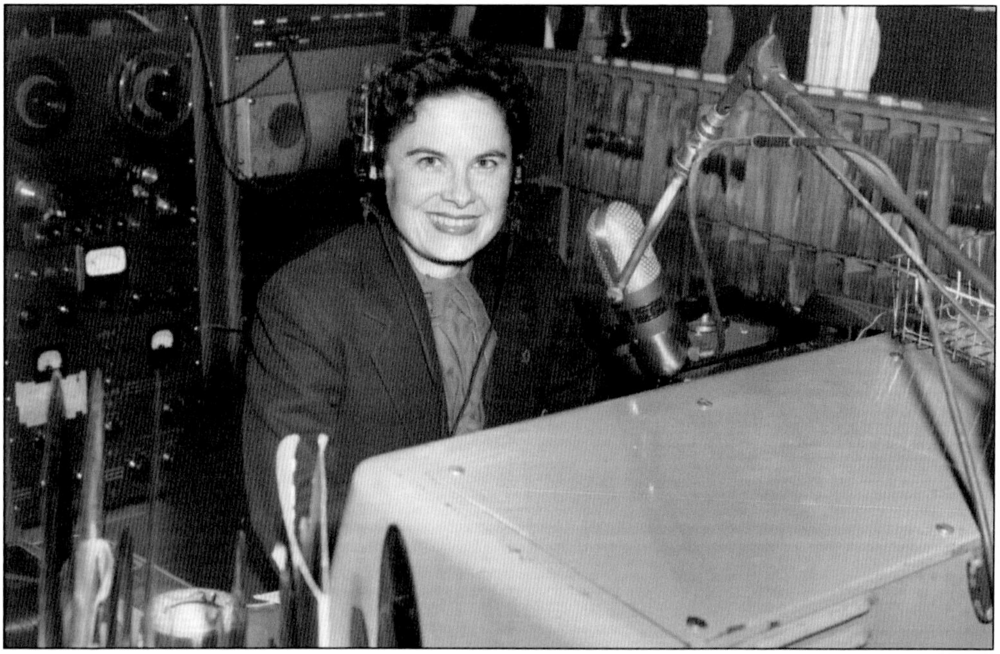

Doris Freeman entered the radio world as WDXI opened on October 31, 1948. She became the first woman to sell radio advertising in Jackson and was the top salesperson. Shown here on the board at the radio station, she was licensed by the FCC as a third-class engineer. (Courtesy Doris Freeman.)

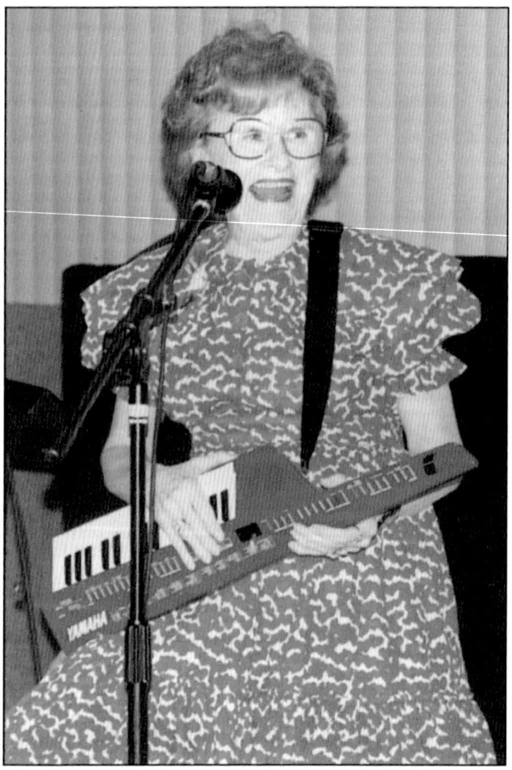

In 1955, she started her television show as Cousin Tuny and continued for 12 years. While she was working for WDXI TV/AM radio, she handled 75 radio sales accounts and did a half-hour bingo show before changing into her hillbilly outfit for her television show with 12 to 20 children. As Cousin Tuny, she appeared with many big-name stars, especially on the telethons that she hosted. (Courtesy Doris Freeman.)

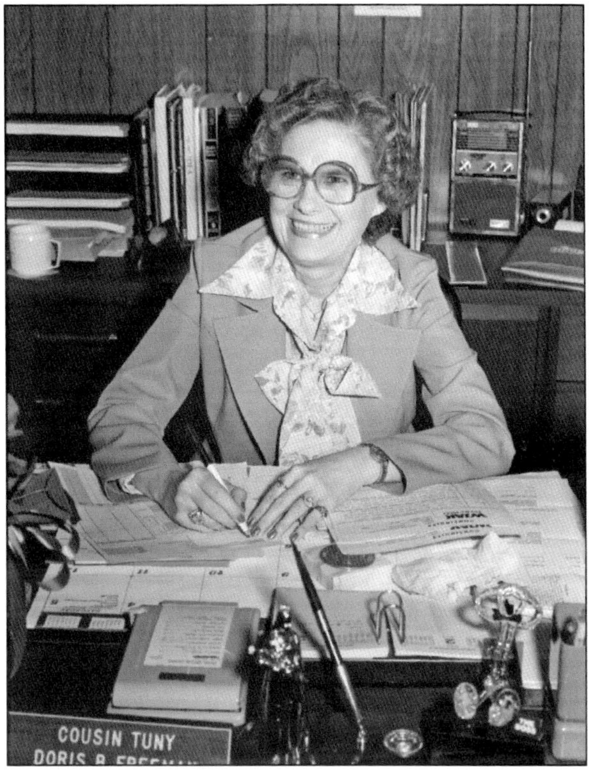

Doris Freeman worked in sales at WJAK radio and then managed the Old Hickory Mall for seven years. She also worked in public relations for the Jackson–Madison County General Hospital, where she originated the mascot "Little General," a white dog with blue spots given to kids who were patients in the hospital and a larger version for public appearances. (Courtesy Doris Freeman.)

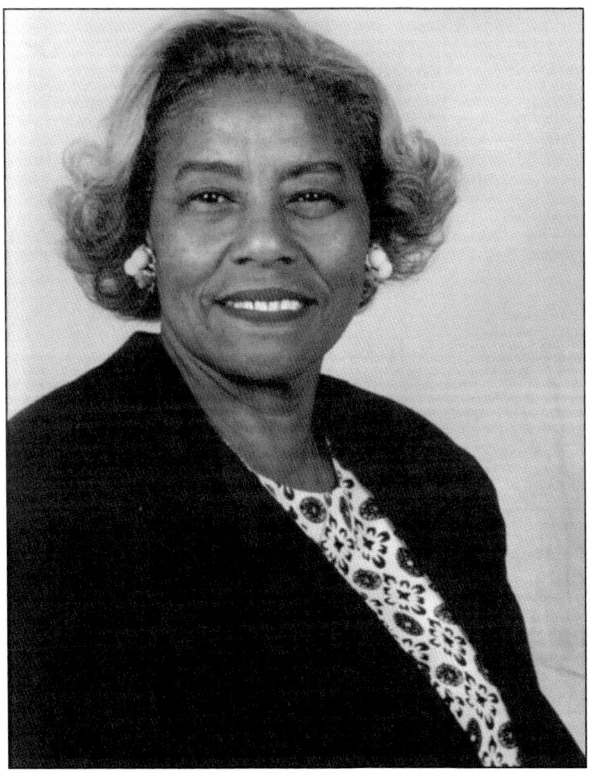

Nell Huntspon started in radio in the mid-1950s on WJAK. She was an on-air personality and also sold advertisements for the station. In 1968, she opened her floral business, Flower Box, but continued to work at WJAK until the mid-1970s. While still running her floral business, she helped obtain the license for Jackson's first talk radio station, WNWS, which began in September 1993. (Courtesy Nell Huntspon.)

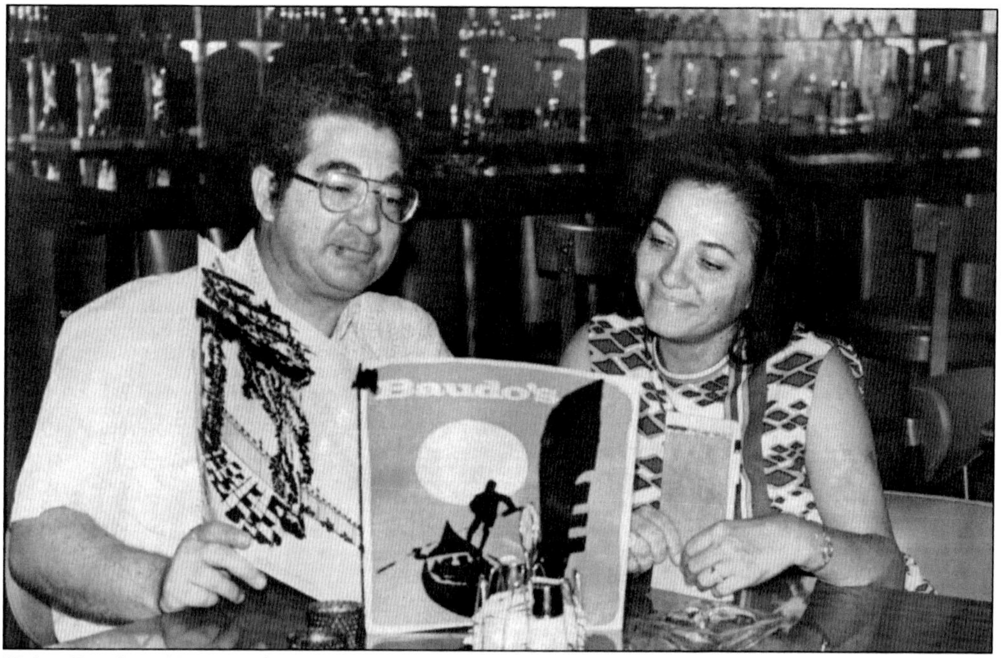

Helen Baudo, of Persian descent, came to Jackson in 1964 from Chicago and missed the ethnic restaurants. She decided that if she could cook for a family of eight, she could enlarge her recipes and open a restaurant. Jackson's first pizzeria, B&H Pizza Parlor, named for Helen's husband, Buzz, and herself, opened in the arcade of Hollywood Shopping Center. (Courtesy Sharon Baudo Smith.)

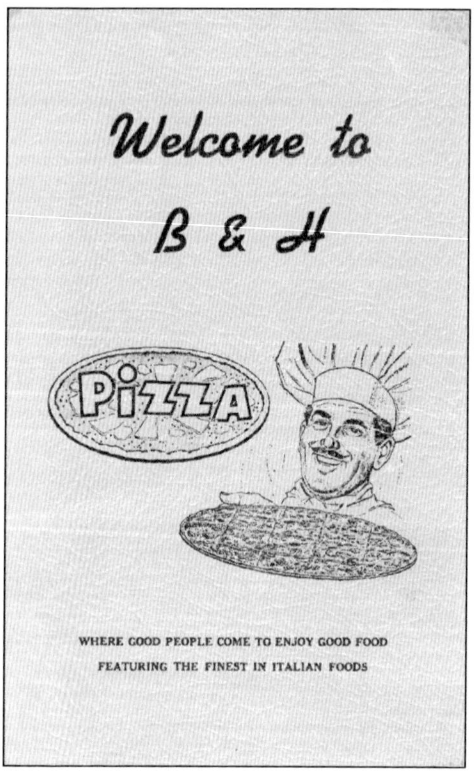

By 1966, the pizza parlor was located on Hollywood Drive and was soon renamed Baudo's. Its expanded menu included steaks, pasta dishes, and candlelight dining. Baudo's remained at that location until 1972, when it relocated to the present site at I-40 and the Highway 45 Bypass. (Courtesy Sharon Baudo Smith.)

Baudo's has always been a family affair, and the tradition continues today, even though Buzz and Helen are retired. In this 1970s photograph are, from left to right, Sharon Baudo Smith (left), who now owns the business; Brenda; Helen; Steve; Randy (age 4), Sharon's son, who now is the head chef; Basil "Buzz;" Jack; and Linda. (Courtesy Sharon Baudo Smith.)

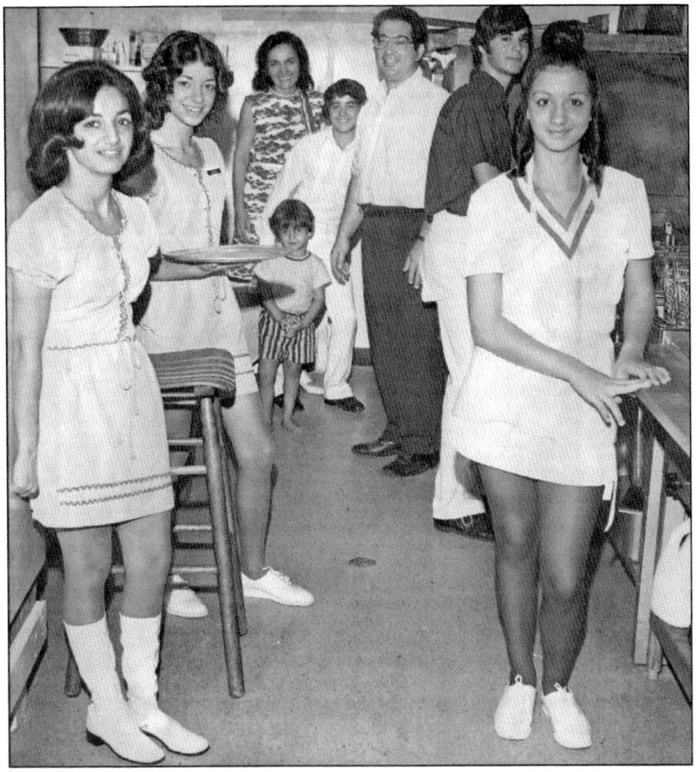

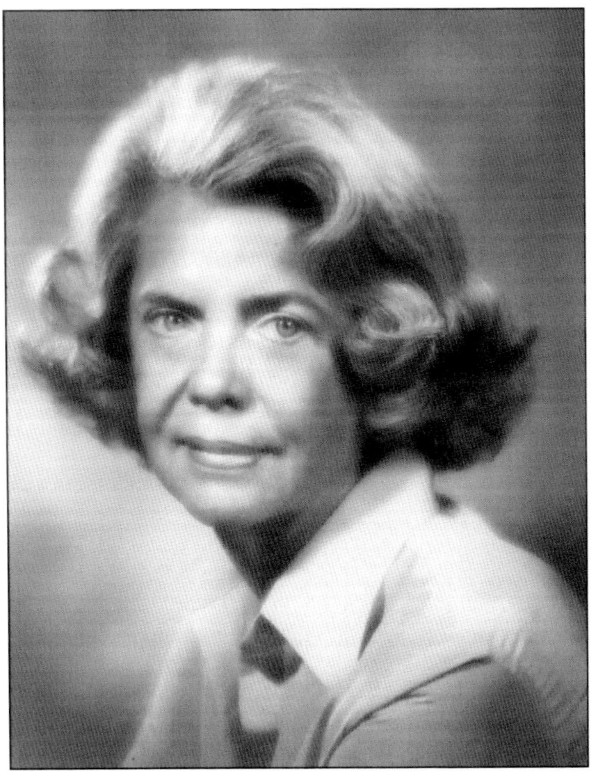

Frances Tomlin Tigrett, co-owner and developer of the Old Hickory Mall in the 1960s, was one of the very few early women in real estate development and was recognized for developing the greatest amount of real estate in West Tennessee. She was also an outstanding supporter of cultural groups and was responsible for bringing a National Public Radio station to Madison County. (Courtesy the *Jackson Sun*.)

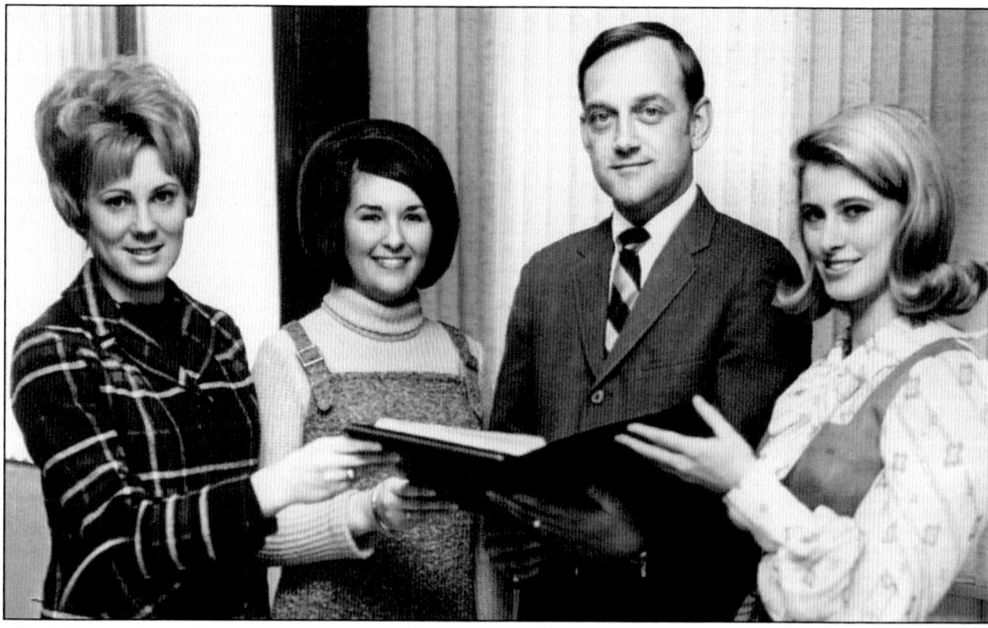

The Miss Madison County pageant, a preliminary to the Miss Tennessee pageant, was sponsored by the South Madison County Jaycees in the 1960s and 1970s. In this February 17, 1969, photograph from the *Jackson Sun*, Murray Williams (second from right), entry chairman for the Miss Madison County pageant, announces the first three entries: from left to right, Linda Lockhart, Terrilyn Arthur Stovall, and Martha Jacqueline Utley. (Courtesy Jackie Utley.)

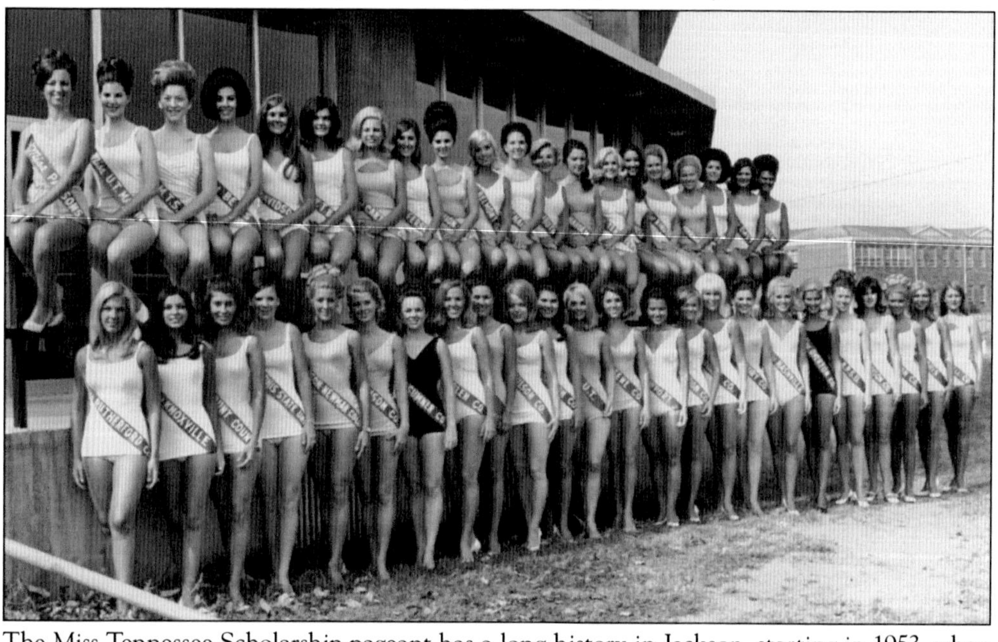

The Miss Tennessee Scholarship pageant has a long history in Jackson, starting in 1953, when it was staged outdoors at Rockroth Stadium. Local contestants in 1969, shown at Oman Arena, include (top row) Suzanne Gobelet, Miss University of Tennessee at Martin (second from left) and Beverly Williams, Miss Union University (ninth from left); (bottom row) Jackie Utley, Miss Madison County (sixth from left). (Courtesy Jackie Utley.)

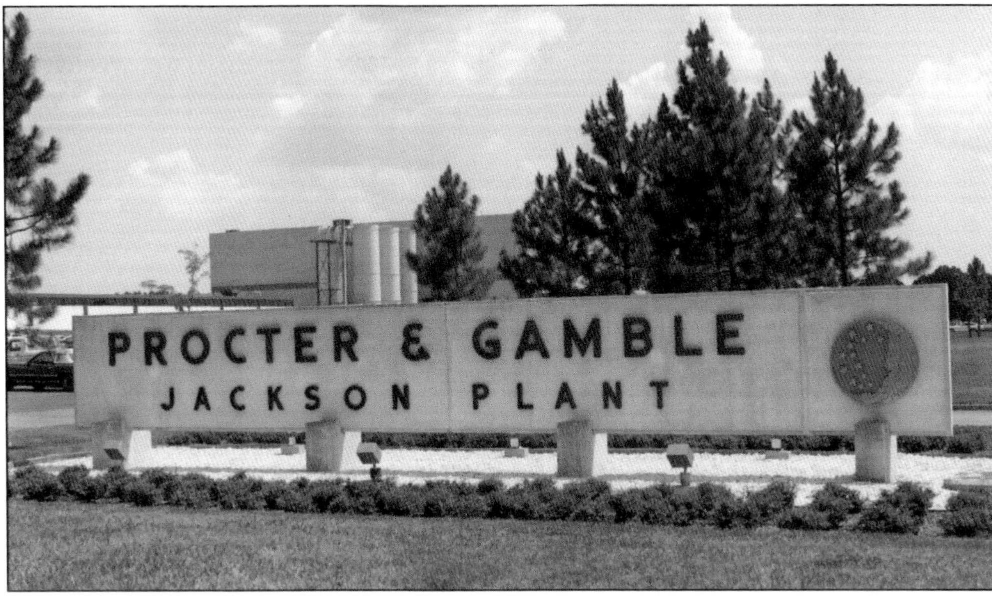

Procter and Gamble's manufacturing plant in Jackson had the company's first female plant manager, Laree Mugler, who came to Jackson as a co-manager of the plant in 1985. She moved on to a P&G position in Shelton, Connecticut, in May 1990. The *Jackson Sun* wrote that she was the city's highest-ranking female executive during the time she was here. (Courtesy Randy Kennedy of Procter and Gamble.)

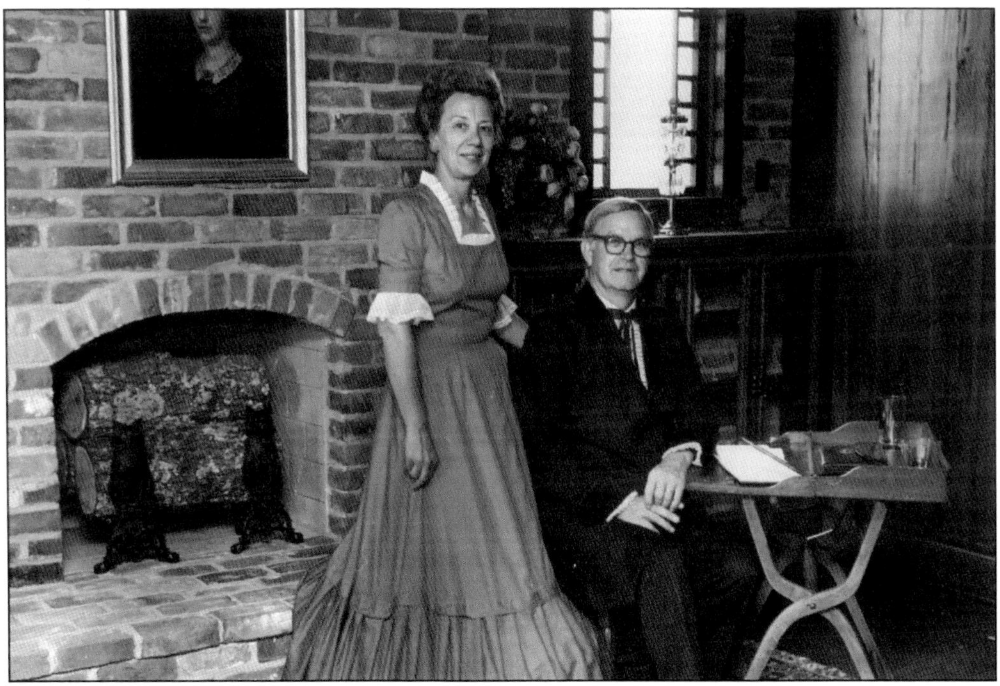

Dorothy "Dee" Middlebrooks and her husband, M. T., restored an old brick building adjacent to their automobile dealership for the 1972 Jackson Sesquicentennial. She and her family moved to Jackson in 1964 when she and her husband bought the Pontiac-Rambler dealership. Dee was one of the first women in the nation to attain a dealership position. (Courtesy Mary Jo Middlebrooks.)

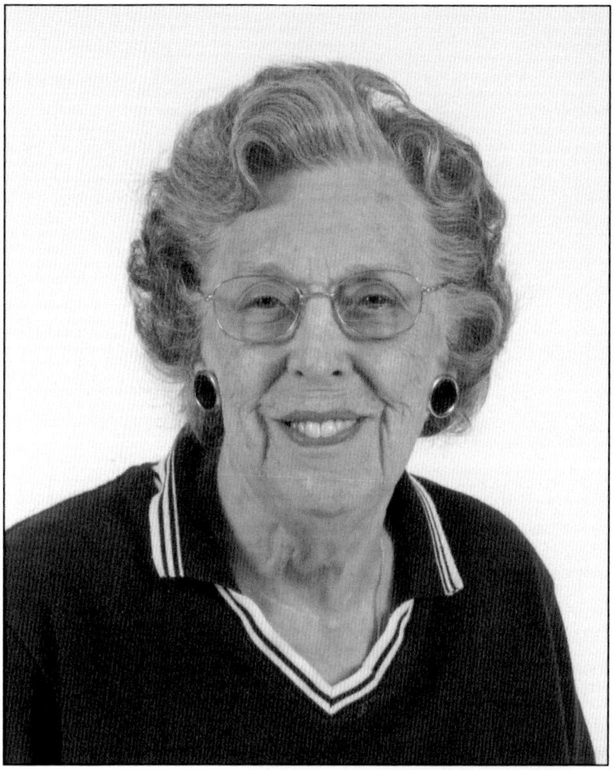

Helen Herron, named manager of Caldwell-Wisdom Insurance firm in 1955, was the first woman elected president of the Insurers of Jackson and became the first woman elected to the state insurers' board since its founding in 1893. She was also the first female president of the Jackson Symphony. She was president of Jackson's Business and Professional Women in 1958 and was named Woman of Achievement in 1964. (Courtesy Lynn Williams.)

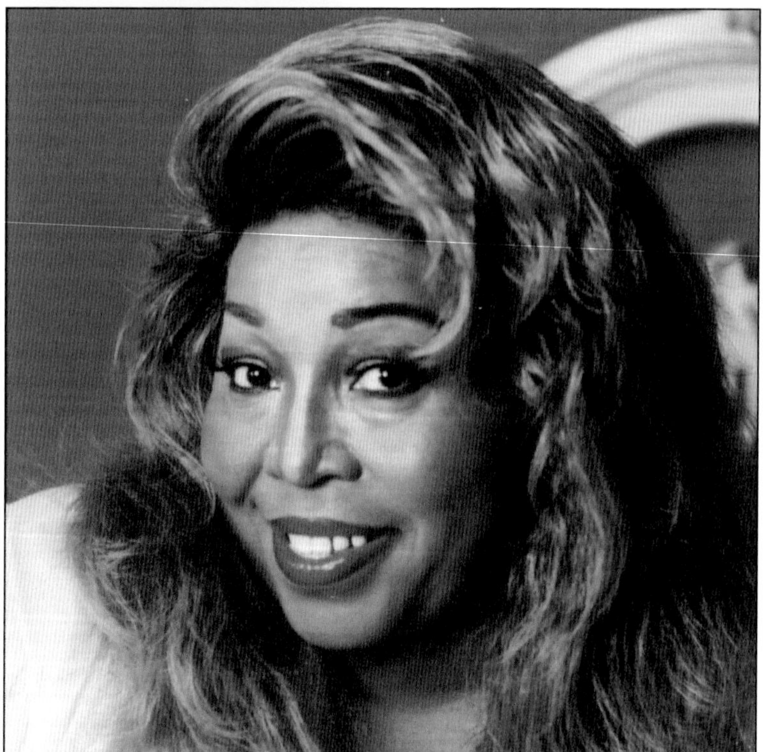

Denise LaSalle, born in Mississippi, is an urban, R&B, and soul singer, songwriter, and record producer. In 1971, while living in Chicago, she had her first success with a self-penned "Trapped in a Thing Called Love." In 1977, she married James E. Wolfe, known as "Super Wolfe," and settled in Jackson. With many gold records, Denise earned the title of "Queen of Soul Blues." Today she writes, records, and performs. (Courtesy Denise LaSalle.)

Neta McKnight stands out in the field of allied health. In 1970, she created Tennessee's first associate degree radiography program at Jackson State Community College. That program produced more than 700 graduates in the 36 years she headed it. In addition to her professional achievements, she has been very active in her community. She was one of four cofounders of the Kiwanis Center for Child Development. (Courtesy JSCC.)

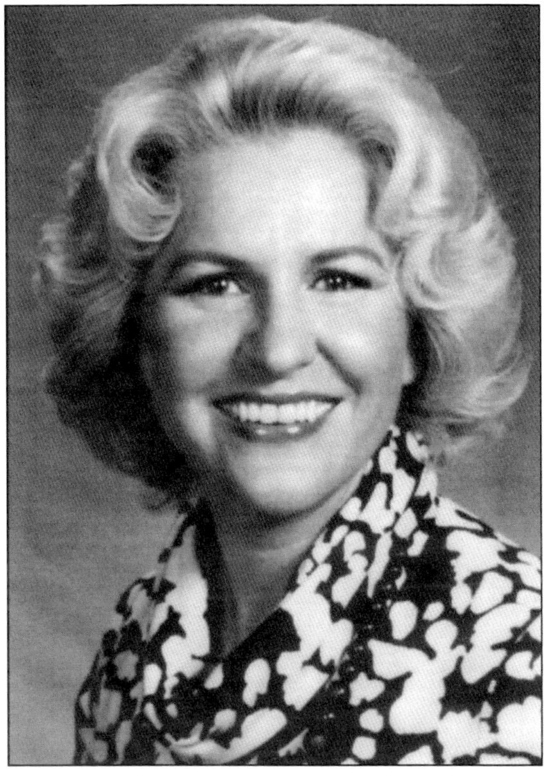

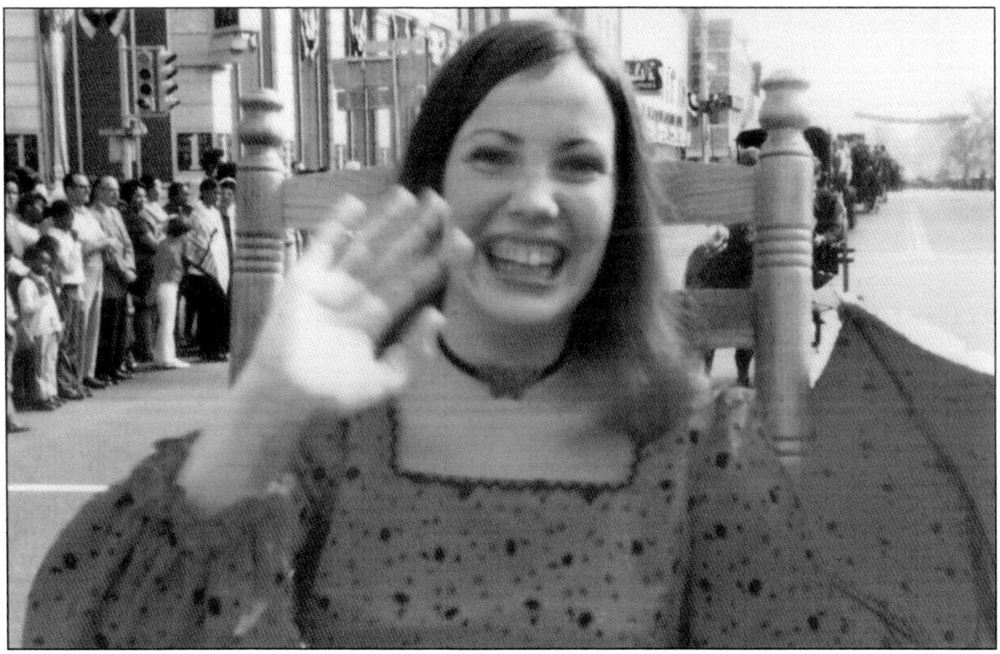

Susan Eliff rocked for five and a half days to win the 1972 Rocking Chair Contest at the Old Country Store. Jean Riles Littrell came in second. The contest drew hundreds of participants and onlookers. Susan is shown in the Rocking Chair parade. (Courtesy Old Country Store and Norwood Jones.)

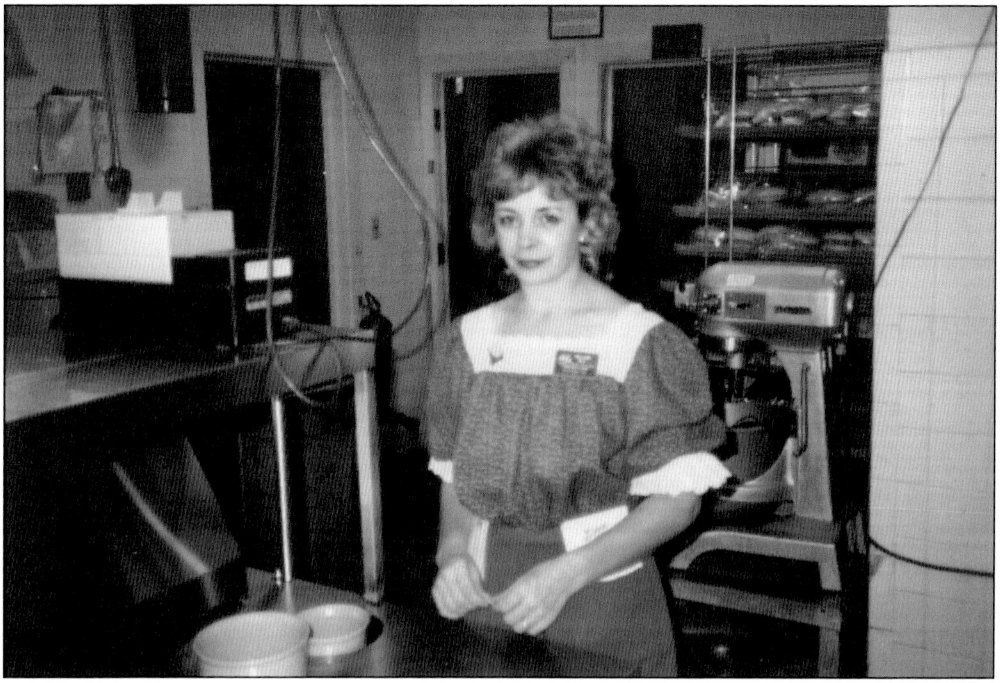

Margie Lemons Mays dressed in a period outfit to help celebrate the 1986 Tennessee Homecoming. Margie, a native of Madison County, has had a successful career as a server at the Old County Store for over 32 years. (Courtesy Old Country Store and Norwood Jones.)

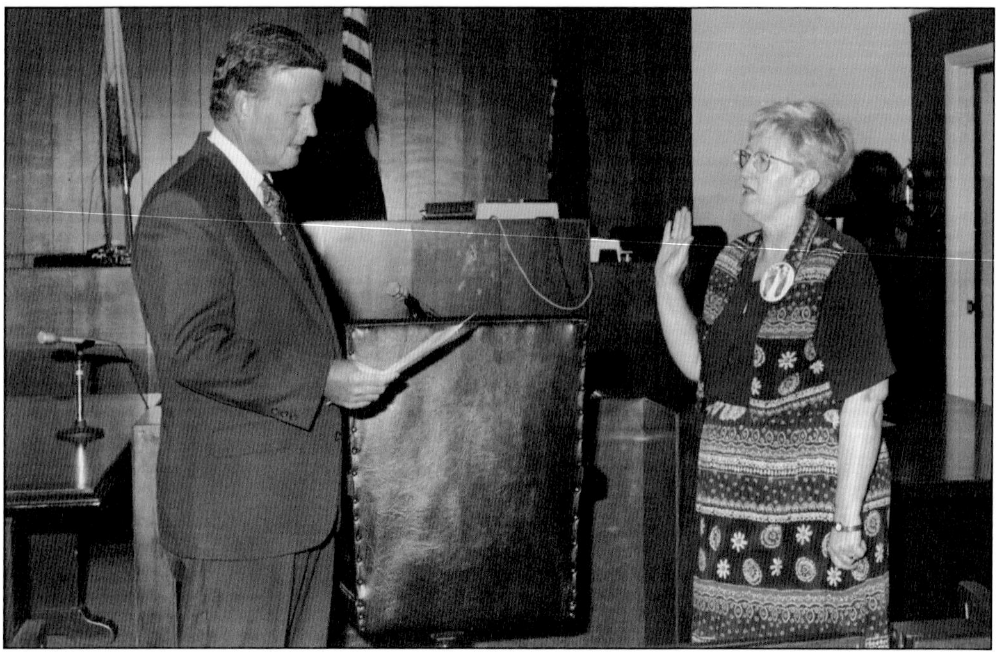

Linda Jennings Higgins made history when she was the first elected city court clerk for the Municipal Court of Jackson. Former mayor Charles Farmer swears in Linda for the job on September 2, 1996. Linda wears a button showing the footprints of her first grandchild, Kelsey Elise Ledford, who was born just six days earlier. (Photograph by Budd Neff, courtesy Linda J. Higgins.)

Five

LIFE IN THE COMMUNITIES

Even in the early days of the 1900s, life in the communities in Madison County was very attractive. Some of the rural attributes were appealing to many citizens.

Life in rural communities such as Beech Bluff, Denmark, Madison Hall, Malesus, Medon, Mercer, Pinson, and Spring Creek was slower and centered mainly on schools and churches. Most of the work involved farming or perhaps running the neighborhood store.

As city life became more involved, many citizens moved to the city to take advantage of all that Jackson had to offer. In addition, Madison County attracted people from other areas with tourist sites, three residential colleges, a business college, a technical school, and finally a community college in 1967. Athletics always held a great interest throughout the entire county.

Many important people have visited Madison County in the 20th century. Theodore "Teddy" Roosevelt, the 26th U.S. president, visited Jackson while running on the Bull Moose ticket for reelection in 1912. Roosevelt served as president from 1901, when Pres. William McKinley was assassinated, and was reelected on the Republican ticket in 1904. According to *Jackson and Madison County: A Pictorial History*, Harry Truman visited Jackson several times, and the last one pictured was in 1960. Lyndon B. Johnson campaigned in Jackson for the vice presidency in 1960. Vice Pres. Hubert Humphrey came to Jackson in 1968 to salute higher education. Vice Pres. George H. Bush, running for president, and his vice presidential candidate, Dan Quayle, came to Jackson in 1988. As a past president, George H. Bush spoke at a scholarship dinner at Union University. The only sitting president to visit Jackson was Bill Clinton, who came in 1996 with Vice Pres. Al Gore. They came to help rebuild black churches in West Tennessee that had been burned by arsonists. Entertainers and prominent speakers have visited Madison County, too, but there were probably more outstanding faces at the funeral of Carl Perkins on January 20, 1998, than had ever gathered here, including all the living members of the Beatles, many rock-and-roll stars, and country singers.

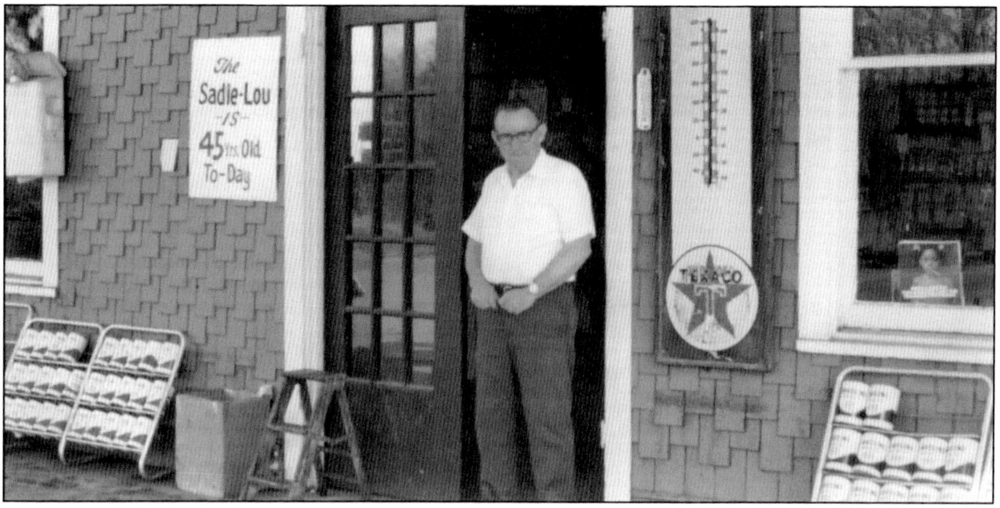

Joe Matthews built the green, wood-shingled Sadie Lou service station at the intersection of the Steam Mill Ferry Road and Riverside Drive in 1929. In this 1974 picture, he stands proudly before the sign that says the Sadie Lou is 45 years old. Joe's brother Marvin (below) worked in the service station, named for their sister, Sadie Lou Matthews, who married Ike Lassiter, the owner of the Wells and Lassiter Dairy. In 1947, Joe added a modern concrete-block building at the back and called it the Sadie Lou Grocery. In the 1950s, he built another, larger grocery store on the other corner of the intersection. Younger brother Floyd Matthews ran that store. The youngest brother, N. T. Matthews, built his cabinet shop and construction business next door to the Sadie Lou Grocery. The intersection became known as "the Sadie Lou Corner." Marvin's oldest son, Buddy, carried on the tradition by building his archery and sports equipment store next to the Sadie Lou service station in the 1960s. (Photograph by William McCommon, both courtesy Kathleen McCommon.)

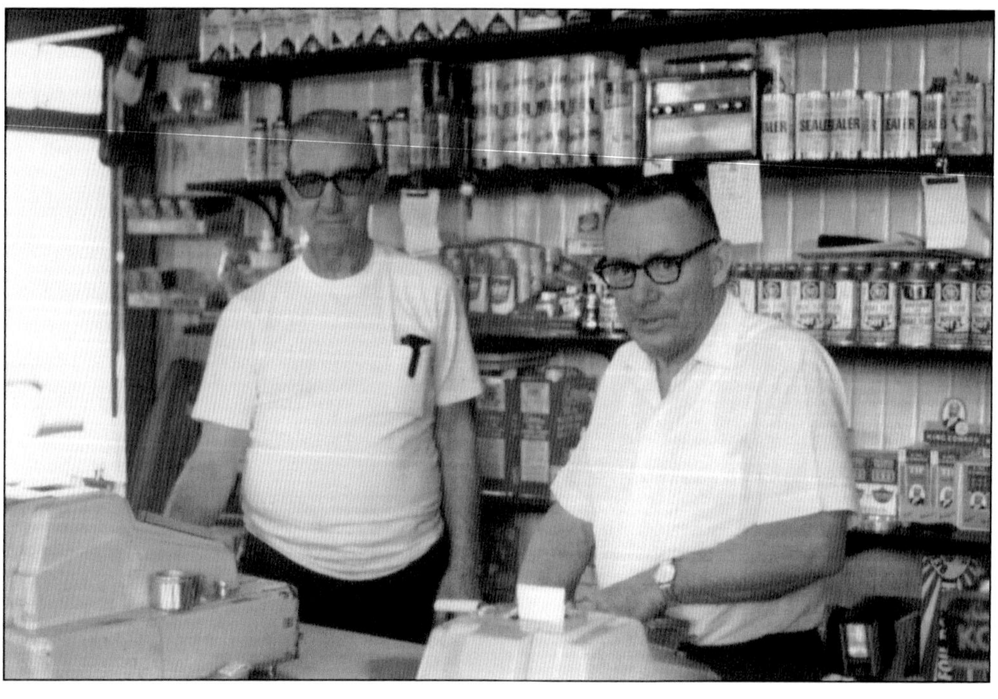

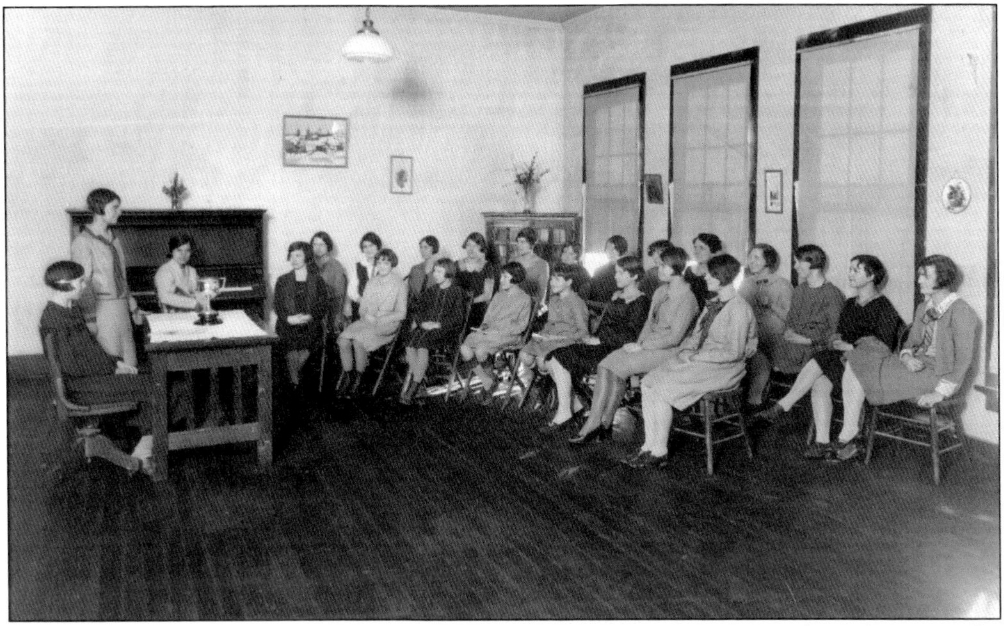

Young women attend a meeting in the Madison Hall Community Center in the early 1920s. The community center (below) was built in 1921 as a school, but the school board agreed to accept the offer from the Community Club and the Woodmen of the World (W.O.W.) to add a third room to the new two-room brick-veneer school building. The club and the W.O.W. paid for the third room, which was to be called the Community Room. The school closed in 1939, and the school board allowed the Community Club to use the entire building. The community center sits on a hill on Steam Mill Ferry Road next to Madison Baptist Church. (Above, courtesy Billie Jennings; below, courtesy William McCommon.)

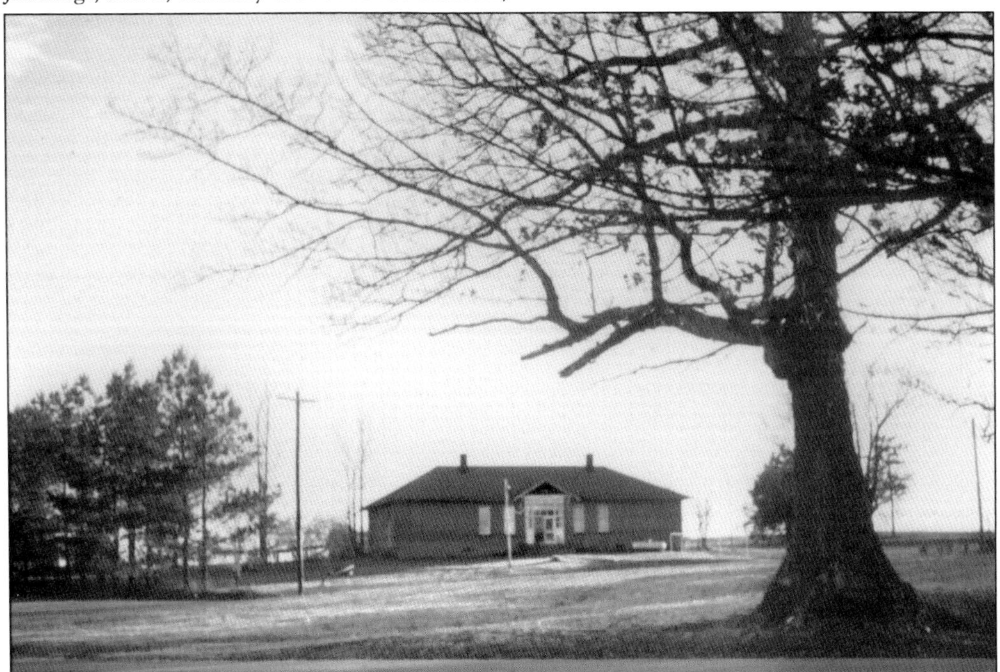

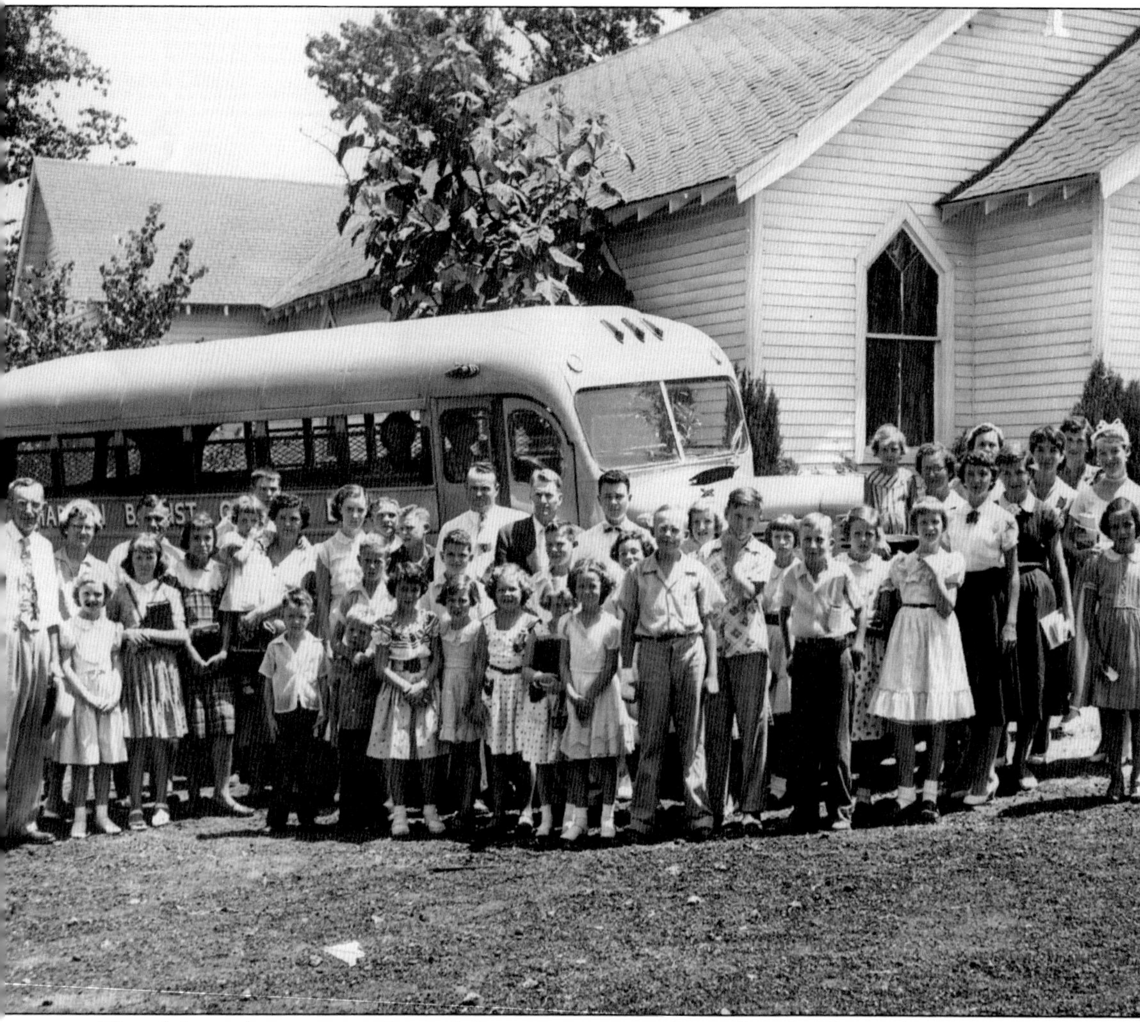

Church buses became popular to help get young people to church. Shown here is the group transported to vacation bible school by the Madison Baptist Church bus in 1954. From left to right are Roy Williams, Dorothy Pratt, Claudia Henderson, Nell Collins, Mr. Pratt, Irene Cox, Ida Nell Nolen holding a small child, James Cox, an unidentified boy in white shirt, Joyce Hall, an unidentified boy in dark shirt, an unidentified boy in white shirt behind him, Sebron Lassiter, Eugene Fortune, Carl Blackwell, Brother T. A. Thacker, Monroe King, Murray Blackwell, five young girls on front are Delma and Pat Norris, Judy Lassiter, Sherry Thacker, Marcia Blackwell, unidentified girl behind, Anthony Collins, Linda Jennings, Joe Collins, Mona Williams, Richard Collins, two unidentified girls in front, Gayle and Mae Collins, Rosalee Jennings, Irene Blackwell, Lutie Williams, Peggy King, Martha Norris, Diane Lassiter, and Thelma Cox in front of her. Madison Baptist Church, established in 1921, stemmed from the first Baptist church in Madison County, the Cane Creek Baptist Church, established in 1822. (Courtesy Billie Jennings and Rosalee J. Gibbons.)

Rural free delivery by the U.S. Postal Service was a boon to Madison County residents who lived on the dirt and gravel roads in the rural areas. Here Rosalee Adele Jennings, age seven in 1946, checks her parents' mailbox on the Old Bolivar Road (later Riverside Drive) in her pedal car. Note the crooked telephone pole but no electrical utilities. (Courtesy Billie Jennings and Rosalee J. Gibbons.)

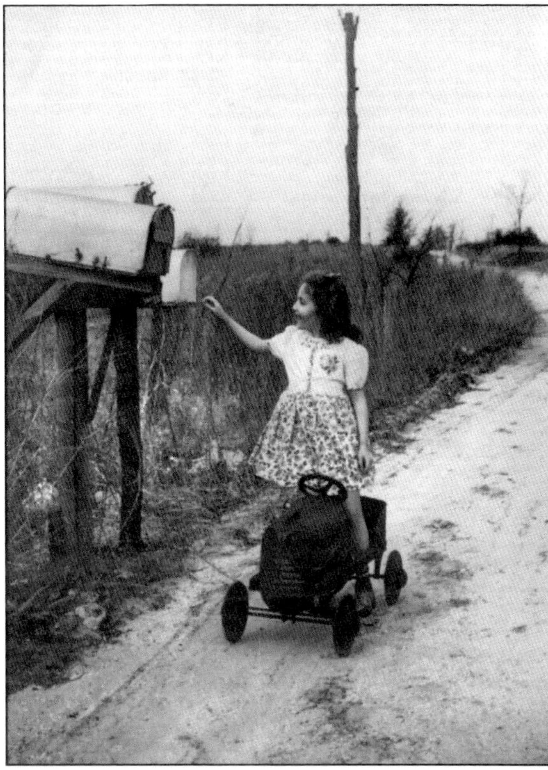

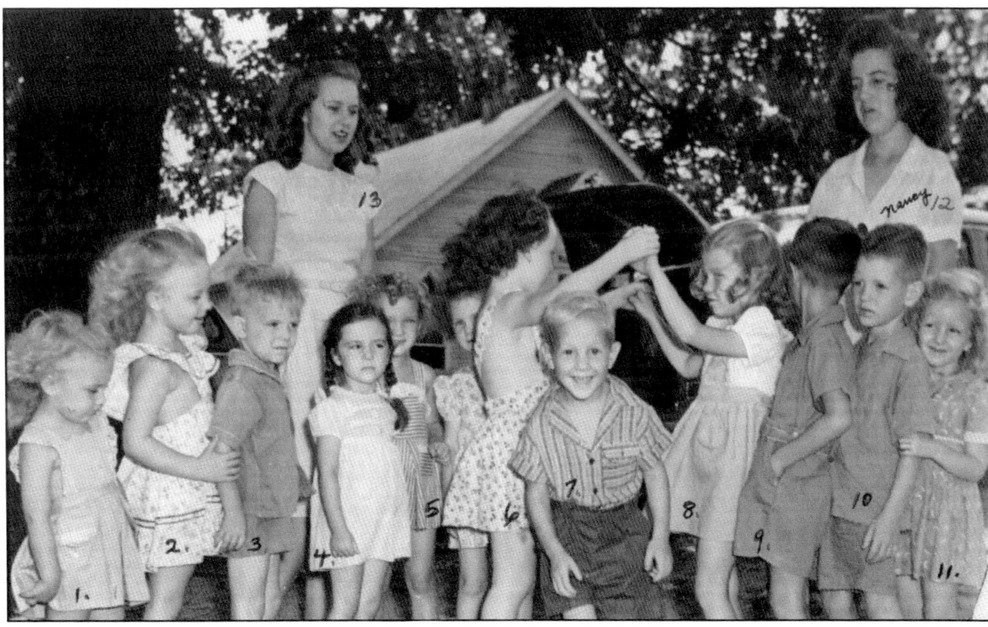

Youngsters are shown playing "London Bridge is Falling Down" at Madison Baptist Church Bible School. From left to right are Mary Evelyn McCommon, Sandra McCommon, Larry Murdaugh, Brenda Matthews, Mary Ann Smith, unidentified, Diane Lassiter, Danny Edwards, Sally Baker, Buddy Matthews, Larry Johnson, and Linda Jennings. Adult leaders are unidentified (left) and Nancy Turner. (Courtesy Madison Baptist Church and Billie H. Jennings.)

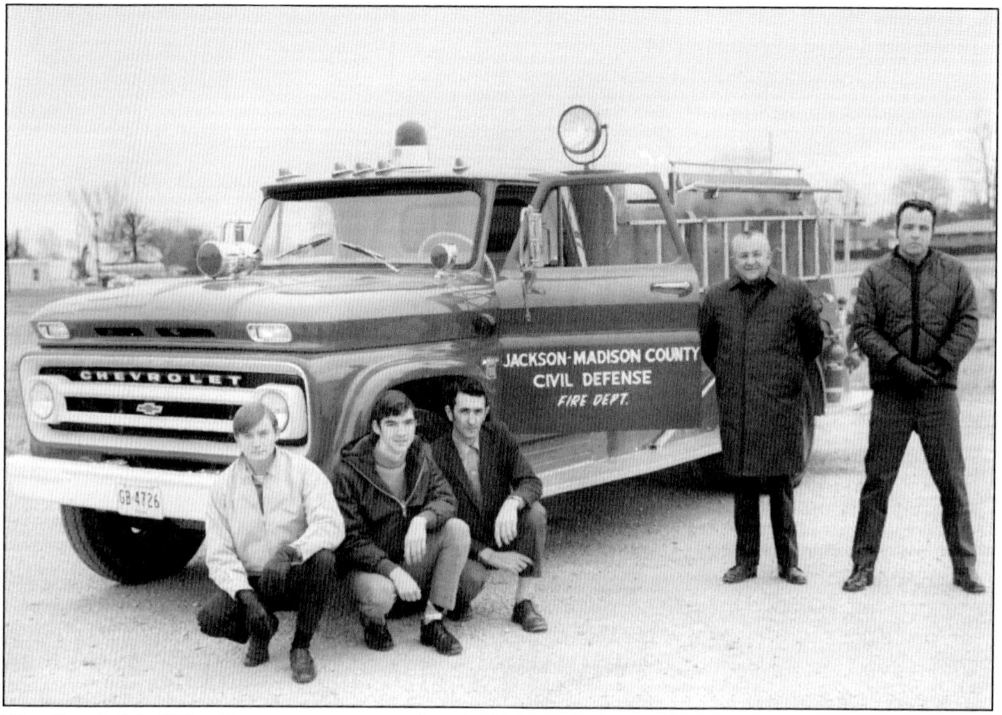

The Beech Bluff Fire Department started in 1975. From left to right are Jim May, Mickey Ellison, Alvin Jones, Murray May, and Bob May. (Courtesy Nina May Jones.)

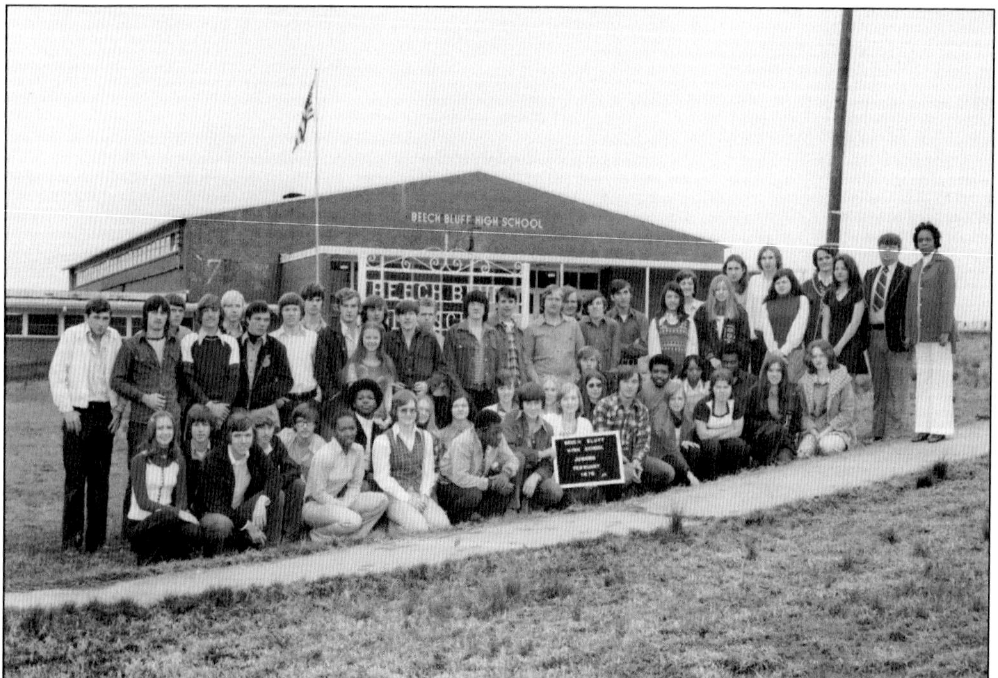

Shown here is one of the last high school classes to graduate from Beech Bluff in 1975. (Courtesy Nina May Jones.)

Steve Carter started delivering mail from the Denmark Post Office at the age of 18 in 1913 after the death of his father, who started delivering the Denmark mail in 1905. The Denmark Post Office was the first post office opened in Madison County in 1820. Carter is pictured around 1940. (Courtesy Louise Stevens.)

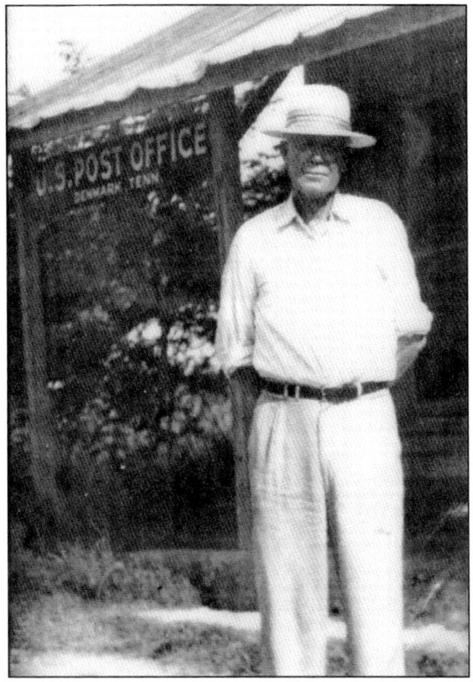

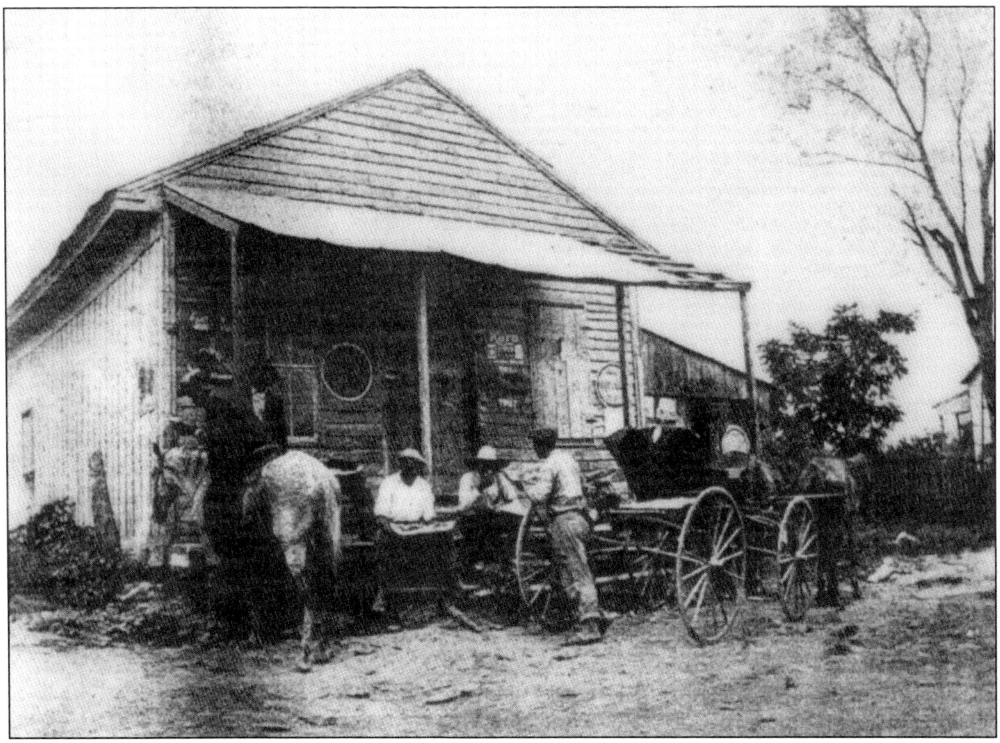

In pre–Civil War days, Denmark was a thriving town with hotels, doctors' offices, academies, several large churches, and a nice-sized population; however, by the beginning of the 20th century, the community had become just another rural town with a post office, a country store, and a cotton gin. (Courtesy Big Black Creek Historical Society.)

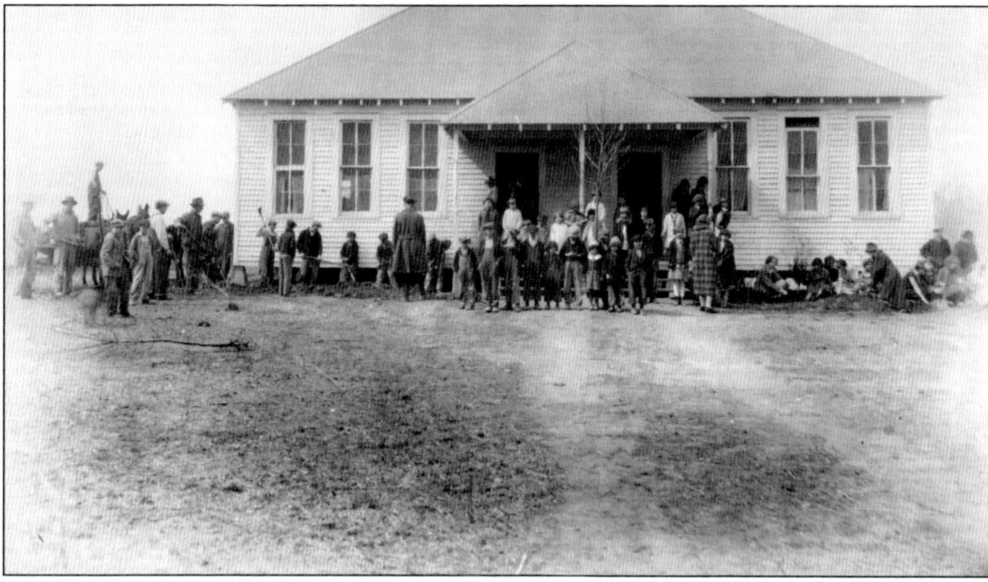

Members of the Harts Bridge community are shown beautifying the school grounds. (Courtesy Billie Jennings and the Madison County Extension Office.)

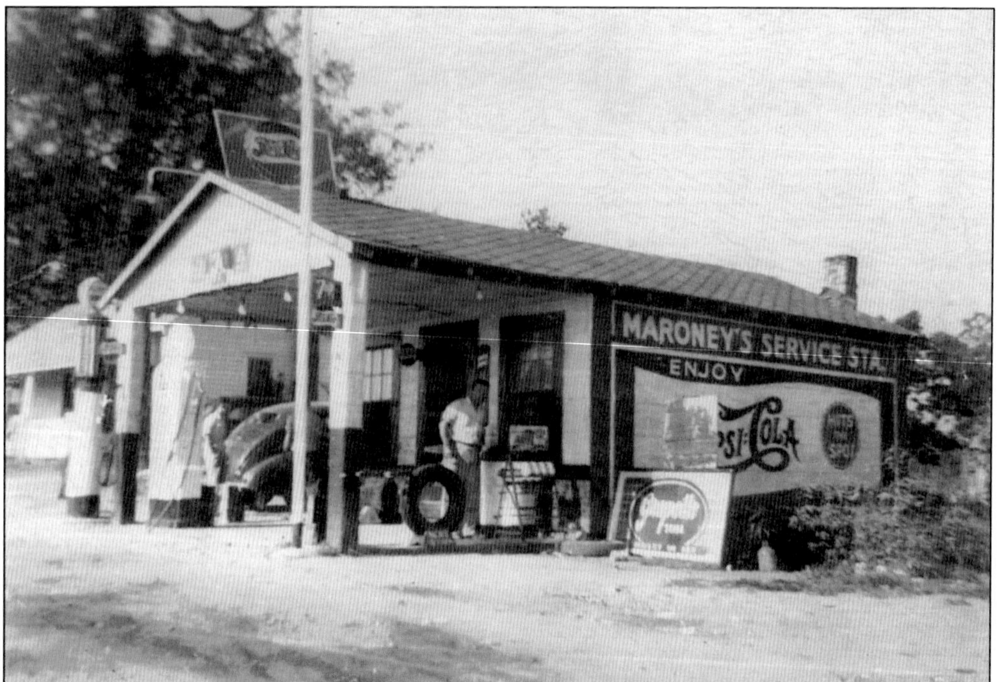

Sidney K. Maroney's service station in Medon, pictured in 1947, was an active place on Highway 18. Medon, ever since being settled in the early 1820s and incorporated in 1852, was a successful stagecoach stop and even had a railroad depot. Today Medon, with an official population of 269 residents, is one of only two incorporated towns in Madison County besides Jackson. (Courtesy of James "Preacher" Maroney.)

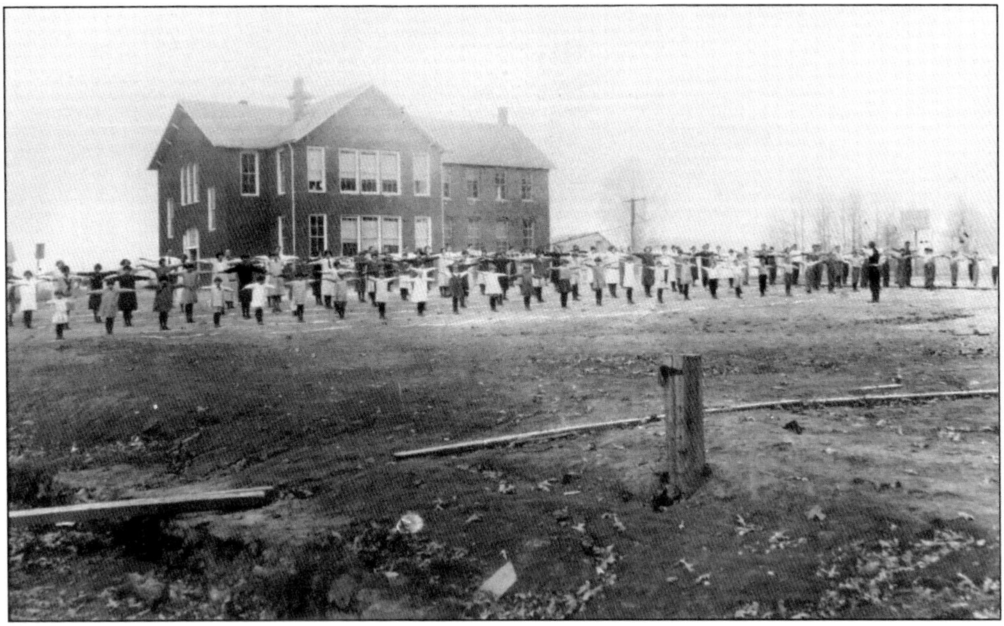

The two-story Malesus School was constructed in 1910, first with stucco and later in the 1920s with brick veneer. The Malesus community, first known as Harrisburg, had a wooden school called Harris' School, which burned in 1910. The two-story structure became a one-story building in 1956 for grades one through eight, and high school students attended the new consolidated county school, called South Side. (Courtesy Margaret H. McGill.)

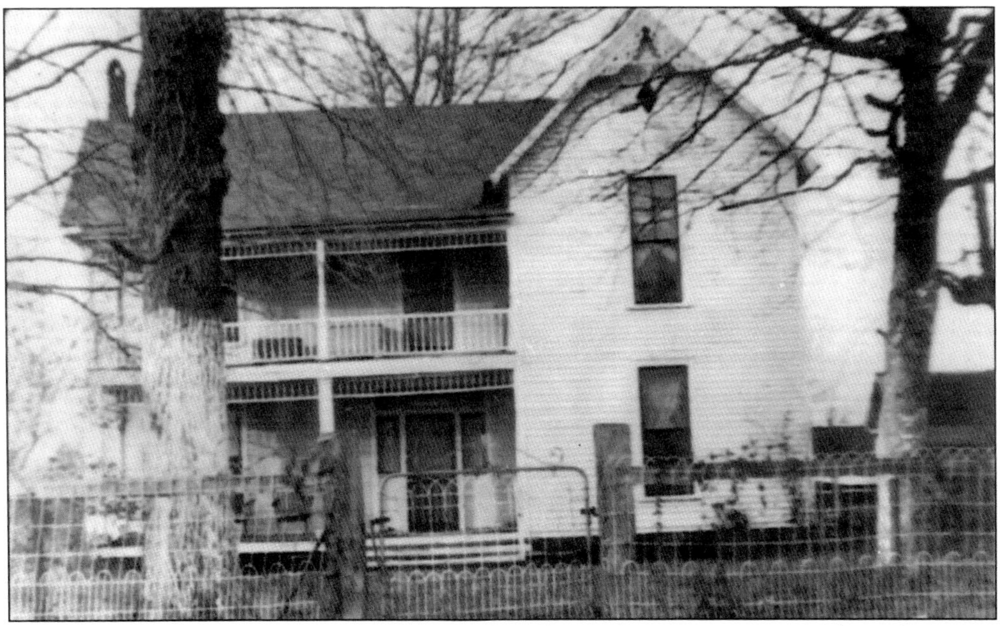

Dr. J. T. and Ida Raines's home was a landmark in the Malesus community. Early in the 1900s, Dr. Raines had his medical practice in a small white building beside the two-story home. The Malesus Missionary Society was organized in 1903 in the house, which was located in front of the Malesus Baptist Church. The Raines's son, Jim, owned the house when it burned in the 1960s. (Courtesy Margaret H. McGill.)

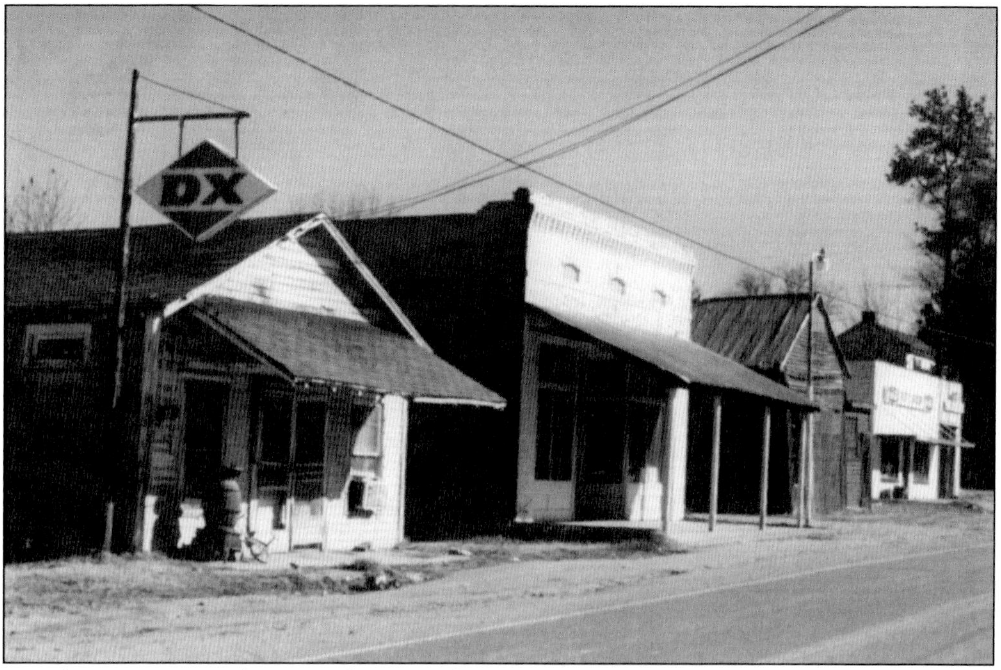

Storefronts in Mercer shown in this 1987 photograph include, from left to right, Ralph Lewis's garage; Rainey's Store, which included Roscoe Overton's garage, the Mercer Co-op, and the fire department; the abandoned building that once held T. W. Robinson's grocery store in 1936; and the 1949 concrete block building that was once a grocery store owned and operated by Troy Burkes, Wade Brown, Ben Wayne Foote, and Mamie Fuller. The picture below shows the Mercer Cotton Gin, which was built beside the railroad tracks that are now gone. (Both courtesy Dr. Henry A. Foote and Ginger Foote Pierpoint.)

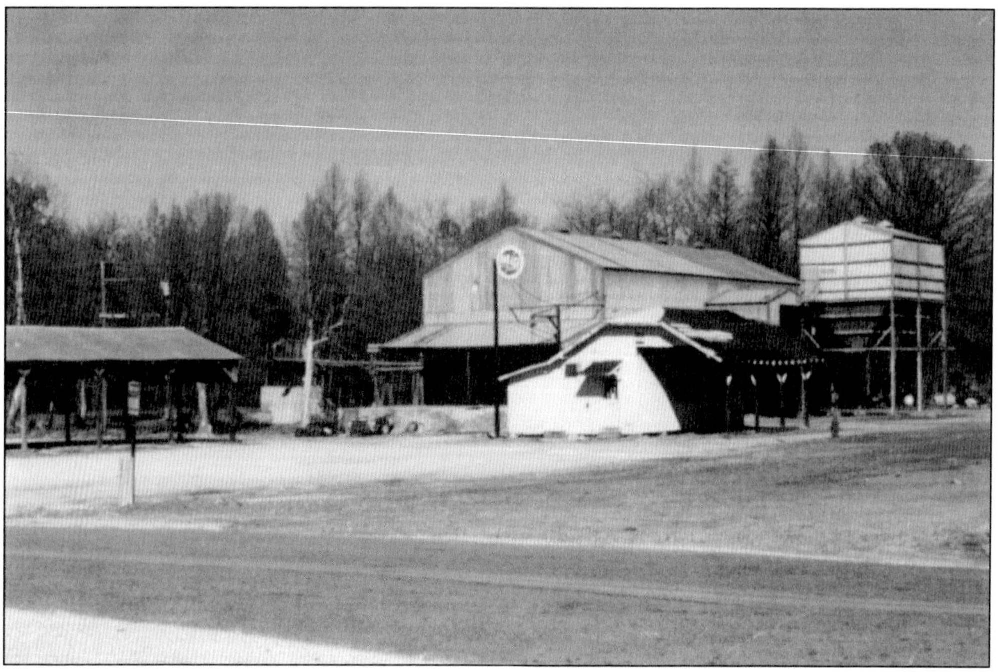

In the Mifflin community early in the 20th century, families didn't need the resources of the city. William Thomas Anderson, born March 23, 1829, and died January 21, 1916, and Elizabeth June Johnson Anderson, born in 1832 and died August 7, 1923, were the grandparents of John Wesley Parham. They lived on Mifflin Road, owned a shoe shop, a gristmill, and a large farm, and were totally self-sufficient. (Courtesy Jane Parham.)

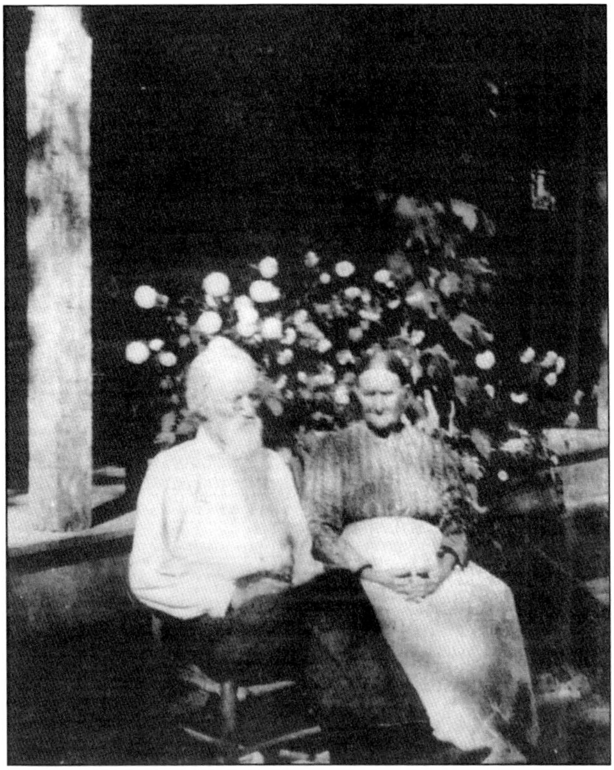

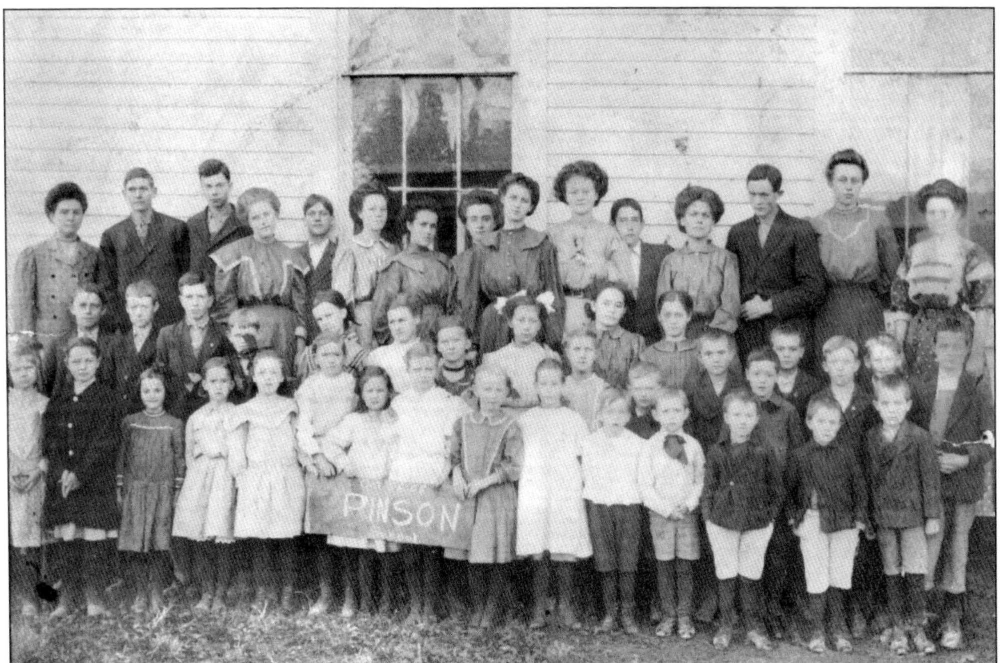

Pinson, a new village on the Mobile and Ohio Railroad, grew rapidly after its settlement in 1866. By 1873, Pinson had a high school with 100 students. The handwritten sign reads, "Oct. 26 08 Pinson School." (Courtesy Linda Wilson Holder and the Pinson Community Cookbook.)

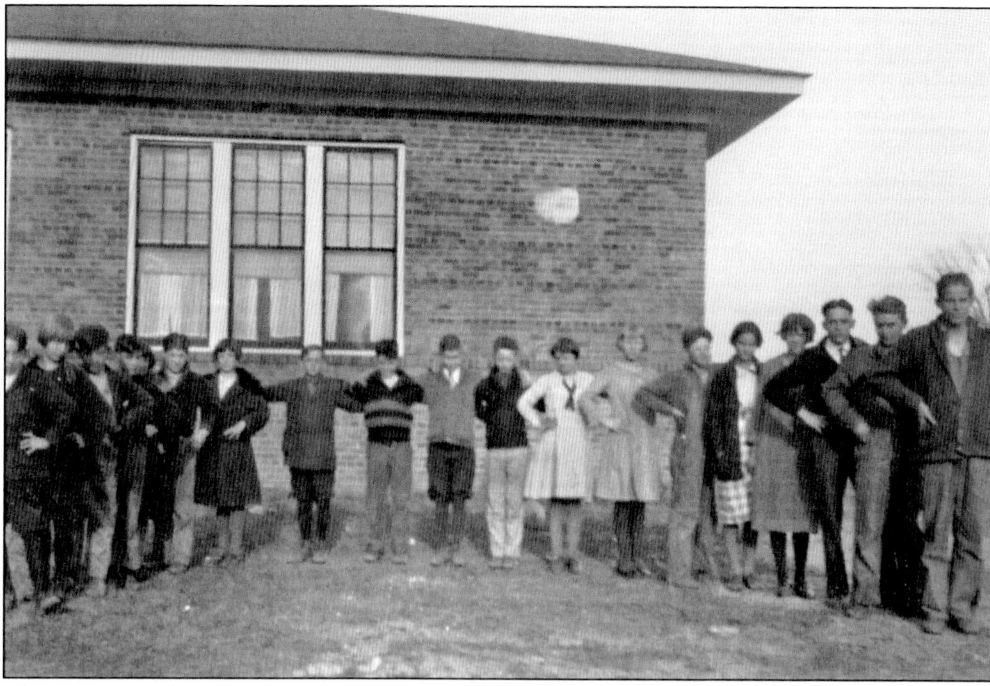

The Pinson School, shown in the 1920s, was built about 1924. In the 1990s, it was closed as a school, but the building still exists. (Courtesy Linda Wilson Holder and the Pinson Community Cookbook.)

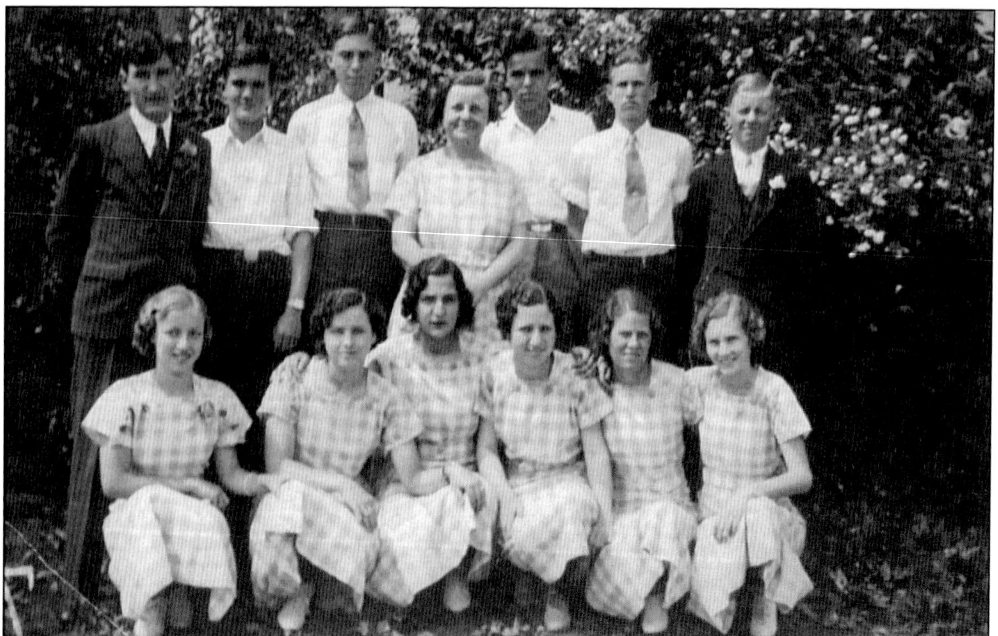

Graduates from Pinson High School in 1935 are, from left to right, (first row) Evelyn Barnette, Ludie Mae Webb, Nadine Isaac, Estelle Arnold, Alma Lea Couch, and Opal Arnold; (second row) Robert Nolen, Hugh Moore, Earl Brown, teacher Myrtle Couch, Wilson Sparks, Grady Arnold, and William Barnette. (Courtesy Robert Nolen.)

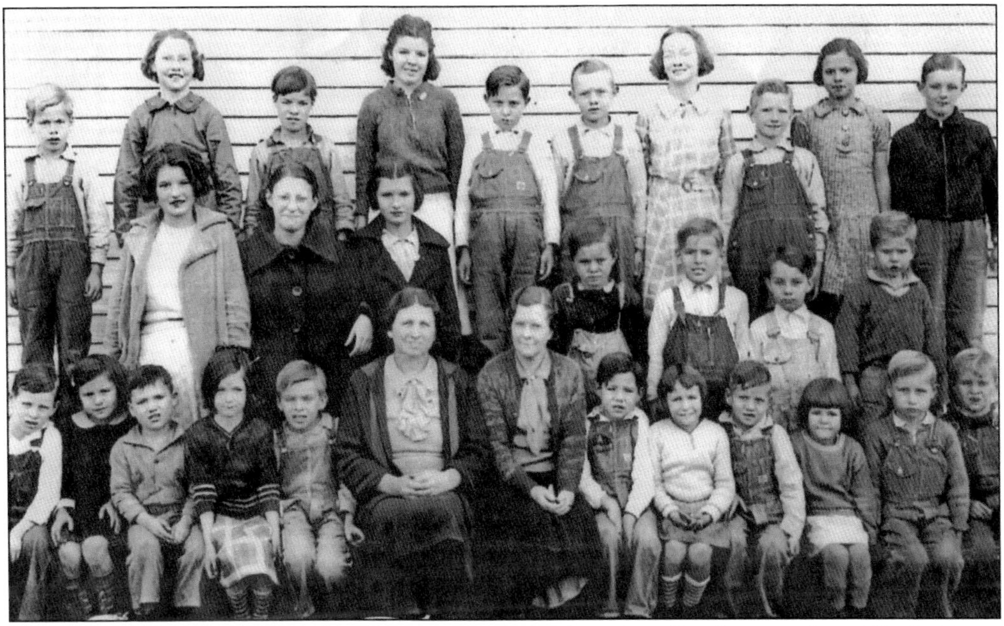

Lanier School, a two-room schoolhouse, was located on Law Road across from Wards Grove Baptist Church in the early 1900s. Those identified here are (first row) Charles Fenner Williams (third from left), Cletus Pillow (fifth from left), teacher Elizabeth Williams (seventh from left), and James Harold Grissom (right); (third row) ? Sikes (third from left), Wayne Pillow (sixth from left), Charlie Caldwell (eighth from left), and Earl King (right). (Courtesy Parnell Landers.)

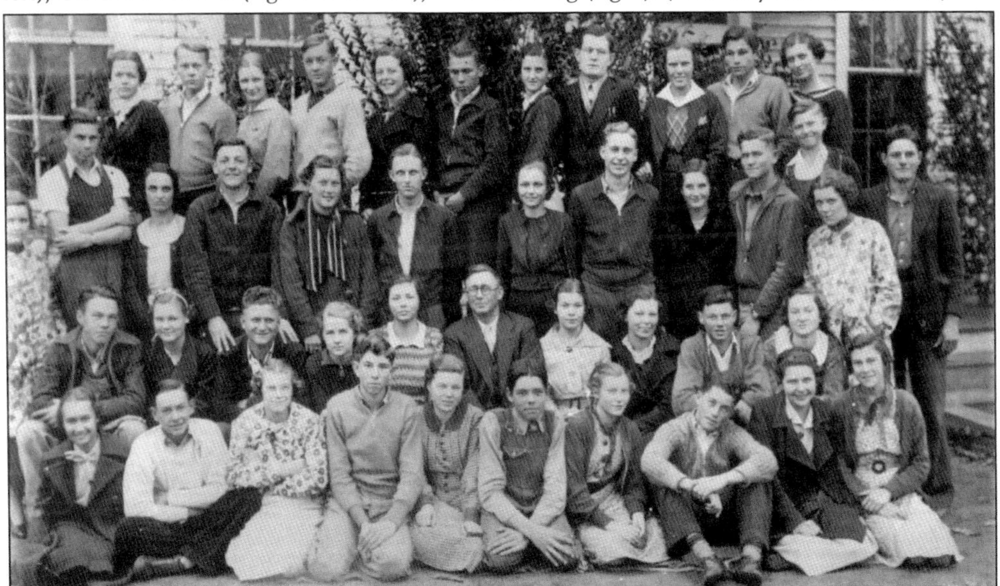

Students at Spring Creek High School in 1936 include (second row) James McLemore (third from left), ? Fly (fourth from left), Virginia Landers (fifth from left), Mildred Settles (seventh from left), and Kathleen Rushing (eighth from left); (third row) Ethel Lawler (third from left), Lawson Specer (fourth from left), Polkie Gateley (fifth from left), Hazel Gurley (seventh from left), ? Hopper (ninth from left), Rupert Caldwell (tenth from left), and Billy Caldwell (right); (fourth row) S. B. Spencer (sixth from left) and Ray Blankenship (tenth from left). (Courtesy Parnell Landers.)

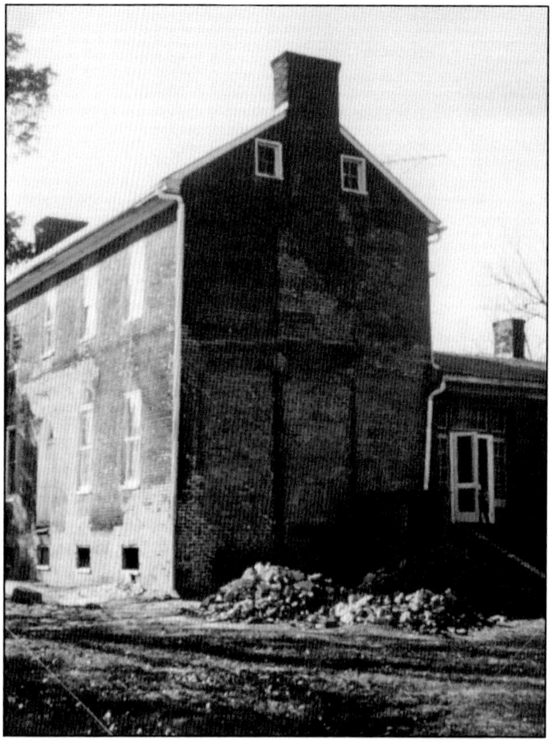

One of the oldest homes still standing in Madison County was built by Mathias DeBerry in 1825, and he named it Rose Hill. His daughter, Sue, changed the name of the estate to Leeper following her marriage. The Leepers remodeled the home in the 1890s. Dan Tankersly, a state representative, purchased the home in 1976, and it is still in private ownership. The name of the estate became part of the new park in the east Madison County area known as Leeper Lane Park, which has walking trails that one day may contain historic markers for the beginnings of Madison County. Below is the Rose Hill School, shown around 1930. The rural school was 3 miles from the city. Today a school built early in 21st century across the street from the original school is named Rose Hill School. (Both courtesy JMCL.)

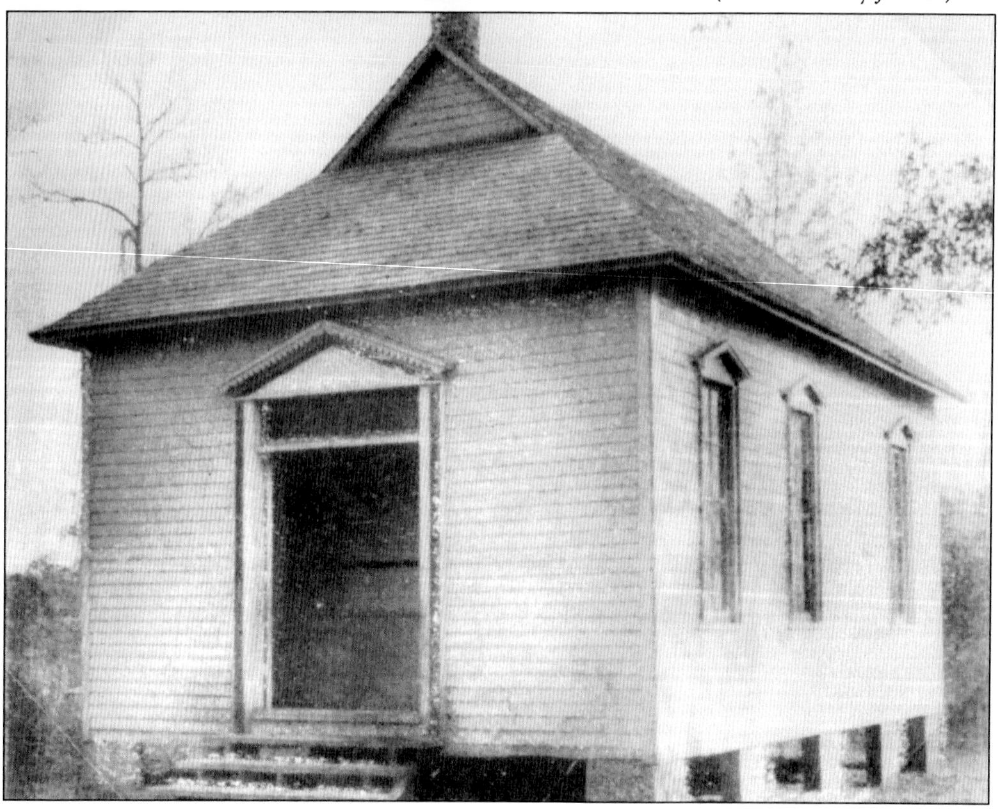

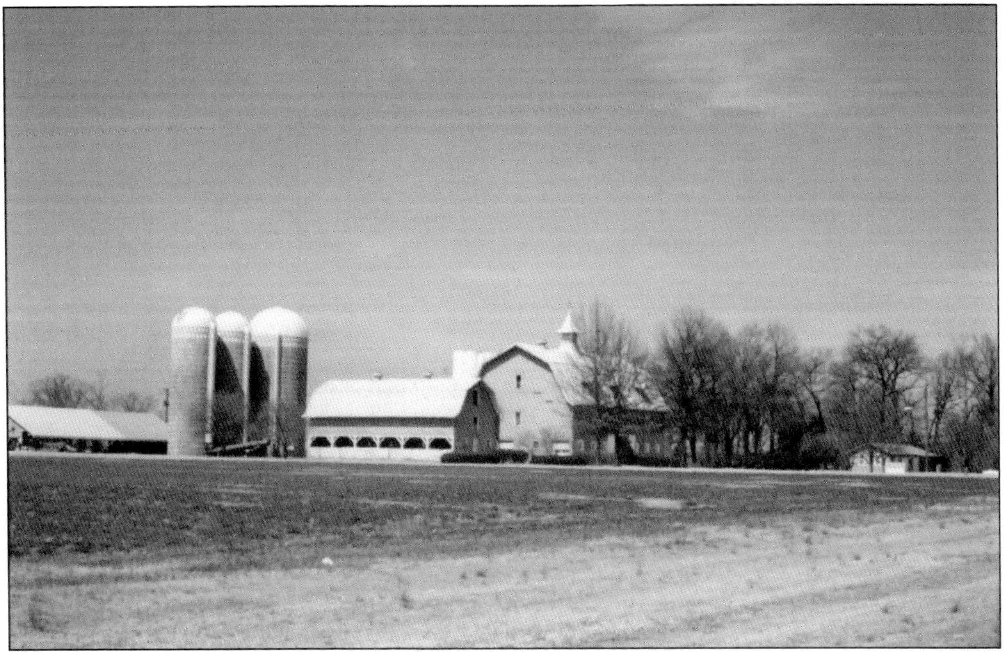

The West Tennessee Experiment Station began in 1908 on 180 acres in the rural portion of the county. The site was selected as the geographical center of West Tennessee. The research farm, now operated by the University of Tennessee, continues to play a major role in serving the local agricultural industry. (Photograph by William McCommon, courtesy Kathleen McCommon.)

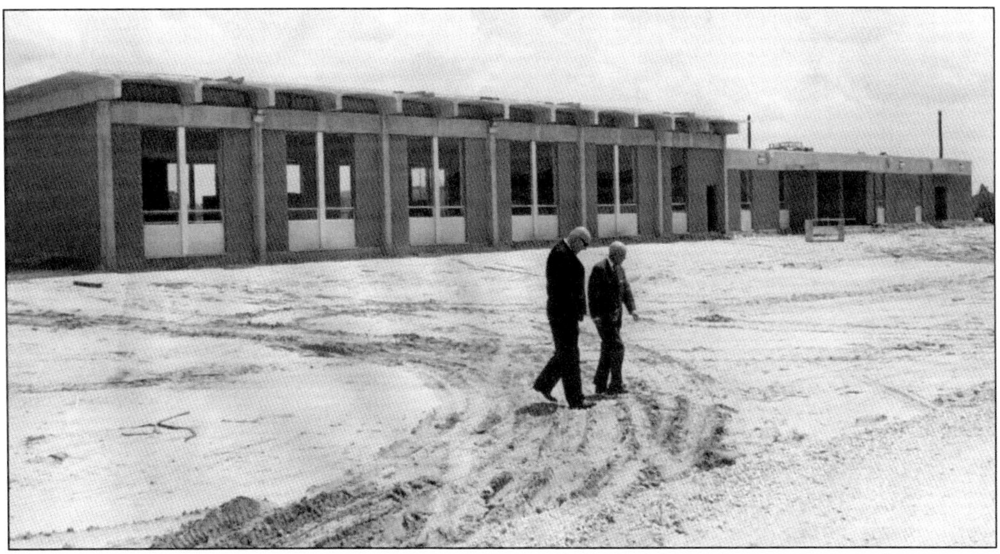

In the mid-1960s, the Tennessee legislature authorized the building of community colleges. Here the first president of Jackson State Community College, Dr. F. E. Wright, talks with the architect Charles Ross, who designed and oversaw the construction of the community college in Jackson. JSCC opened in 1967. (Courtesy JSCC Library.)

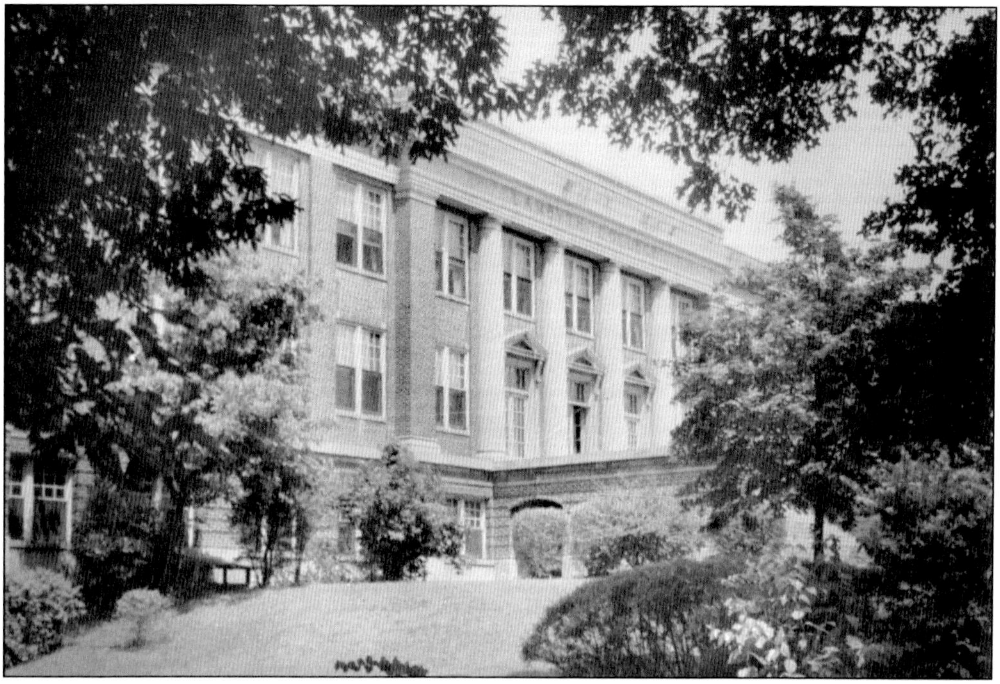

Lambuth College opened in the building constructed in 1924 on what is now Lambuth Boulevard. Before 1924, an elaborate building erected in 1843 was still in use by the Memphis Conference Female Institute on Royal and Chester Streets. (Courtesy JMCL.)

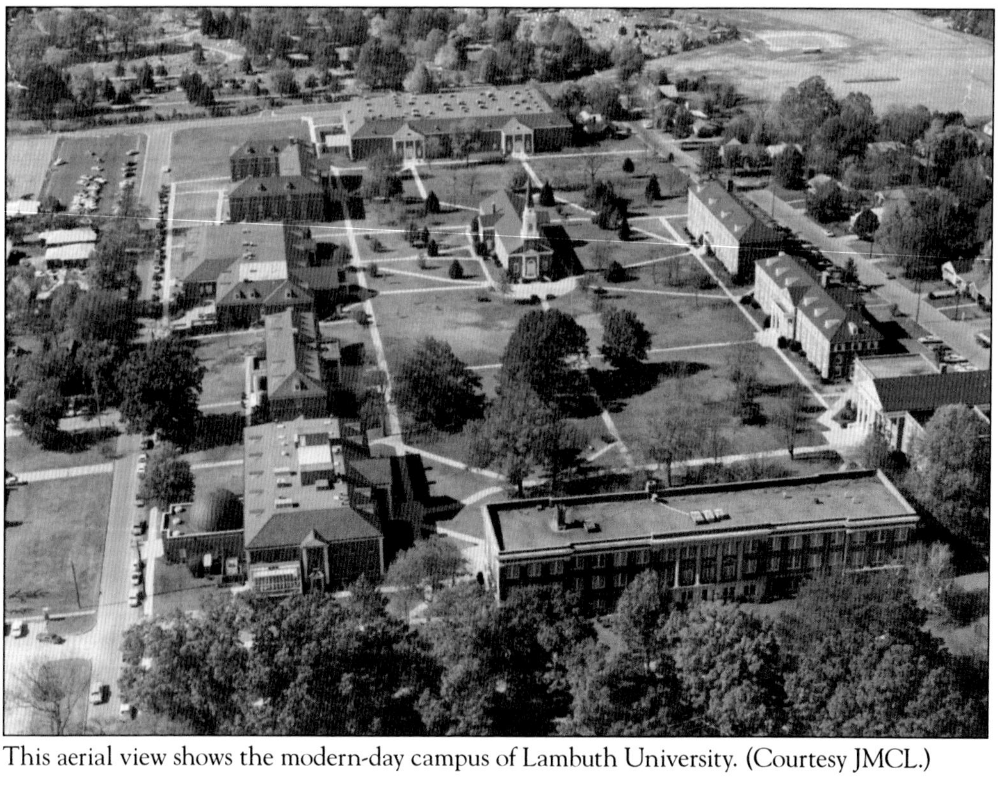

This aerial view shows the modern-day campus of Lambuth University. (Courtesy JMCL.)

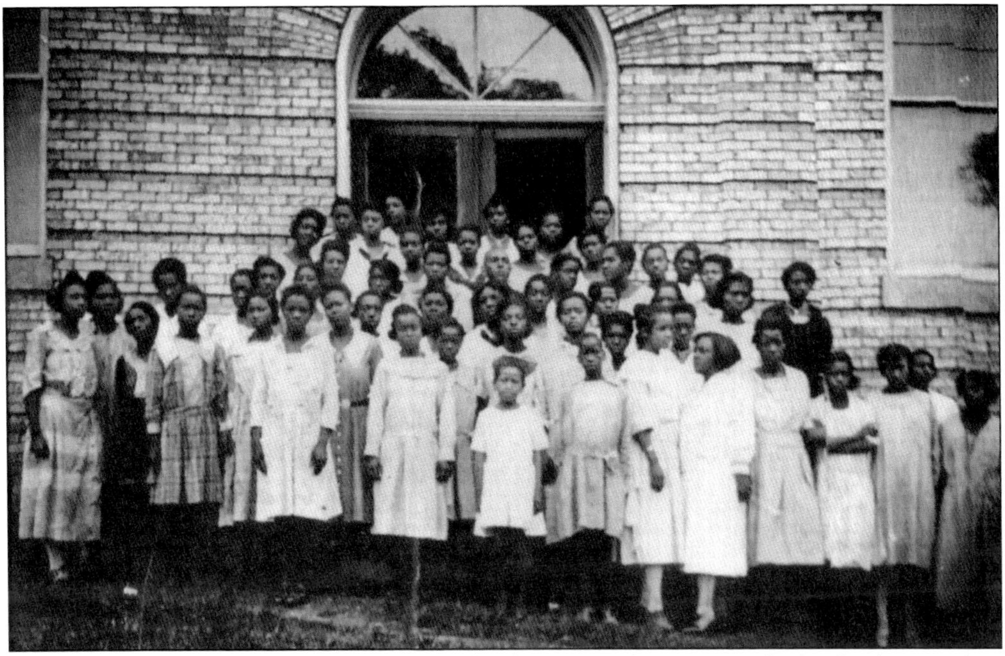

Lane College, established in 1882 as a high school, continued to operate a high school curriculum along with its college courses until 1933. Shown here is a 1921 class that appears to have both high school and college students outside the historic administration building, which is now on the National Register of Historic Places. (Courtesy Lane College.)

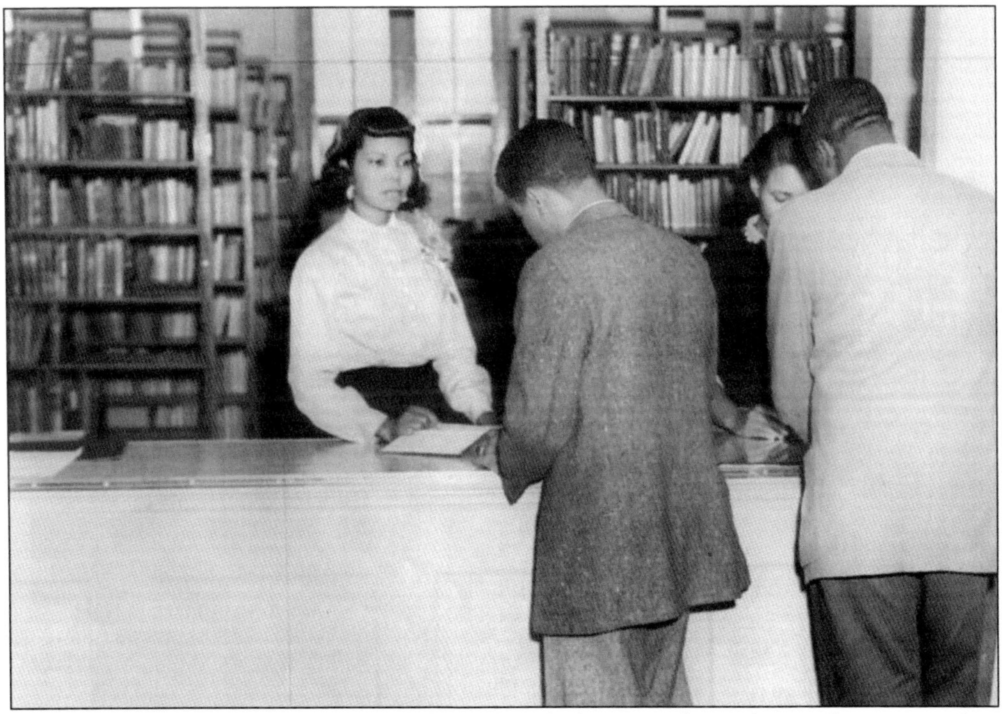

In the 1950s, students took advantage of the well-stocked Lane College Library. The new president in 1950 was Dr. C. A. Kirkendoll. (Courtesy Lane College.)

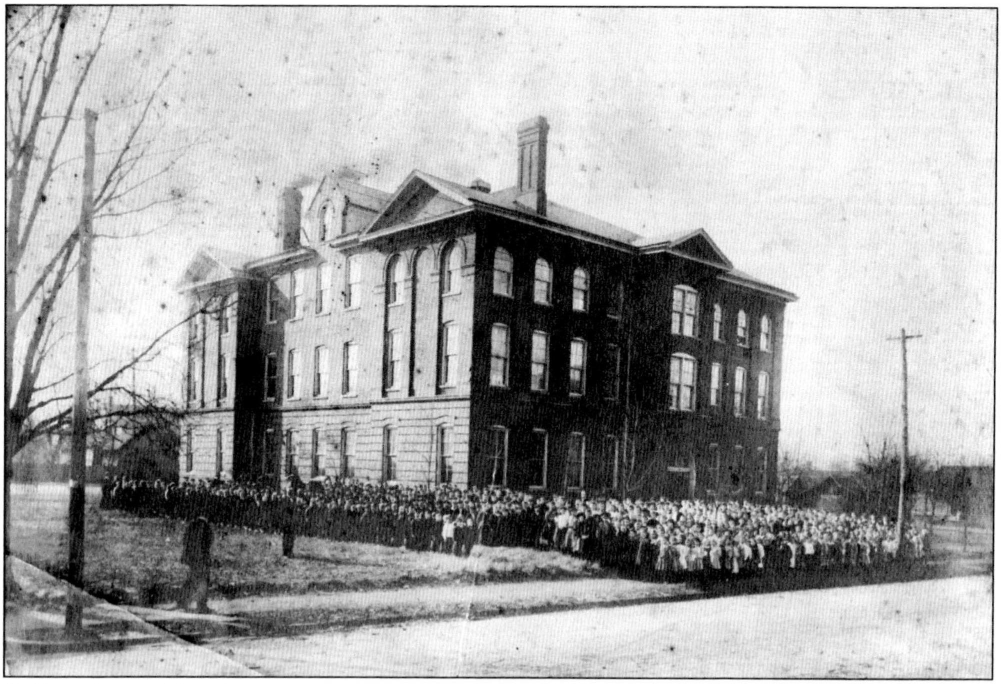

College Street School is pictured as it appeared in 1909. It closed as an elementary school in 1950. Union University moved its chemistry classes into the building and used it until the university moved to its new location on Highway 45 Bypass in 1975. (Courtesy JMCL.)

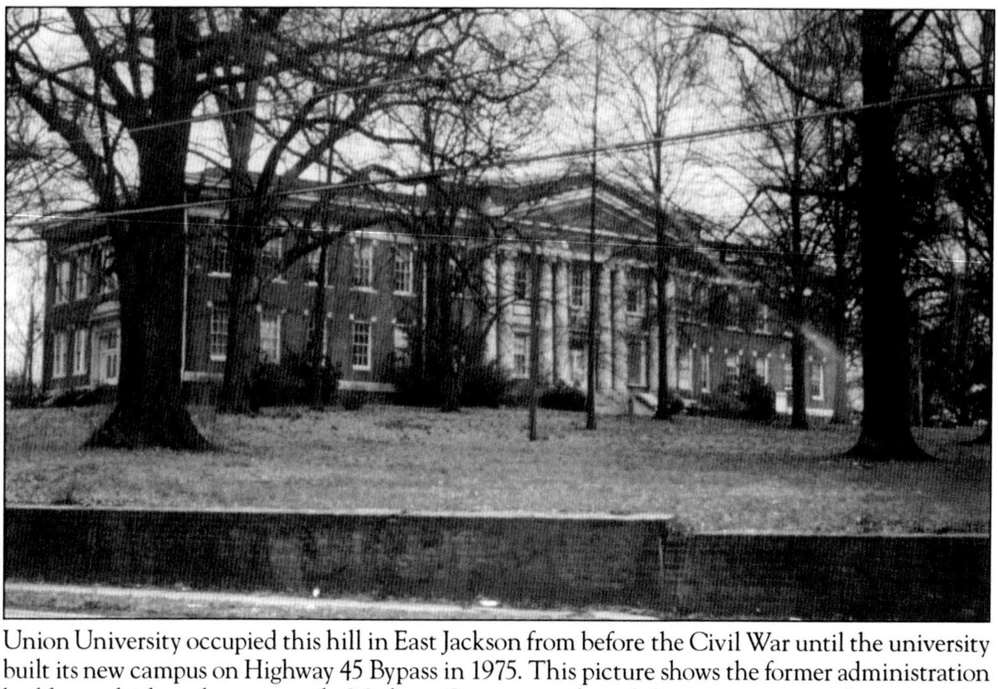

Union University occupied this hill in East Jackson from before the Civil War until the university built its new campus on Highway 45 Bypass in 1975. This picture shows the former administration building, which no longer stands. Madison County purchased the east campus and is using it for Juvenile Court and Services and the Sheriff's Administration offices. (Photograph by William McCommon, courtesy Kathleen McCommon.)

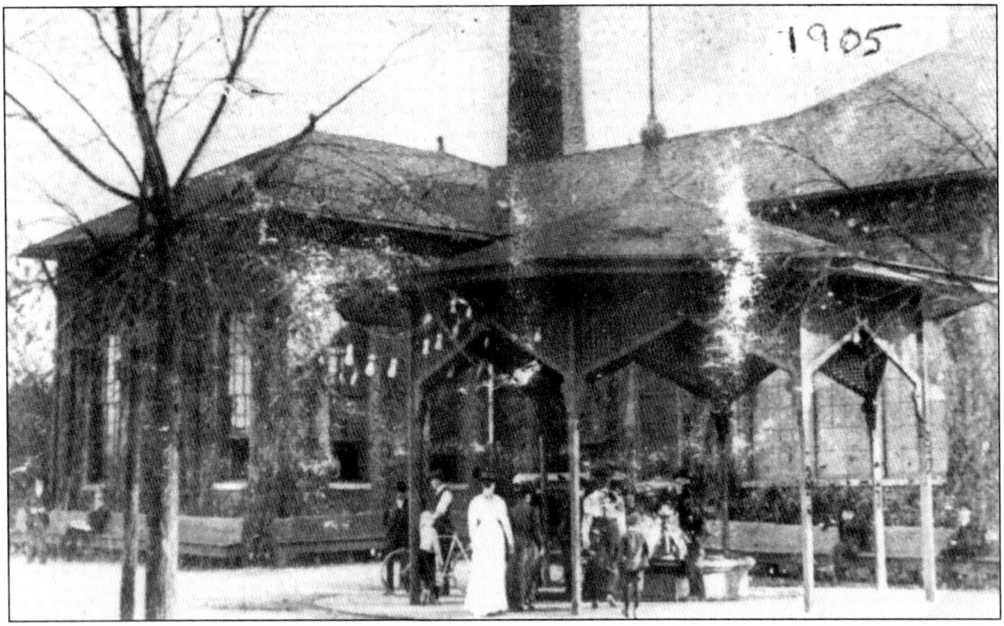

Beginning early in the 20th century, Jacksonians thought they had one of the "most popular watering places in the South." This was the electro-chalybeate well dug in 1904 at 604 South Royal Street next to the 54-acre Lancaster Park. Even though the site did not attract out-of-town tourists, "The park was the main recreational area of Jackson for almost 40 years," describes Curtis McMillan in 1980. (Courtesy JMCL.)

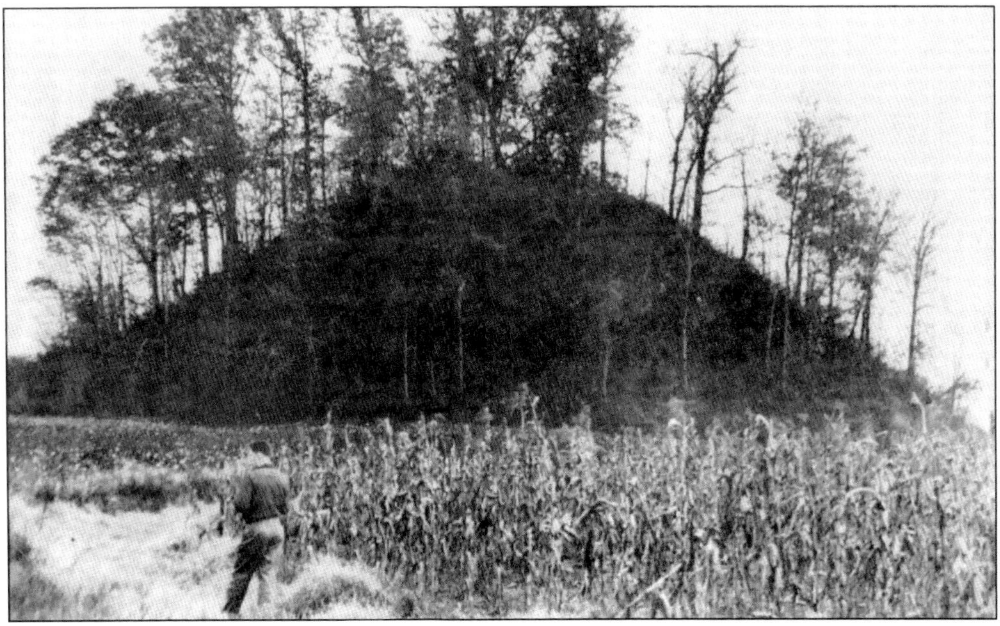

Pinson Mounds Archaeological Area is located in southeastern Madison County. Saul Mound, shown here, measures 72 feet high and is the second-tallest mound in the United States. In 1967, the area became a state park and was placed on the National Register of Historic Places. Excavations revealed that the mound builders were ancestors of the Native Americans who hunted in this area. (Courtesy Mrs. John Nucholls.)

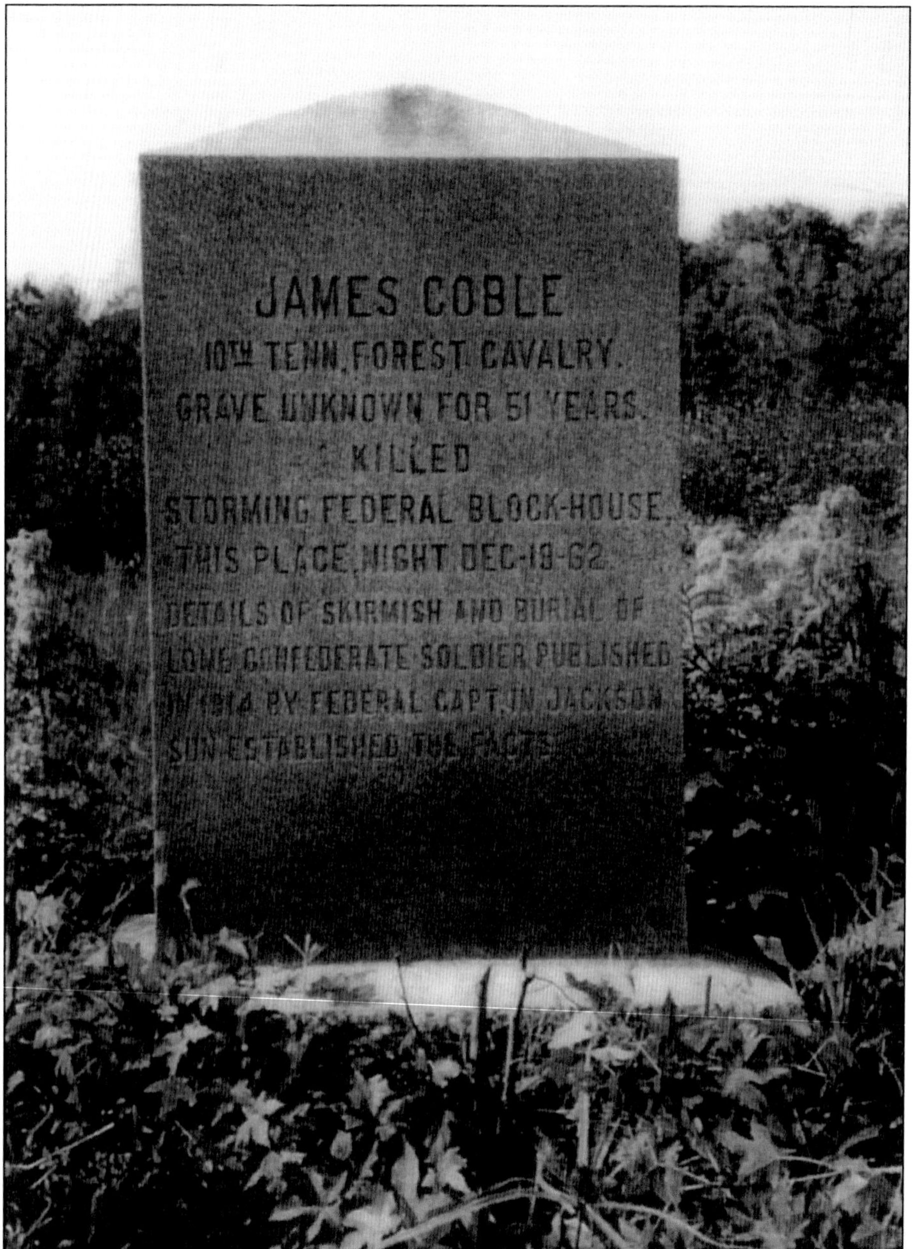

A lone Confederate gravestone marks the burial of James Coble of the 10th Cavalry, who was killed storming a Federal blockhouse on the M&O railroad tracks just off Harts Bridge Road on December 19, 1962. Coble's burial remained unknown for 51 years, until a Federal captain published information about the attack, the death, and the burial of the soldier in the *Jackson Sun* where descendants of Coble read the account, realized who it was, and placed the marker. E. M. Stansell, on whose farm the monument exists, hopes to add the gravestone to the Civil War Trails in Madison County. Other Civil War tourist sites include the Britton Lane Battle Park, the skirmish at Salem Cemetery, and Riverside Cemetery. (Courtesy E. Maurice Stansell Sr.)

This bell in the yard of the historic Denmark Presbyterian Church called people to worship for over 100 years. The two-story church building, constructed in 1854, still stands due to the complexity of the post-and-beam construction. In the early 1990s, the church was named to the National Register of Historic Places. The church attracts Civil War battle re-enactors, students, and those interested in history. (Courtesy JMCL.)

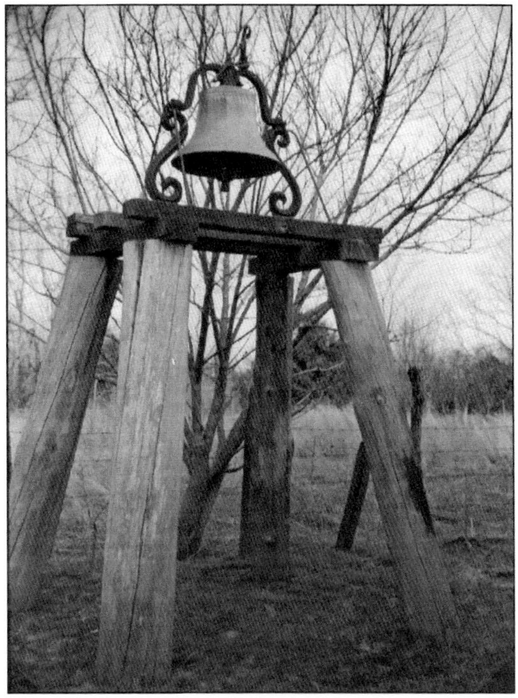

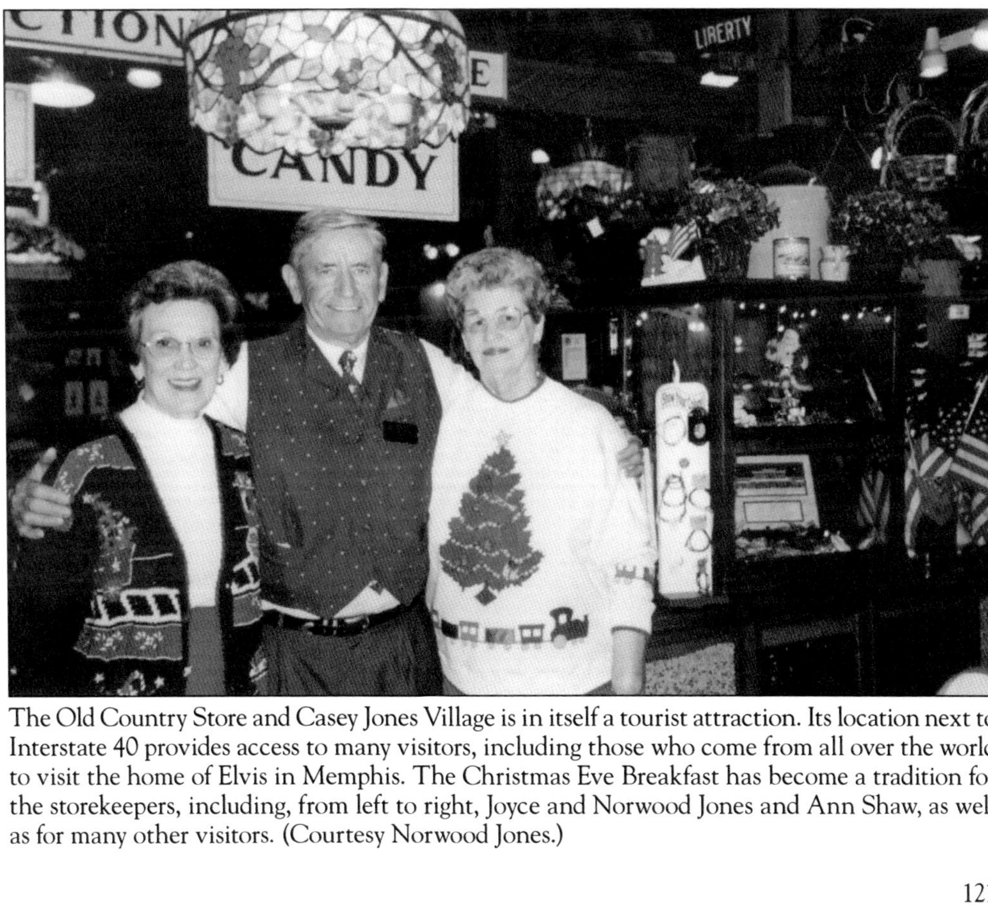

The Old Country Store and Casey Jones Village is in itself a tourist attraction. Its location next to Interstate 40 provides access to many visitors, including those who come from all over the world to visit the home of Elvis in Memphis. The Christmas Eve Breakfast has become a tradition for the storekeepers, including, from left to right, Joyce and Norwood Jones and Ann Shaw, as well as for many other visitors. (Courtesy Norwood Jones.)

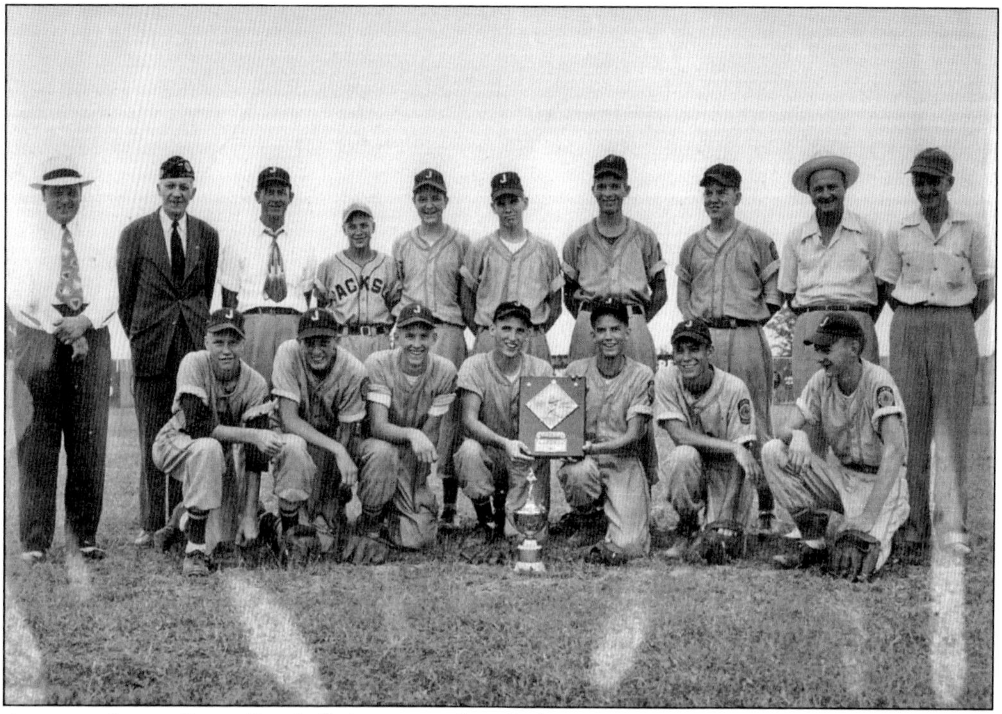

American Legion Junior Baseball champions from Jackson were state runners-up and were awarded their trophy by Ford Motor Company. (Courtesy E. Maurice Stansell Sr.)

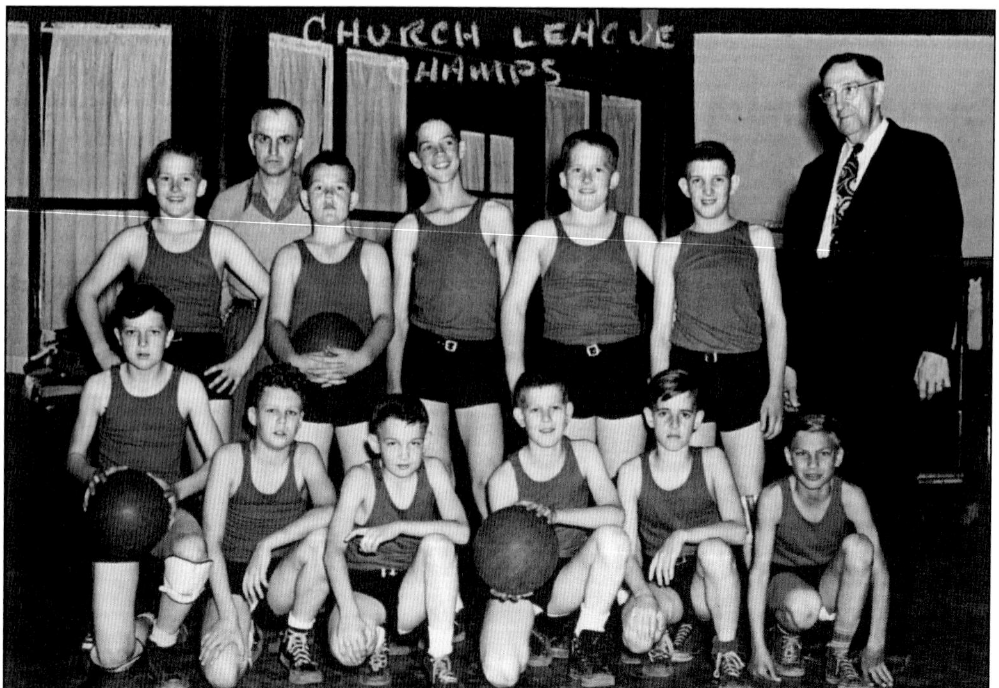

Churches got involved in sports, too. Here are the 1947–1948 Church League champions. (Courtesy of E. Maurice Stansell Sr.)

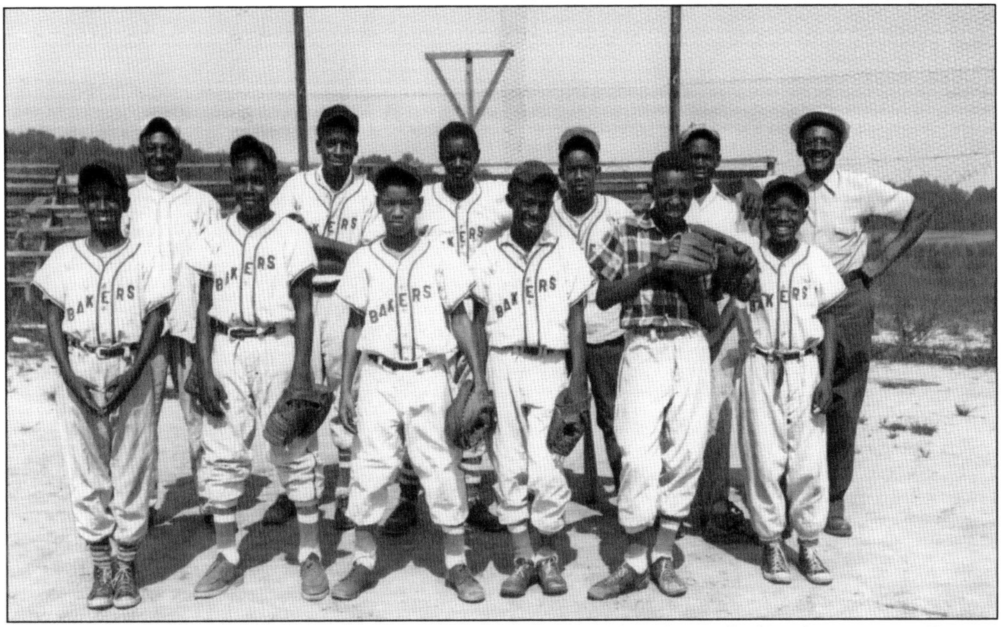

The Black Little League team played their games in the field at the end of Butler Street in Bemis. All the players were from Bemis. From left to right are (first row) Corin Spann, Roy Bell Jr., George Thomas, Herman Ivyn, Johnny McNuckles, and Willie Spann; (second row) F. J. Frank Spann, George Butler, Mike Mercer, Rod Motty, Willie B. Walker, Romy Dodd, and manager D. Dodd. (Courtesy Bemis Historical Society.)

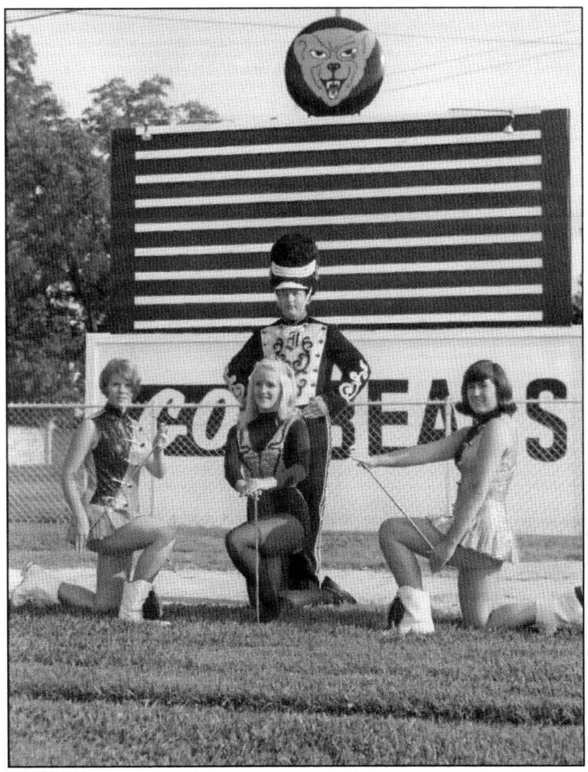

During the last year of Jackson High School, the Golden Bears Band drum major was Mike Winslow (standing), and the majorettes, from left to right, are unidentified, head majorette Melinda Middlebrooks, and featured twirler Jan Caylor. (Courtesy Old Country Store and Norwood Jones.)

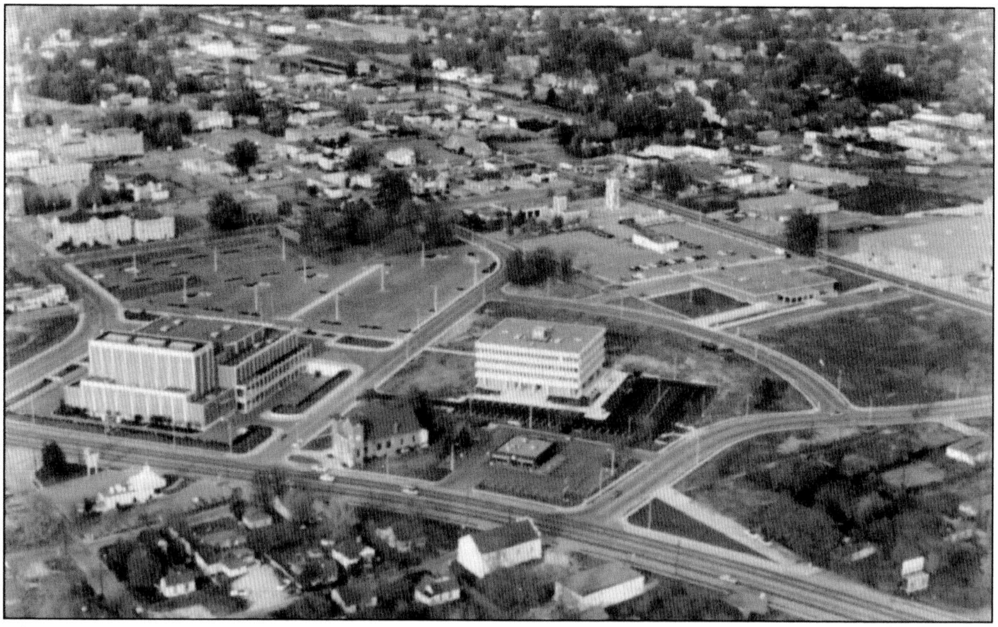

The new civic center, opened in 1973 and shown in this aerial view, brought many new opportunities for entertainment, including the Jackson Symphony, which had been organized in 1961 but had never had an adequate place to perform. The Miss Tennessee Scholarship pageant adopted the civic center as home. Following the death of rockabilly singer Carl Perkins, the city council voted to rename the civic center in his memory. (Courtesy JMCL.)

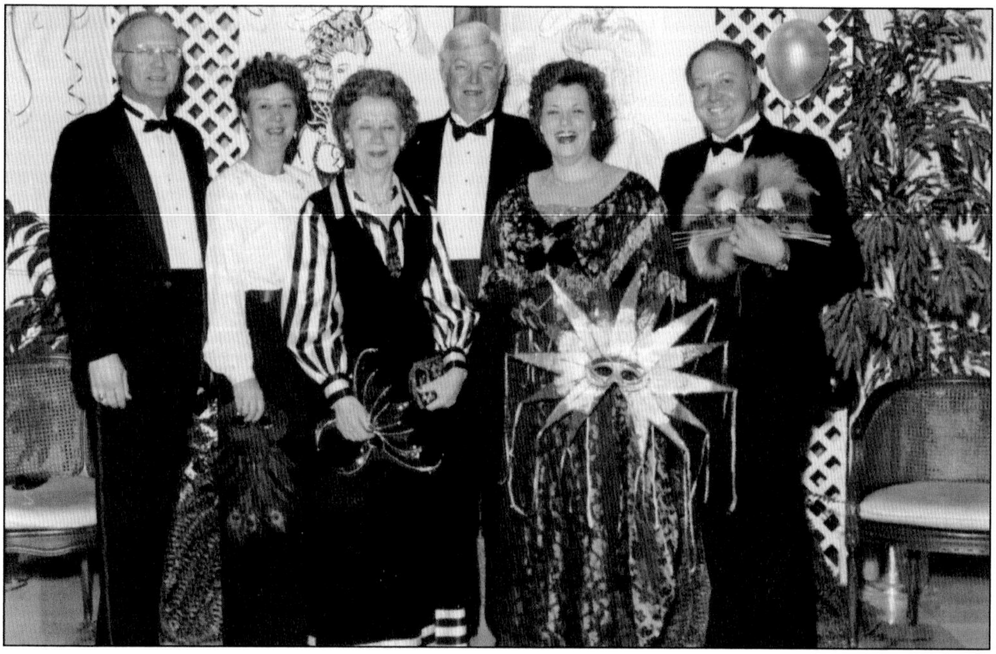

The Jackson Symphony League annually sponsors the debutante ball as a fund-raiser for the symphony. Here at the 1987 masked ball are, from left to right, Charles N. Roth, Georgia Middlebrooks Roth, Dorothy "Dee" Middlebrooks, M. T. Middlebrooks, Mary Jo Middlebrooks, and Ernie H. Gray. (Courtesy Mary Jo Middlebrooks.)

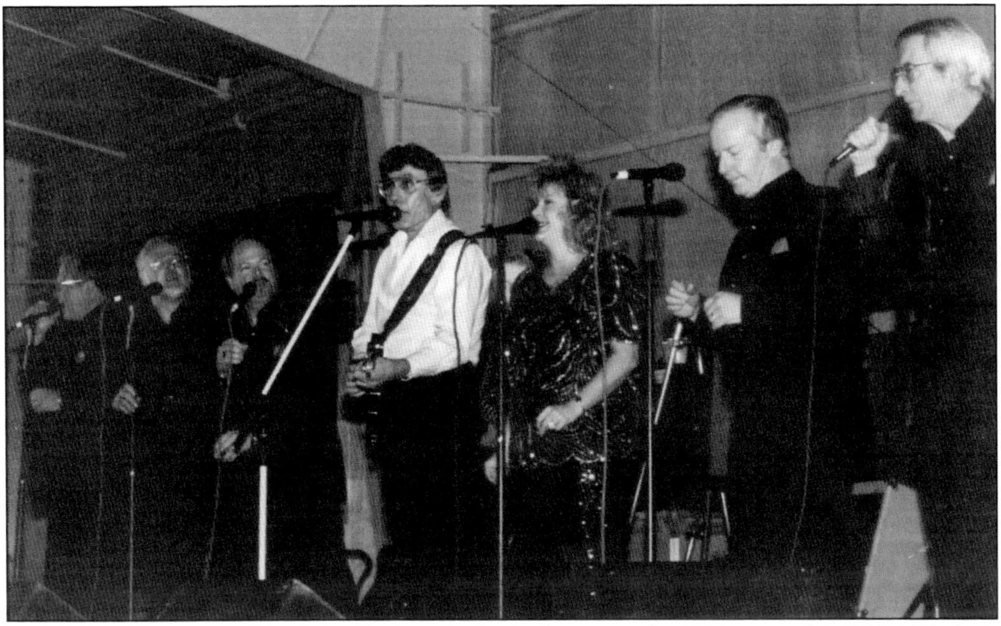

The Delecardos, a popular a cappella singing group that started in 1981, joined with Carl Perkins for a one-time performance in 1996. From left to right are Jerry Campbell, Ron Canter, Steve Little, Perkins, Christy Little, Bill Way, and Cecil Cravens. Five are still together and perform frequently. They all kept their day jobs, including being an educator, a judge, an insurance man, a radio and television host, and a music store owner. (Courtesy Cecil Cravens.)

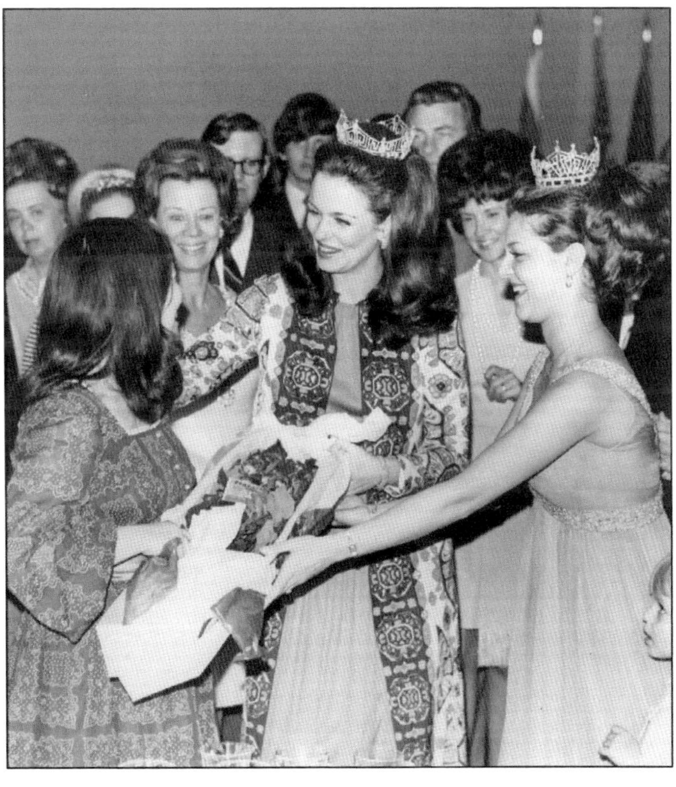

In 1971, Miss America Phyllis George came to Jackson. The Jackson Chapter of alumnae of George's sorority, Zeta Tau Alpha, hosted a reception at the Holiday Inn. Looking over George's right shoulder with a big smile is Dorothy "Dee" Middlebrooks. (Courtesy Mary Jo Middlebrooks.)

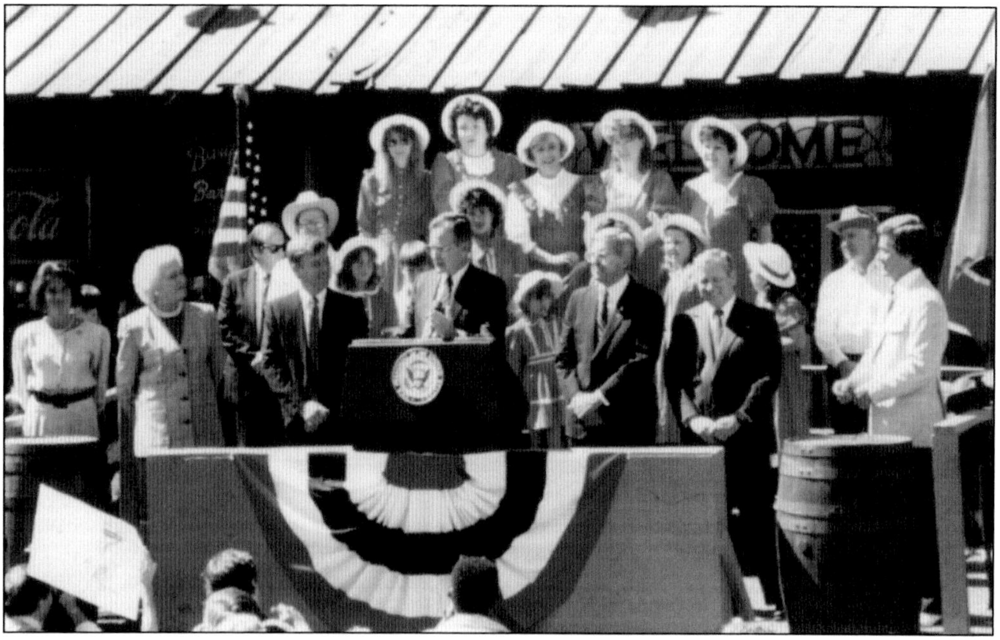

In 1988, Vice Pres. George H. Bush, who was the Republican presidential candidate, and his vice presidential selection, Dan Quayle, visited Jackson at the Old Country Store, where hundreds crowded into the Casey Jones Village to hear the candidates who would be elected in November 1988. (Courtesy Norwood Jones.)

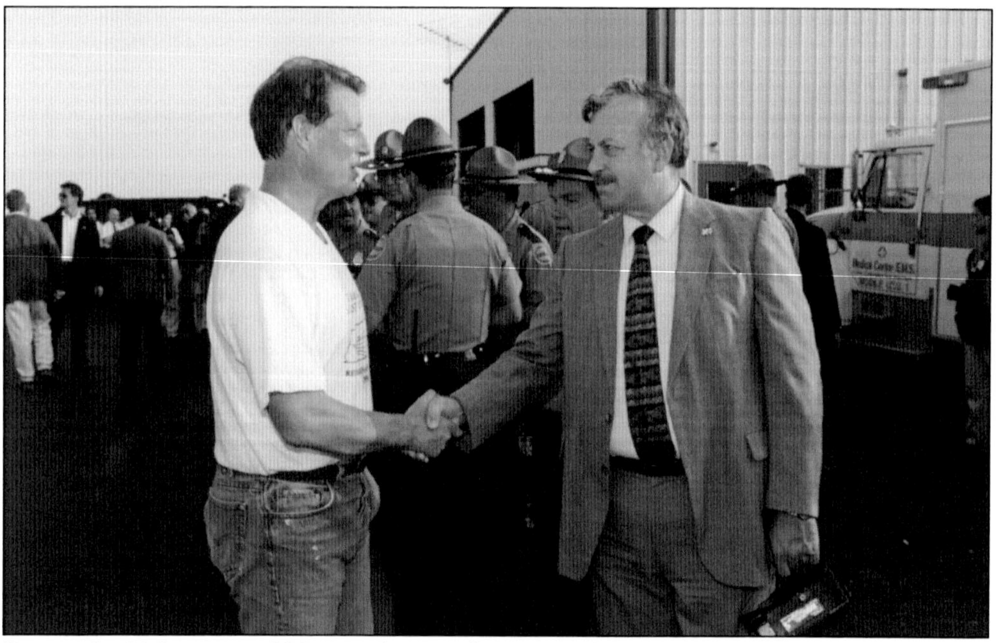

During the 20th century, U.S. presidents and vice presidents visited Jackson. The latest was a "working visit" by Pres. Bill Clinton, his wife, Hillary, Vice Pres. Al Gore, and his wife, Tipper, as they came to help rebuild some churches that had been burned by arsonists. Here Vice Pres. Al Gore is greeted at the Jackson Airport in 1996 by police captain Richard L. Higgins. (Courtesy Richard L. Higgins.)

Bibliography

"Agriculture: Member Reviews Demonstration Club's History." The *Jackson Sun*. Sunday, December 3, 1939.

Borner, Barbara K. *Reflections: A Pictorial History of Madison County*. Marceline, MO: D-Books Publishing, 1998.

"Business and Industry, 150 Years." The *Jackson Sun*. Friday, September 11, 1998.

Carter, Mitch, Marion Smothers, and Emma Inman Williams. *Jackson and Madison County: A Pictorial History*. Norfolk, VA: The Donning Company, 1988.

Jackson's Business: A Chronology of Business Enterprise in the Jackson Area of West Tennessee. Business History Project cosponsored by the Lambuth College Center for the Study of American Business and the Jackson Area Chamber of Commerce. Coordinated by Laurie Mercier and directed by Dr. Clint Daniels. Jackson–Madison County Library, Tennessee Room, special collection.

Pinson Community Cookbook. Kearney, NE: Morris Press Cookbooks, 2008.

Tigrett, John Burton. *Fair and Square*. Nashville, TN: Spiridon Press, Inc., 1998.

Williams, Emma Inman. *Historic Madison*. Jackson, TN: McCowat-Mercer Press, 1946.